Computer Ethics

Computer Ethics

Cautionary Tales
and Ethical Dilemmas in Computing

Tom Forester
and Perry Morrison

The MIT Press
Cambridge, Massachusetts

Fourth printing, 1993

First MIT Press edition, 1990
© 1990 Massachusetts Institute of Technology
Published in the UK by Basil Blackwell, Oxford, England

Printed and bound in the United States of America by Maple-Vail, Inc.

Library of Congress Cataloging-in-Publication Data
Forester, Tom.
    Computer ethics : cautionary tales and ethical dilemmas in
computing / Tom Forester and Perry Morrison.
        p.   cm.
    Includes bibliographical references.
    ISBN 0-262-06131-7 (HB), 0-262-56065-8 (PB)
    1. Electronic data processing–Moral and ethical aspects.
I. Morrison, Perry.   II. Title.
QA76.9.M65F67   1990b
174'.9004–dc20   89-71358   CIP

Contents

Preface and Acknowledgements

The aim of this book is two-fold: (1) to describe some of the problems created for society by computers and (2) to show how these problems present ethical dilemmas for computer professionals and computer users.

The problems created by computers arise, in turn, from two main sources: from hardware and software *malfunctions* and from *misuse* by human beings. We argue that computer systems by their very nature are insecure, unreliable and unpredictable – and that society has yet to come to terms with the consequences. We also seek to show how society has become newly vulnerable to human misuse of computers in the form of computer crime, software theft, hacking, the creation of viruses, invasions of privacy, and so on.

Computer Ethics has evolved from our previous writings and in particular our experiences teaching two courses on the human and social context of computing to computer science students at Griffith University. One lesson we quickly learned was that computer science students cannot be assumed to possess a social conscience or indeed have much awareness of social trends and global issues. Accordingly, these courses have been reshaped in order to relate more closely to students' career goals, by focusing on the ethical dilemmas they will face in their everyday lives as computer professionals.

Many college and university computer science courses are now including – or would like to include – an ethics component, but this noble objective has been hampered by a lack of suitable teaching materials. *Computer Ethics* has therefore been designed with teaching purposes in mind in an effort to help rectify the shortage of texts. That is why we have included numerous up-to-date references, as well as scenarios, role-playing exercises and 'hypotheticals' in the suggestions for further discussion at the end of each chapter. The creative teacher should be able to build on these.

Readers will notice that we have not adopted an explicit theoretical framework and have avoided philosophical discussion of ethical theory. The reason is that this book is but a first step, with the simple aim of sensitizing undergraduate computer science students to ethical issues. Neither will readers find a detailed account of the legislative position around the world on the various topics discussed. This is because in each country the legal situation is often complex, confused and changing fast – and again this is not the purpose of the book.

Finally, a note on sources. First, we have to acknowledge an enormous debt to Peter G. Neumann, whose 'Risks to the public in computer systems' sections in *Software Engineering Notes*, the journal of the Association of Computing Machinery's Special Interest Group on Software (ACM-SIGSOFT) have provided inspiration, amusement and a vast amount of valuable information. Long may he continue. Second, we have to caution that many of these and other sources are newspaper and media reports, which, like computers, are not 100 per cent reliable.

Tom Forester and Perry Morrison

Computer Ethics

1 Introduction: Our Computerized Society

Some Problems Created for Society by Computers
– Ethical Dilemmas for Computer Professionals and
Users

Computers are the core technology of our times. They are the new paradigm, the new 'common sense'. In the comparatively short space of 40 years, computers have become central to the operations of industrial societies. Without computers and their associated communication systems, much of manufacturing industry, commerce, transport and distribution, government, the military, health services, education and research would grind to a halt. Computers are certainly the most important technology to have come along this century and the current technological revolution may in time exceed the Industrial Revolution in terms of social significance. Our dependence upon computer and communication systems will grow still further as we enter the next millennium. Yet as society becomes more dependent on computers, we also become more and more vulnerable to computer malfunctions and to computer misuse – that is, to malfunctioning hardware and software and to misuse by human beings.

Some Problems Created for Society by Computers

The problems with computers and communications technology – commonly referred to jointly as 'information technology' (IT) – can be viewed in terms of scope, pervasiveness and complexity. First, information technology enables enormous quantities of information to be stored, retrieved and transmitted at great speed on a scale not possible before. This is all very well, but it has serious implications for data security and personal privacy (as well as employment) because computers are basically insecure. Second, information technology is permeating almost every aspect of our lives, including many areas previously untouched by technology. But unlike other pervasive technologies such as electricity, television and the motor car, computers are on the whole less reliable and less predictable in their behaviour. Third, computer systems are often incredibly complex – so complex, in fact, that they are not always understood even by their creators. This often makes them completely unmanageable.

Unmanageable complexity can result in massive foul-ups or spectacular budget 'runaways': for example, Bank of America in 1988 had to abandon a $20 million computer system after spending five years and a further $60 million trying to make it work. Allstate Insurance has seen the cost of its new computer system rise from $8 million to a staggering $100 million and estimated completion delayed from 1987 to 1993. The Pentagon, the City of Richmond, the States of New Jersey and Oklahoma, Geophysical Systems Corp. and Blue Cross/Blue Shield of Wisconsin have all suffered major recent 'runaways'. Moreover, the problem seems to be getting worse: in 1988 the American Arbitration Association took on 190 computer disputes, most of which involved defective systems. The claims totalled $200 million – up from only $31 million in 1984.[1] Complexity can also result in disaster: no computer is 100 per cent guaranteed because it is virtually impossible to anticipate all sources of failure. Yet computers are regularly being used for all sorts of critical applications such as saving lives, flying aircraft, running nuclear power stations, transferring vast sums of money and controlling missile systems – and this can sometimes have tragic consequences.[2]

In fact, computers have figured one way or another in almost every famous system failure of recent times, from Three Mile Island, Chernobyl and the Challenger space shuttle disaster, to the Air New Zealand Antarctic crash and the downing of the Korean Air Lines flight 007, not to mention the sinking of *HMS Sheffield* in the Falklands' war and the shooting down of the Iranian airbus by the *USS Vincennes* over the Persian Gulf. Popular areas for computer malfunctions include telephone billing and telephone switching software, air traffic control systems, bank statements and bank teller machines, electronic funds transfer systems and motor vehicle licence databases, although industrial robots and police computers have contributed their fair share to the long list of foul-ups. Indeed, programming or design errors have resulted in the ozone hole at the South Pole remaining undetected for years, the failure of weather forecasters to predict Britain's Great Storm of October 1987 and the chaos in the 1986 Brazilian general election.[3] (Although computers have often taken the 'blame' on these occasions, the ultimate cause of failure in most cases is, in fact, human error.)

Every new technology creates new problems (as well as new benefits) for society and information technology is no exception. But digital computers have rendered society especially vulnerable to hardware and software malfunctions. Industrial robots go berserk while heart pacemakers and automatic garage door openers are rendered useless by 'electronic smog' emitted from point-of-sale terminals, personal computers and video games.[4] Automated teller machines (ATMs), pumps at gas stations and fast-food outlet terminals are closed down because of unforeseen software snafus. It is reported that British businesses suffer around 30 major mishaps a year, involving losses running into millions of pounds. These are malfunctions caused by machine or human error and do not include human misuse in the form of fraud and sabotage. The cost of failures in domestically produced software in the UK alone is conservatively estimated at US $900 million per year.[5] In 1988, Dr John Collyer, a computer expert at the UK Ministry of Defence's Royal Signals and Radar Establishment (RSRE) warned that faulty microchips would start killing people in a big way within the next four years, while in 1989 a British Computer Society committee reported that much software was now so complex that current skills in safety assessment were inadequate and therefore the safety of people could not be guaranteed.[6]

Computers and communications technologies in turn are vulnerable to fires, floods, earthquakes and power cuts, as well as attacks from outside hackers and sabotage from inside employees. For example, a major fire which occurred in the Setagaya telephone office in Tokyo on 16 November 1984 destroyed 3,000 data communication and 89,000 ordinary telephone circuits resulting in total direct and indirect business losses of 13 billion yen.[7] In November 1987, a saboteur entered telecommunications tunnels in Sydney, Australia, and carefully severed 24 cables which knocked out 35,000 telephone lines in 40 Sydney suburbs, bringing down hundreds of computers, ATMs and POS, telex and fax terminals with it. Some businesses were completely out of action for 48 hours as engineers battled to restore services at a cost of thousands of dollars. Had the saboteur not been working with an out-of-date plan, the whole of Australia's telecommunications system could have been blacked out.[8]

In Chicago in 1986, a disgruntled employee at *Encyclopaedia Britannica*, angry at having been laid-off, merely tapped into the encyclopaedia's data base and made a few alterations to the text being prepared for a new edition of the renowned work – like changing references to Jesus Christ to Allah and inserting the names of company executives in odd positions. As one executive commented, 'In the computer age, this is exactly what we have nightmares about.'[9] A year later, another saboteur shut down the entire National Association of Securities Dealers' automatic quotation service (NASDAQ) for 82 minutes, keeping 20 million shares from being traded. The saboteur in question was an adventurous squirrel, who had caused a short circuit in Trumbull, Connecticut, where NASDAQ's main computer is situated. Meanwhile over in Denmark, a strike by 600 computer personnel paralysed that country's government for four months in 1986, causing the ruling party to call an early general election.[10]

The very existence of computers – and their ability to malfunction or to be abused – has created a whole new range of social problems or issues with which we need urgently to grapple. These include:

- the unauthorized use of hardware
- the theft of software
- disputed rights to products
- the use of computers to commit fraud
- the phenomenon of hacking and data theft
- sabotage in the form of viruses
- responsibility for the reliability of output (there is no warranty on software)
- making false claims for computers and
- the degradation of work.

Some of these issues are entirely new – in other instances, computers have merely created new versions of 'old' moral issues such as right and wrong, honesty, loyalty, responsibility, confidentiality and fairness. However, it is these issues which we intend to highlight in succeeding pages of this book.

Ethical Dilemmas for Computer Professionals and Users

Because computing is a relatively new and open field, the computer profession as such has had neither the time nor the organizational capability to establish a binding set of moral rules or ethics. Older professions, like medicine and the law, have had literally centuries to formulate their codes of conduct. And there is another problem, too: computer usage, unlike the practice of medicine or the law, goes outside the profession. We are all computer users now, and we are all to some extent faced with the same ethical dilemmas and conflicts of loyalty. Many of these dilemmas – like whether or not to copy software – are new 'grey areas' for which there is little in the way of accepted rules or social conventions, let alone established case law.

The ethical questions faced by computer professionals and computer users are numerous, but they include:

- Is copying software really a form of stealing? What sort of intellectual property rights should software developers have?
- Are so-called 'victimless' crimes (against, e.g., banks) more acceptable than crimes with human victims? Should computer professionals be sued for lax computer security?
- Is hacking merely a bit of harmless fun or is it a crime equivalent to burglary, forgery and/or theft?[11] Or are hackers to be seen as guardians of our civil liberties?

- Should the creation of viruses be considered deliberate sabotage and be punished accordingly?
- Does information on individuals stored in a computer constitute an intolerable invasion of privacy? How much protection are individuals entitled to?
- Who is responsible for computer malfunctions or errors in computer programs? Should computer companies be made to provide a warranty on software?
- Is 'artificial intelligence' a realistic and a proper goal for computer science? Should we trust our lives to allegedly artificially intelligent 'expert' systems?
- Should we allow the workplace to be computerized if it de-skills the workforce and/or increases depersonalization, fatigue and boredom?
- Is it OK for computer professionals to make false claims about the capabilities of computers when selling systems or representing computers to the general public? Is it ethical for computer companies to 'lock-in' customers to their products?
- Should, indeed, computer professionals be bound by a Code of Conduct and if so, what should it include?

In partial answer to the last question, the current state of play in the United States, for example, is that the Association for Computing Machinery (ACM) has a code of professional conduct; the Institute of Electrical and Electronics Engineers has adopted a code of ethics; the Data Processing Management Association (DPMA) also has a code of ethics; and the International Federation for Information Processing (IFIP) is in the process of developing one based on an international survey of opinion in the computing community. The British Computer Society (BCS) agreed codes of practice and conduct in 1983, while the Australian Computer Society (ACS) adopted a code of ethics in 1987.[12] In 1989, European computer societies, under the auspices of the Dutch Computer Society, began a process designed to formulate a Europe-wide code of practice. But it is fairly true to say that few of these worthy statements have or will have much force behind them, given that membership of these organizations is in general not compulsory. Enforcement is therefore difficult to non-existent.

One problem in developing ethical guidelines for the computer profession is that it does not have the status of professions like medicine or the law. Deborah G. Johnson, who has written extensively on the subject of computer ethics, likens the status of computer professionals to that of engineers. Mostly, she says, they work as employees rather than in their own right. While they have esoteric knowledge, they typically have quite limited autonomy. They often work in teams rather than alone and on small segments of large projects. They are usually distant from the effects of their work and they do not have a single unifying and regulating professional organization. Like engineers, she says, they have four basic types of obligations:

1   obligations to society;
2   obligations to their employers;
3   obligations to their clients;
4   obligations to co-professionals and even professional organizations.

Conflicts can occur between every type of obligation (employer–client, employer–co-professionals, etc.), as well as within each category (e.g., between two different clients), but it is the conflict between computer professionals' obligations to their employer and their obligation to society that has received the most attention through the publicity given to 'whistleblowing' cases.[13]

Yet despite their lower social status, the use of information technology for storing vital financial, marketing, personnel, health, research and military information puts new forms of power in the hands of computer professionals, from the humble operator to the top systems developer. This power is not specifically sought, but nevertheless computer professionals do find themselves in positions of power over employers, clients, co-professionals and the general public – and it is power which can be easily abused by those without scruples or those who easily fall victim to temptation.

Employers can be held to ransom by disgruntled employees who have the ability to change passwords or insert software 'time bombs' or 'logic bombs' which can knock out entire systems on a given date. For example, a programmer with a Minneapolis company was charged with extortion after threatening to trigger a 'time bomb' in the firm's computer system unless he received $350 per week until he found another job; a controversial DC government financial analyst changed the password to the Treasurer's office computer and refused to tell his superiors because he disagreed with their policies; and an employee of an Ontario company planted a 'logic bomb' in the company's computer designed to erase the entire system on a certain date – he was unhappy about a delayed salary increase.[14]

Clients are at the mercy of systems designers who alone know how a system works, consultants whose services may not strictly be necessary and computer companies who can virtually write their own bills. Society as a whole is vulnerable to the actions of computer professionals because most of the general public do not understand the dangers or implications of projects under the professionals' command. Because information is money and information is power, the information technology revolution has placed computer professionals under severe temptation: whether or not to abuse this power of access to confidential and valuable information is one of the most important ethical dilemmas facing members of the new profession.

Computing educators therefore have a special responsibility to ensure that future generations of computer professionals are aware of the social problems caused by computers and are aware of the ethical conflicts they will face every day in their future roles as computer professionals. Tomorrow's graduates will also to some extent be considered 'experts' or spokespersons for the industry, interpreting computers to the wider world, and they will be creators of systems which will have major implications for organizations, the workplace and society in general.[15]

Computing educators should not merely be in the business of training technicians. They should be producing articulate information technologists – technologists endowed with communication skills, 'people skills' and possessing an appreciation of the social and ethical implications of information technology. They must prepare people for the messy real world, not the tidy, imaginary one inside a VDT screen.[16] They therefore have a duty to stimulate discussion about these issues and to generate awareness of the choices available to us. This book is a contribution to that task.

Notes

1 *Los Angeles Times*, 7 February 1988, p. 1 and *Los Angeles Times*, 29 June 1988 (from the ACM SIGSOFT's *Software Engineering Notes*, vol. 13, no. 3, July 1988, p. 4); articles by Jeffrey Rothfeder in *Business Week*, 7 November 1988 and 3 April 1989.

2 Peter Mellor, 'Can you count on computers?' *New Scientist*, 11 February 1989; David Bellin and Gary Chapman (eds), *Computers in Battle – Will They Work?* (Harcourt Brace Jovanovich, Boston, MA, 1987); Charles Perrow, *Normal Accidents: Living With High-Risk Technology* (Basic Books, New York, 1984).

3 *The New York Times*, 29 July 1986, p. C 1; *Computer News* (UK), 22 October 1987 and *New Scientist*, 3 March 1988; *Daily Telegraph*, 3 November 1986.

4 See, for example, Barry Fox, 'Electronic smog fouls the ether', *New Scientist*, 7 April 1988. For a more general discussion of vulnerability, see Jan Holvast, 'Vulnerability of information society', in Roger Clarke and Julie Cameron (eds), *Proceedings of SOST '89* (Australian Computer Society, Sydney, Australia, 1989).

5 *The Guardian*, 10 November 1986; Roger Woolnough, 'Britain scrutinizes software quality', *Electronics Engineering Times*, 13 June 1988.

6 *The Australian*, 2 February 1988 (reprinted from *The Times*); and *The Australian*, 21 February 1989.

7 Barry Fox, 'Corrupt power corrupts computer data', *New Scientist*, 29 October 1987; Katherine M. Hafner et al., 'Is your computer secure?' *Business Week*, 1 August 1988; Naruko Takanashi, Atsushi Tanaka, Hiroaki Yoshii and Yuji Wada, 'The Achilles' Heel of the information society: socioeconomic impacts of the telecommunication cable fire in the Setagaya Telephone Office, Tokyo', *Technological Forecasting and Social Change*, vol. 34, 1988, pp. 27–52.

8 'Saboteur tries to blank out Oz', *The Australian*, 23 November 1987, p. 1.
9 'Laid-off worker sabotages encyclopedia', *San Jose Mercury News*, 5 September 1986 (from *Software Engineering Notes*, vol. 11, no. 5, October 1986, p. 28).
10 'Stray rodent halts NASDAQ computers', *New York Times*, 10 December 1987, p. 33 and 'Computer strike forces Denmark poll', *The Australian*, August 20 1987 (from a UPI report).
11 In a recent court case in Britain, a 22 year-old hacker claimed that he had penetrated British Telecom's *Prestel* information system 'in order to make it more secure'. The prosecuting counsel replied: 'It's a bit like a burglar claiming all the credit for improved house security because the householder has put locks on the windows.' He claimed that the hacker was also guilty of forgery because he had used someone else's computer identification, which was 'equivalent to signing someone else's name without their consent' (*The Times*, London, 16 April 1986).
12 See Hal Sackman, 'Toward an IFIP code of ethics based on participative international consensus', in Roger Clarke and Julie Cameron (eds), *Proceedings of SOST '89*. For details of the BCS, DPMA, ACM and IEEE codes of ethics, see Deborah G. Johnson and John W. Snapper (eds), *Ethical Issues in the Use of Computers* (Wadsworth, Belmont, CA, 1985). For the others, contact the organizations concerned – indeed, this is advisable in all cases if up-to-date versions are required.
13 Unpublished paper by Deborah G. Johnson, 'The social responsibility of computer professionals', Department of Science and Technology Studies, Rensselaer Polytechnic Institute, Troy, NY, September 1988. See also a philosophical discussion of ethical theory in relation to computing in Deborah G. Johnson, *Computer Ethics* (Prentice-Hall, Englewood Cliffs, NJ, 1985); also Donn B. Parker, *Ethical Conflicts in Computer Science and Technology* (AFIPS Press/SRI International, Menlo Park, CA, 1981) and Donn B. Parker, Susan Swope and Bruce N. Baker, *Ethical Conflicts in Information and Computer Science, Technology and Business*, a report prepared for the National Science Foundation, Washington, DC, 1988); and W. Michael Hoffman and Jennifer Mills Moore (eds), *Ethics and the Management of Computer Technology* (Oelgeschlager, Gunn and Hain, Cambridge, MA, 1982).
14 *Minneapolis Star and Tribune*, 23 May 1985; *Washington Post*, 9 February 1986; *Globe and Mail*, Toronto, 3 November 1987.
15 For pleas along these lines, see Marcia Ascher, Ithaca College, Ithaca, NY, 'Ethical conflicts in the computing field: an undergraduate course', *Computers and Society*, vol. 16, no. 1, 1986; J. J. Buck BloomBecker, 'Computer ethics: an antidote to despair', *Computers and Society*, vol. 16, no. 4, 1986; Thomas J. De Loughry, 'Failure of colleges to teach computer ethics is called oversight with potentially catastrophic consequences', *The Chronicle of Higher Education*, 24 February 1988, p. A15; Delmar E. Searls, Asbury College, Wilmore, KY, 'Teaching computer ethics', *SIGCSE Bulletin*, vol. 20, no. 3, September 1988; and J. Daniel Couger, 'Preparing IS students to deal with ethical issues', *MIS Quarterly*, June 1989.
16 VDT (Visual Display Terminal) is used throughout this book rather than the UK expression VDU (Visual Display Unit) because it is the more common term in the rest of the world.

2 Computer Crime

The Rise of the High-Tech Heist – Is Reported Crime
the Tip of an Iceberg? – Targets of the Computer
Criminal – Who are the Computer Criminals? –
Improving Computer Security – Suggestions for
Further Discussion.

On Christmas Eve, 1987, a 26 year-old clerk at Lloyds Bank in Amsterdam, Frans Noe, ordered that sums of $8.4 million and $6.7 million be transferred via the SWIFT international funds transfer system from the Lloyds branch in New York to an account he had opened with the Swiss Bank Corporation in Zurich. The young Dutchman then flew to Switzerland to collect the money. But owing to an unforeseen computer malfunction, the transfer of the $6.7 million failed to go through. Returning after Christmas, fellow employees saw the failed transaction on their screens and reported it. Noe was subsequently arrested and returned to Amsterdam, where he then threatened to leak news of his security breach to the press unless the bank dropped all charges against him. In May 1988 the 'flying' Dutchman was jailed for 18 months for breaking into a computer system and his two accomplices got 12 months each.[1]

The Rise of the High-Tech Heist

Computers have created opportunities for crime that never existed before. History shows that the growth of crime is strongly related to opportunity and changes in technology generate both new types of crime and new techniques of detection.[2] Consequently both criminals and crime-busters compete to stay one jump ahead of each other. The invention of the computer – and more recently the rapid spread of personal computers and 'distributed processing' – has provided ample opportunity for new kinds of crime. The huge increase in the number of people with computer skills also means that there are many more potential computer criminals. In fact, the new technology is, in a sense, democratizing white-collar crime, because it enables even the humblest programmer, operator or clerk (like Frans Noe) to participate in sophisticated frauds that were once pretty much the preserve of top management. In his book, *Technocrimes: the Computerization*

9

of Crime and Terrorism (1987), August Bequai even argues that organized crime and the Mafia are using computers for record-keeping, not to mention extortion, blackmail and sabotage – and that the very future of Western society is now threatened by computerized crime and high-tech terrorism.[3]

The arrival of automated teller machines (ATMs) provides a good example of how a new technological device creates new opportunities for fraudulent activity. The number of ATMs in the USA grew from 4,000 to over 50,000 between 1975 and 1985.[4] The value of transactions is believed to have grown about ten-fold and with it ATM fraud has correspondingly mushroomed into a major growth industry. Plastic card abuse of all kinds has grown in parallel: in 1985, for instance, cheque card fraud alone cost UK banks £26 million. Foreign currency and other financial frauds have also grown in parallel with the rapid growth of electronic funds transfer (EFT) systems, while the widespread use of information systems in manufacturing and distribution has made possible the illegal diversion of goods on a scale not possible before.

Still more opportunities for high-tech high jinks have been provided by an even newer technology, cellular mobile telephones: in March 1987, 18 New Yorkers were arrested on charges of illegally reprogramming memory chips in their mobile phones in order to make calls without being charged for them. The fraud had cost the local mobile phone company about $40,000 per month. It was the first time anyone in the world had been arrested for this type of offence. Commenting on the case, Laurence A. Urgenson, the chief assistant US attorney for the Eastern District of New York, said: 'Every new technology carries with it an opportunity to invent a new crime.'[5] In the same year, US Sprint, one of AT&T's new competitors in the long-distance phone market, unmasked another new type of fraud in which a group of hackers had used computers to identify and steal US Sprint authorization codes. The codes had then been sold to a large number of individuals and companies who, between them, had allegedly helped themselves to over $20 million worth of long-distance calls.[6]

Computer crime has been defined broadly as a criminal act that has been committed using a computer as the principal tool. Some have also talked in terms of a distinction between 'computer-related' fraud (in which the computer is purely coincidental) and 'computer-assisted' fraud (in which the computer is used to commit the fraud), while others have argued that a genuine computer fraud is one which could not take place *without* the use of a computer. If we accept this 'tight' definition, then the real computer fraud needs computer expertise and greater skills to perpetrate than do the computer-assisted and computer-related frauds. But when most people talk about computer crime, they are usually referring to the fact that a computer has either been the object, subject or instrument of a crime.[7]

Computer crime can take the form of the *theft of money* (for example, the transfer of payments to the wrong accounts), the *theft of information* (for example, by tapping into data transmission lines or databases at no cost), or the *theft of goods* (by their diversion to the wrong destination). Two techniques of computer theft are *The Salami*, which involves spreading the haul over a large number of transactions like slices of salami (for example, a bank clerk might shave a trivial sum off many customer accounts to make up a large sum in his or her own account) and *The Trojan Horse*, which involves the insertion of false information into a program in order to profit from the outcome (for example, a false instruction to make payments to a bogus company). Theft is undoubtedly the most common form of computer crime: of the 191 cases reported to the Australian Computer Abuse Research Bureau (ACARB), for example, 111 involved theft of some kind.[8]

Computer crime can take the form of *unauthorized use* or access to information systems or the modification of programs to benefit the fraudster. Techniques include *Piggybacking*, which involves tapping into communication lines and riding into a system behind a legitimate user with a password and *Data Diddling*, which entails swapping one piece of data for another. Computer crime can also take the form of *hacking, sabotage* and *blackmail*. Hacking or computer burgling involves breaking in to other people's systems for fun or with intent to blackmail or commit sabotage. Techniques include *Scavenging* for stray data or 'garbage' for clues that might unlock the secrets of a system; *Zapping*, which means penetrating a computer by unlocking the master key to its program and then destroying it by activating its own emergency program; *Worms* or worm programs entail the deletion of portions of a computer's memory, thus creating a hole of missing information; and *Time Bombs* or *Logic Bombs*, which involve the insertion of routines which can be triggered later by the computer's clock or a combination of events. When the 'bomb' goes off, the entire system – perhaps worth millions – will crash; *Viruses* are self-replicating programs which can have a similar effect (see chapter 4).

Computer crime should not present an ethical dilemma for computer professionals or computer users. Theft is theft and fraud is fraud and both are generally accepted by our society to be morally wrong. Criminal activity is not a new problem. But what is new is that the widespread use of information systems has placed great temptation in the hands of ordinary programmers and systems developers, who are often, among other things, the only people who know how a particular system works. For a minority of computer professionals, it is a temptation and an opportunity which is hard to resist – especially if they see a systematic way to 'cover-up' their crime which makes detection of their crime difficult or impossible. Computers have also had the effect of further *depersonalizing* crime: in explaining their illegal activities, some guilty computer professionals have talked about so-called 'victimless' crimes (for example, against large corporations or banks) as being somehow more acceptable than crimes with human victims. But this is hardly a justification.

Is Reported Crime the Tip of an Iceberg?

The true extent of computer crime is not known, can't be known and never will be known. The American Bar Association (ABA), in a major report published in 1984, concluded that losses arising from computer crime sustained by US business and government institutions were 'by any measure, huge'. Their survey of 300 top US corporations suggested that annual losses in each company could range from $2 million to as high as $10 million. 'If the annual losses attributed to computer crime sustained by this relatively small survey group are conservatively estimated in the range of half a billion dollars, then it takes little imagination to realize the magnitude of the annual losses sustained on a nationwide basis', said the report.[9] More recently, the Cleveland accounting firm Ernst and Whinney estimated that the losses sustained by US companies in total amount to between $3 billion and $5 billion a year. Of the 240 companies surveyed, more than half admitted that they had been a victim of computer fraud.[10]

In the UK, an Audit Commission survey of 1,200 organizations, published in 1988, found that reported computer crimes had risen in value from around £1 million in 1981 to around £3 million in 1987. Nine out of ten respondents believed that they had not suffered from computer fraud. Yet a large number of the 118 frauds detected were only discovered by accident. Only 38 of the 118 cases resulted in prosecutions. Meanwhile a 1986 survey of 50 British companies by insurance brokers Hogg Robinson led them to estimate that frauds involving computers were costing UK firms £40 million a year and others have suggested that total UK losses are a lot higher. In France, an association of French insurance companies estimated that problems with computer systems were costing French firms about $1.1 billion a year, and 44 per cent of this was accounted for by fraudsters, hackers and disgruntled employees (the rest were caused by accidents, such as fire, malfunctions and human error).[11]

Are these estimates correct or do they merely represent the tip of an iceberg? Or is there *no* iceberg of undetected computer crime lurking below the surface of society? There are two main reasons why many experts believe that the amount of computer crime is much greater than we think. First, it is clear that many crimes go completely undetected because so many are discovered by accident and because so many are, by their very nature, simply very hard to detect. An official guide produced for US Federal Agencies in 1986 stated that detected computer crimes are less than 1 per cent of the total. Second, very few computer frauds are made public because companieś – especially banks and other financial institutions – are loath to admit that their security systems are fallible. Publicity of this nature is disastrous for public relations and it could lead to the loss of customer confidence, so they prefer to cover things up.

Of those crimes that *are* detected only a small percentage arrive in court: for example, a 1986 survey by the Los Angeles-based National Center for Computer Crime Data found that fewer than 100 cases of computer fraud in the USA had actually been prosecuted in the preceding two years. IBM security analyst Robert Courtney told the US Office of Technology Assessment (OTA) in 1985 that of the 1,406 computer crime cases known to him, 89 per cent were never taken to judicial process and convictions were obtained in only 18 per cent of the remainder.[12] Hugo Cornwall, in his book, *Datatheft* (1987), lists some reasons why non-reporting of computer crime is so widespread: '. . . there is very little benefit to the victim. The law is unlikely to be able to undo the damage caused, the criminal is unlikely to be convicted, much staff time is likely to be tied up assembling evidence (if it can be collected at all), and wider knowledge of the crime is likely to harm the future prospects of the victim organization.'[13]

What is therefore clear is that nobody is very sure about the true extent of computer crime – but most analysts who have looked at the problem seem to think it is large and growing. Even if the percentage of installations affected may be small, the sum involved in the 'average' computer crime is probably much larger than in conventional robberies – according to the FBI, for instance, the average computer crime is worth about $600,000. As to the future, the American Bar Association report concluded: 'It would seem beyond dispute that computer crime is today a large and significant problem with enormous potential for becoming even larger and more significant', while Hugo Cornwall writes: 'Datacrime deserves to be as much a social issue as more traditional areas of "law and order" such as crimes against the person, crimes against property and the maintenance of public peace.'[14]

Targets of the Computer Criminal

Banks and financial companies are major targets for high-tech criminals. Banks are vulnerable to frauds committed by insider employees and to frauds committed by outsiders playing 'vault invaders'. Of the computer crimes detected in a British survey by BIS Applied Systems, 37 per cent were in the financial sector, while over 50 per cent of the crimes measured by value reported to the Australian Computer Abuse Research Bureau were in banking and finance.[15]

The increased reliance of the financial sector on electronic funds transfer (EFT) systems – it is said that over $200 billion changes hands daily in the New York banks' automated payments system – has greatly increased the opportunities for crime. If the electronic authorization codes used in EFT fall into the wrong hands, huge sums of money can be moved about – including out of the country – in a matter of seconds. For example, in a famous case in 1979, Stanley Mark Rifkin, a computer consultant to the Security Pacific National Bank, visited the bank's wire transfer room where he learned the EFT codes. Later, posing as a branch manager, he phoned the Los Angeles bank and used the codes to transfer money, in amounts of less than $1 million, to a New York bank. Then he instructed the New York bank to send the money – by now totalling $10.2 million – across to a Swiss bank account. Having flown to Switzerland, he converted the money into diamonds and then returned to the USA. It was only when he boasted openly of his feat that he was caught and convicted.

What is probably the largest-ever computer crime in history involved a foreign exchange contract fraud. In 1987, it became apparent that the Volkswagen company in West Germany had lost around $260 million in a fraud which took place in 1984. Very little is known about the fraud, except that it entailed tampering with programs and the erasure of tapes. It is also known that VW sacked the head of its foreign exchange department and suspended four others, along with the heads of the financial transfer department and the cash and currency clearing sections.

Some of the biggest frauds ever attempted have involved EFT and banks. In early 1988, a huge sum (variously reported to be between $33 and $54 million) was illegally transferred from the Union Bank of Switzerland branch in London to a private bank account in the small Swiss town of Nyon, near Lausanne. The stunt would have succeeded except for a computer glitch at the Swiss end which forced the bank that day to make manual checks of payment instructions that normally would have been processed automatically. Suspicions were aroused and the Swiss police were waiting to pounce on the man who arrived to collect the cash. Further arrests followed.[16] A similar attempt in 1986 to transfer by EFT the sum of $8.5 million from the London branch of the US investment bank, Prudential-Bache Securities, to another Swiss bank account was foiled after the bank hastily obtained a court injunction in Switzerland to stop the money being paid out. In September 1987, two men admitted conspiracy to defraud in a London court and were sentenced to three years and 18 months respectively. While in May 1988 seven men were arrested in New York after an attempt to embezzle $70 million by creating phony transactions transferring money out of First National Bank of Chicago accounts of Merrill Lynch, United Airlines and Brown-Forman. The amounts exceeded the threshold of permissible transactions, but the perpetrators had been able to control the telephone response that requested authorization. The transaction was detected when the Merrill Lynch account became overdrawn.[17]

Speaking at a British Computer Society Security Committee seminar, Detective-Inspector John Austen of the Computer Crime Unit at New Scotland Yard, London, highlighted the threat to EFT systems from both criminals and terrorists: 'EFT now represents 83 per cent of the value of all things paid for – money transferred – in Britain. Money, as an invisible export, is a major part of our GNP. Foreign exchange markets in London transfer $200 billion daily using EFT via satellite. The transactions take a very short time, and once complete there is no calling them back. A lot of people are aware of this. And many, both here and abroad, are prepared to steal from EFT systems. The rewards are tremendous. Companies, and even the economies of smaller countries, could be crippled by a sustained hit on EFT systems. Terrorists, such as the Middle East factions, the IRA and the Red Army Faction are particularly aware of this – and they need money. The Red Army Faction has already, unsuccessfully, made moves to intercept EFT in Germany. They and others will try again.' [18]

ATM fraud has also become increasingly common in recent years. In 1987, for example, a 35 year-old former ATM repairman, Robert Post, was apprehended after illegally obtaining $86,000 out of New York City ATMs. He'd spy over customers' shoulders to get their PINs (Personal Identification Numbers) and whenever someone left their receipt, he'd take it and discover their account number. Then he'd go home, forge a card using a $1,800 machine he'd bought, and return to the ATM and make withdrawals. He was caught because his encoding of the account number and the PIN, while good enough to work in the machine, was flawed. Manufacturers Hanover managed to program its network to detect the flawed cards and capture them. After capturing two and verifying that they were fake, they reprogrammed the machine to notify security when one was being used, and dispatched guards to catch Mr Post. Interestingly, when questioned about his crime, Post said he was not like someone who mugs a customer and steals a card: 'I'm a white-collar criminal,' he proclaimed, adding that he was surprised that the bank had not offered him a consulting job![19]

In the UK, City of London police in 1987 arrested four suspected ATM fraudsters after finding no less than 1,864 cash cards in their possession.

Their arrest followed a denial by the major high street banks that their ATMs posed a security risk after TV viewers had seen a cash card fraud demonstrated on national television. In the US in 1988, someone successfully used a Security Pacific National Bank master card to steal $237,000 from 300 customer accounts and a plot to defraud Bank of America and other banks on the Plus System of ATMs out of $14 million over one weekend was only foiled at the last minute by an insider tip-off. Police found 7,000 counterfeit ATM cards in the possession of computer programmer Mark Koenig and four accomplices. Meanwhile from New Zealand came the astonishing tale of a schoolboy called Simon who outsmarted a United Building Society ATM by using cardboard from a lollipop packet to transfer NZ $1 million into his account. All the 14-year-old did was to slip the cardboard into a deposit envelope and insert it into the machine, while punching up $1 million. When Simon checked his account a few days later, he was amazed to find that the $1 million had been credited. So he withdrew $10. When no alarms went off or police appeared, he withdrew another $500, but suddenly got cold feet and put it back again. A few days later, Simon withdrew $1,500 but his nerve failed again and he told one of his teachers, who took him along to the United Building Society for a chat with the manager. His headmaster commented that Simon had not been considered one of the brightest pupils . . . 'at least until now.'[20]

But it's not just banks that are the target of computer criminals. Computer thieves have also been attracted to insurance companies, where there is scope for manipulating computers to pay out on fictitious claims and to grant bogus premium refunds. One of the largest computer crimes ever discovered involved an insurance company – only this time it was the employers rather than employees who were responsible: from 1965 to 1971, Equity Funding Inc. used its computers to generate thousands of phony insurance policies that were later sold to reinsurance companies for a total of over $27 million.[21] In a more recent case of systematic fraud by a company, Hertz Corp. allegedly overcharged customers who damaged rental cars and were liable for repair charges. Hertz's computers were apparently programmed to generate two estimates – one for the actual repairs at discount rates and one with the higher price which was sent to customers and insurers. According to the story, Hertz had already issued refunds of about $3 million and it is estimated that they may have collected $13 million through these questionable practices. In 1989, Continental Can was accused of using a secret computer program to determine which employees should be fired before they had worked long enough to be eligible for pension benefits.[22]

Brokerage houses and government departments are not immune to computer-based financial fraud. In 1986 a New York brokerage house decided to speed up the operation of its IBM system at peak hours by switching-off the applications-level software that recorded information for the audit trail of each transaction. Knowing this, a crafty clerk selflessly volunteered for overtime, during which he sold the stock holdings of many customers and credited the money to 22 phony bank accounts he had set up. The money subsequently made its way to Switzerland and the clerk disappeared without trace. To this day, the company has no clear idea of who has lost what and has appealed to customers to come forward and provide details of their losses, but one report puts the total cost of the scam at $28.8 million.[23] In a recent case in California, four employees of the Defense Contract Administration Services Region (DCASR) office in El Segundo were accused of having rigged the DCASR computer to issue a cheque for $9.5 million to one of them individually as payment for a legitimate invoice from a legitimate contractor. A bank officer became suspicious when the person trying to deposit the check wanted $600,000 in cash on the spot, and called in the police.[24]

Computers are being used to steal goods by altering inventories and re-directing items, which can then be sold for cash. Computer records can be doctored to make it seem that goods have been damaged and disposed of, shipped to a customer but returned, or have simply gone missing. For example, an 18 year-old college student, Jerry Schneider, posed as a magazine reporter doing a story on Pacific Telephone's parts-distribution system. In this way, Schneider learned that requests for parts came in via touch-tone phones and were delivered to any location. With a foolproof method for convincing the company's computer that his instructions were legitimate internal orders for parts, Schneider collected enormous quantities of parts at specific pick-up points, which he then sold through his new company, Creative Telephone. By the time Schneider was turned in by a Creative employee, over $1 million worth of phone equipment had gone missing from Pacific Telephone.[25]

Theft of information stored in computers is another growth industry. In a famous case some years ago, three computer operators attempted to sell *Encyclopaedia Britannica*'s list of 2 million customers to a direct mail company, while in 1984 the Waterford Glass Company in Ireland had 25 computer discs stolen which held unique instructions for their glass-cutting machines. These probably made their way to counterfeiting factories in the Far East.[26] Many a computer professional has been induced to part with commercial information which has value to a competitor company. Computerized mailing lists or lists of potential or actual customers can change hands for considerable sums of money. Some are acquired legitimately, some are not. In fact, 'database marketing' is a rapidly expanding area – and it explains why consumers who have purchased a product or service from company A are then deluged with mail shots not only from company A, but also from companies X, Y and Z. This explains why the volume of junk mail has grown enormously, particularly to well-off customers or residents of well-off areas, and why postal services are once again becoming profitable – despite the predictions about 'paperless' electronic mail replacing conventional surface mail.

Changing the information stored is an equally serious form of computer abuse. Recent cases have included the New York college students who paid other students doing vacation work for the college to change the grades on their college records and the alleged alteration of driving licence records at Britain's national Driver and Vehicle Licensing Centre (DVLC) in Swansea, South Wales, so as to erase traffic violations and other offences. This licence 'cleaning' service was allegedly on sale in London pubs and clubs.

There have also been cases of the deliberate destruction of information stored on computer as a form of commercial or even political sabotage. For example, in 1986 someone entered the Capitol Hill computer systems of two Republican congressmen, Ed Zschau of California and John McCain of Arizona, and destroyed records of letters sent to constituents and mailing lists. One break-in took place over the lunch hour, the other late at night. The police were called in and they recommended better controls in future. But Ed Zschau said: 'The entering of my computer was tantamount to someone breaking in to my office, taking my files and burning them . . . the police would be more concerned if this were a physical break-in. Because people don't see the files overturned or a pile of ashes outside the door, it doesn't seem as bad . . . But it is equally devastating.'[27]

Who are the Computer Criminals?

The theft of computer time, usually in the form of the unauthorized use of an employer's computer, is another grey area in which there are no easy answers. Unauthorized use is technically 'theft' of processing and storage power, yet most employers turn a blind eye to employees using the company's computers in moderation for such purposes as preparing individual tax returns or biorhythm charts or doing the mailing list for the local church. Unauthorized use rarely leads to prosecutions, but at some point such activity could be deemed excessive and therefore improper. Using company computers for financial gain such as private consulting work is clearly unethical, unless the employee's employment contract (for example, with a university) specifically allows for it. Sackings for this kind of computer abuse are not unheard of, although managers have to tread warily for fear of destroying staff morale.

The thorny problem of unauthorized use demonstrates how new possibilities opened up by new technologies can lead otherwise honest and loyal employees down the slippery slope to more serious misconduct and perhaps outright criminal behaviour. Indeed, from the studies that have been done by US computer crime specialists such as Donn Parker and Jay BloomBecker, a picture has emerged of the 'typical' computer criminal as being a loyal, trusted employee, not necessarily possessing great computer expertise, who has been tempted, for instance, by the discovery of flaws in a computer system or loopholes in the controls monitoring his or her activity. Like most fraud, it is the opportunity more than anything else that seems to generate this kind of aberrant behaviour.

In a review of the major British studies of computer crime, Keith Hearnden found that the vast majority (80 per cent) of crimes involving computers were carried out by employees rather than outsiders. While 25 per cent of all crimes were carried out by managers or supervisers-and 24 per cent by computer staff, a surprising 31 per cent were committed by lowly clerks and cashiers who had little in the way of technical skills. Moreover, nearly all computer criminals were first-time offenders who were motivated, says Hearnden, by greed, pressing financial worries and other personal problems such as alcohol or drug dependency. Love and sex can also provide a powerful stimulus: in one case, a 23 year-old male bank clerk became infatuated with a 32 year-old woman. In trying to impress her with expensive gifts, travel and good living, he spent his way through £23,000 stolen from four bank accounts, covering the theft by transferring cash through a computer from seventeen other accounts. He then lost £10,000 in casinos, trying to repay the money. By the time he was finally caught, the woman had deserted him![28]

There is a commonly held view that the typical computer criminal is something of a whiz-kid, with highly developed computing skills and a compulsive desire to beat the system. But Hearnden shows that the substance for this image is absent: 'Not many crimes . . . demonstrate high technical ingenuity on the part of the perpetrator. Most exhibit an opportunistic exploitation of an inherent weakness in the computer system being used.' Ball states that most computer criminals '. . . tend to be relatively honest and in a position of trust; few would do anything to harm another human, and most do not consider their crime to be truly dishonest.' While Cornwall says we must understand the process by which 'nice suburban people with jobs that give them access to sensitive information, systems and data are able to justify to themselves and their friends the committing of certain types of criminal act.'[29]

Jay BloomBecker has listed eight motivations that can lie behind computer crimes. Some computer criminals, he says, think of crime as a game and see the computer environment as a kind of 'playpen' for their own enjoyment. Others see computer systems as a 'land of opportunity' where crime is easy, or a 'cookie jar' which will readily solve pressing financial or personal problems. Some see computer and/or communication systems as a kind of 'soapbox' for political expression, while others see them as a 'fairyland' of unreality; a 'toolbox' for tackling new crimes or modernizing traditional crimes; or a 'magic wand' that can be made to do anything. Finally, crimes involving sabotage are often based on a view that the computer environment is a 'battle zone' between management and alienated employees.[30] This latter perspective has found backing in a recent US survey which found, for instance, that 63 per cent of accountants and 75 per cent of computer professionals believed that employees steal because 'They feel frustrated or dissatisfied about some aspect of their job.'[31] This could be an accurate reflection of the lack of autonomy, minimal job variety and poor management communications often endemic in computer work.

Others have surmised that the intellectual challenge of fooling a system plays an important role in motivating individuals to commit computer crimes, while still others have emphasized that computer crimes involve very little physical risk (unlike, for example, a bank hold-up); that computer crimes can be committed alone, without talkative associates, thus further reducing the risk of detection; and that (as in BloomBecker's 'fairyland') computer crimes can often appear not to be a criminal act – shuffling numbers around in a remote and abstract way is not quite the same as handling gold bars or huge piles of paper money.[32]

Improving Computer Security

The growth of computer crime calls for new kinds of security measures, measures which can be costly and can involve the use of computers. But improved security often lags behind the discovery of new crimes – computer security experts are forever trying to shut the stable door after the horse has bolted. Many companies are still extremely lax about computer security, often believing that computer frauds could never happen to them. Market researchers Computer Intelligence estimate that a mere 10 per cent of IBM mainframes had data security software in 1982 and this figure had only grown to 35 per cent by late 1988.[33] Yet vulnerability to computer break-ins has increased because the operations of so many companies – especially in the service sector – are now entirely dependent on computers. A good illustration of poor security is provided by the recent case of Herbert Zinn, a 17 year-old Chicago high school student who broke into AT&T's computer systems using a personal computer in his bedroom. Some reports say he say he copied software worth $1 million, including material on AT&T computers at military bases. AT&T spokespersons blamed the lapse on employees who had not followed proper security procedures, rather than their security system.[34]

'The problem with computer security is that everyone talks about it but not enough people do anything about it,' says one New York analyst. Bank security and industrial security are well understood – it is comparatively easy to stop cash or materials going out of the door – but the need for computer security is less well appreciated and the task of protecting information is much more difficult. A 1988 study by the accountants Coopers and Lybrand, for example, found that only one out of a sample of 20 top European companies was 'adequately secure.' Most computer security experts lay the blame for poor security squarely at the door of top management. Often they don't understand their computer systems, they can't be bothered, they don't wish to restrict ease of use, or they don't appreciate what their information is worth. But there are signs that the whole issue is now being taken more seriously: in 1987, for instance, the leading British banks and building societies launched a major review of their security measures.

Computer security can be greatly improved by the adoption of relatively simple, common-sense measures. Passwords allowing access to systems, for instance, can be made less obvious and memorable by avoiding such passwords as partners' names. Passwords should be issued only to the absolute minimum of people requiring access. A 1986 survey by British insurance broker Hogg Robinson found that the words chosen for passwords were mostly useless and very easy for colleagues to guess. Top of the list in Britain was 'Fred', followed by 'God', 'Pass' and 'Genius', while many chose the names of their spouses or family pets. (In America, apparently, the favourite password is 'Love', closely followed by 'Sex' – indicative of an obsession which is absent in the British ratings.)[35]

A growing market is now developing for access-control software that closes password loopholes. This software restricts users – individually identified by passwords and codes – to only those files they are authorized to use. Even then, the software permits the users to perform only authorized functions, such as adding or deleting information, and they can no longer browse through parts of the system which they are not entitled to enter. One obvious and major limitation with access-control software, however, is that it does not protect a company against frauds committed by employees while going about their legitimate tasks – and as we have seen, a high proportion of computer crimes occur in this way.

Many companies are installing dial-back or black-box systems to protect their assets. When a user calls into a computer, a black box intercepts the call and asks for a password. The unit then disconnects the call, looks up the password in the directory and calls the user back at his or her listed telephone number: fraudsters calling from another number will be screened out. A large mainframe may have hundreds of 'ports' of entry from remote stations and each one has to be protected by these dial-back systems which can cost many hundreds of dollars.

Scrambling devices and encryption software are additional, expensive items which scramble messages for transmission so that only the legitimate recipient can understand them. Anyone tapping into, say, a bank's communication line or eavesdropping on the electromagnetic waves emitted from a computer or piece of electronic equipment will pick up only a jumbled list of zeros and ones. Encryption devices in the form of DSPs (Digital Signal Processors) are being used increasingly to scramble voice and data messages over telephone networks. Voice encryption is obviously vital in the military and in security agencies. However, even the best encryption codes can be broken – and so the codes have to be changed frequently – like every hour, for example. This is what the Pentagon sometimes does with very sensitive information. It is also spending $200 million under its 'Tempest' program to eliminate or muffle electromagnetic signals from machines used by the military, security agencies and defence contractors.

Audit control software packages are also available which can monitor transactions or the use of a computer. These enable auditors to trace and identify any operator who gains access to the system and when this occurred, such as after-hours. Audits can also highlight an abnormal number of correction entries, which often indicates the trial-and-error approach of fraudulent activity. But a major problem is that the demand for auditors with computer skills is high, and there are not enough who are capable of outsmarting crooked computer personnel.

Computers are also being used increasingly in the fight *against* crime, both conventional crime and computer-based crime. A British company has developed software which enables a computer to browse through vast amounts of financial data looking for possible connections which might indicate insider trading or foreign exchange fraud. A similar system is at work on the New York Stock Exchange. A British firm of management consultants used computers to search for illegal multiple share applications made during the UK government's privatization programme. And an Australian insurance company has developed a system which searches through its claims files attempting to associate random items of information about the company's customers. It is credited with unmasking scores of fraudulent injury claims.[36] The vast amounts of so called 'transactional' information – records of phone calls, air travel, credit card purchases etc. – stored on computers are providing a fertile field for crime-busters. One spectacular recent example was the discovery that all the messages passed between Colonel Oliver North and his collaborators in the illegal sale of arms to Iran and the illegal transmission of aid to the Contras in Nicaragua were faithfully recorded on a local area network they used called PROFS (IBM's Professional Office Systems Network). So much for 'covert' action.

Another weapon in the fight against crime is 'biometrics', or the digitizing of biological characteristics. These include not only fingerprints, but also voices, the veins of the back of the hand and the pattern of blood vessels in the retina. Police forces all over the world are now using computerized fingerprint identification systems which have a remarkable record of cracking hitherto unsolved cases, while fingerprint scanning devices are now being used to control access to computer rooms, to bank vaults and to military bases. An Oregon company is marketing a retinal scanner rather like the one used in the James Bond film 'Never Say Never Again'.

Some argue that improving computer security is a management problem rather than a technical problem. Careful vetting of employees in the first place can be a great help. Then sensible security procedures, starting with rules for password usage and including sophisticated access-control systems, should be formulated and rigidly enforced. Obviously the latest technology should be used where possible, but it is no guarantee of total security. Ultimately the best security might be to manage employees effectively, because in the final analysis even the best security systems cannot stop the determined fraudster. Employers must be able to rely on the goodwill of their employees.

Suggestions for Further Discussion

You may wish to think about the following, hypothetical scenario.

Imagine a scenario involving a systems analyst working for a major multinational corporation, Megatronics International Inc. The company's interests include mining, agribusiness, petrochemicals, international finance, Third World manufacturing, tourism and property development. Imagine, too, that after some while the systems analyst begins to become aware of the extent to which this corporation is involved in illegal and unethical activities. For example, the available systems suggest that money laundering and tax avoidance are being regularly practiced.

In addition, the analyst has become aware of the extent to which the company derives most of its profit from manufacturing plants in less-developed countries – plants which demonstrate massive profits but very little return in the form of salaries, plant modernization, working conditions or pollution controls. He investigates one particular country – 'Lower Tse Tse' and discovers that its military dictatorship has willingly entered into a highly exploitative agreement with Megatronics. The deal provides inadequate wages to the local employees and no pollution restrictions, thereby causing widespread sickness among the surrounding villages. Meanwhile, the government and its cronies receive large kickbacks and bribes, cars, private aircraft and expensive homes – all courtesy of Megatronics.

This disturbs our systems analyst greatly and the more he digs, the more he comes to appreciate the extent and scope of Megatronics's unethical and illicit activities. Soon after he has furtively broken security codes to examine confidential documents, an envelope appears on his desk each week containing several hundreds of dollars in cash. The implication the analyst draws from this is that his activities have been noticed and that an effort is now being made by those higher in the organization to buy his silence.

The systems analyst stores the cash, refusing to spend it and not knowing who it should be returned to. Meanwhile, the security system has been changed and all substantial files are being regularly encrypted. Only authorized individuals are allowed access to certain files and these are re-encrypted after they have been worked on.

Now imagine this man's dilemma: he knows that he is being watched and that his future employment (and perhaps even his health!) may be in jeopardy. He also knows that it would be almost impossible to bring the company to account by calling in the authorities. His knowledge of the system tells him that all audit trails would disappear in a few minutes. So he plots his own vengeance by planning an elaborate theft of company funds.

First, he manages to obtain his supervisor's password by peering over her shoulder one day. Then, finding an isolated terminal, he logs into her account and begins siphoning off funds received from Third World manufacturing installations. Then, after establishing a bank account for himself in Switzerland, he transfers all monies to this account, tenders his resignation and flies to Europe to collect the money.

Finally, in an act of poetic justice, he contacts Amnesty International and presents them with several million dollars with which to assist their efforts in Africa. In particular, the analyst asks that they focus on Lower Tse Tse. After several years, the glare of international attention from Amnesty helps bring about the downfall of the Lower Tse Tse dictatorship and ends the exploitative arrangement with Megatronics. A new contract is drawn up and the people once more begin to enjoy more of the fruits of their labour.

Readers may wish to ponder the ethical aspects of such a scenario.

Notes

1 From reports in *Software Engineering Notes*, vol. 13, no. 2, April 1988, p. 5 and *The Australian*, 24 May 1988.
2 Jay S. Albanese, 'Tomorrow's thieves', *The Futurist*, September-October 1988, p. 25 and Hugo Cornwall, *Datatheft: Computer Fraud, Industrial Espionage and Information Crime* (Heinemann, London, 1987), p. xi.
3 August Bequai, *Technocrimes: the Computerization of Crime and Terrorism* (Lexington Books, Lexington, MA, 1987).
4 Albanese, 'Tomorrow's thieves' and Tom Forester, *High-Tech Society* (Basil Blackwell, Oxford, and MIT Press, Cambridge, MA, 1987), pp. 219–22 and 261–8.
5 *The New York Times* News Service, 27 March 1987, cited in *Software Engineering Notes*, vol. 12, no. 2, April 1987, pp. 8–9.
6 *Communications Week* (USA), 31 August 1987.
7 R. Doswell and G. L. Simmons, *Fraud and Abuse of IT Systems* (National Computing Centre, Manchester, UK, 1986), pp. 32–5.
8 *The Australian*, 1 September 1987.
9 *The Financial Times*, 22 October 1984.
10 *PC Week*, vol. 4, no. 21, 26 May 1987 and *Business Week*, 1 August 1988, p. 51.
11 *The Australian*, 5 January 1988 and 26 April 1988; *The Independent*, 30 October 1986.
12 *Business Week*, 1 August 1988, p. 53.
13 Cornwall, *Datatheft*, p. 46
14 Ibid., p. xiii. See also Jeffrey A. Hoffer and Detmar W. Straub, 'The 9 to 5 underground: are you policing computer crimes?' *Sloan Management Review*, Summer 1989, pp. 35–43.
15 *The Financial Times*, 3 January 1986 and *The Australian*, 1 September 1987.
16 *The Australian*, 11 July 1988 and *Information Week*, 11 July 1988, cited in *Software Engineering Notes*, vol. 13, no. 3, July 1988, p. 10.
17 *The Financial Times*, 2 September 1986 and *The Australian*, 15 September 1987; *Software Engineering Notes*, vol. 13, no. 3, July 1988, p. 10.
18 *Computer News* (UK), 15 January 1987.
19 *The Wall Street Journal*, 18 May 1987, cited in *Software Engineering Notes*, vol. 12, no. 3, July 1987, p. 11; and *Computing Australia*, 10 August 1987.
20 *The Chicago Tribune*, 15 August 1986, cited in *Software Engineering Notes*, vol. 11, no. 5, October 1986, pp. 15–16; 'Are ATMs easy targets for crooks?' *Business Week*, 6 March 1989; and *The Los Angeles Times*, 11 February 1989, cited in *Software Engineering Notes*, vol. 14, no. 2, April 1989, p. 16.
21 Leslie D. Ball, 'Computer crime', in Tom Forester (ed.), *The Information Technology Revolution* (Basil Blackwell, Oxford and MIT Press, Cambridge, MA, 1985), p. 534, reprinted from *Technology Review*, April 1982.
22 *Software Engineering Notes*, vol. 13, no. 2, April 1988 and *Computing Australia*, 22 May 1989.
23 *Digital Review*, 6 April 1987, p. 75.
24 *Evening Outlook*, Santa Monica, CA, 4 February 1988.
25 Ball, 'Computer crime' in Forester, *The Information Technology Revolution*, pp. 534–5.
26 Cornwall, *Datatheft*, p. 102.

27 *The New York Times* News Service, 21 March 1986, cited in *Software Engineering Notes*, vol. 11, no. 2, April 1986, p. 15.

28 Keith Hearnden, 'Computer criminals are human, too', in Tom Forester (ed.), *Computers in the Human Context* (Basil Blackwell, Oxford and MIT Press, Cambridge, MA, 1989), pp. 415–42.

29 Ibid., p. 420; Ball, 'Computer crime', in Forester, *The Information Technology Revolution*, p. 536; Cornwall, *Datatheft*, p. 135; and 'Technological ability not needed to commit crime', AAP report in *The Australian*, 14 March 1989.

30 Jay BloomBecker, 'Introduction to computer crime', in J. H. Finch and E. G. Dougall (eds), *Computer Security: A Global Challenge* (Elsevier, North-Holland, 1984).

31 Hearnden, 'Computer criminals are human too', in Forester, *Computers in the Human Context*, pp. 420–1.

32 Other useful taxonomies of computer crime have been provided by Donn B. Parker, *Fighting Computer Crime* (Scribner, New York, 1983) and Detmar W. Straub and Cathy Spatz Widom, 'Deviancy by bits and bytes: computer abusers and control measures', in J. H. Finch and E. G. Dougall, *Computer Security*.

33 Katherine Hafner et al., 'Is your computer secure?' *Business Week*, 1 August 1988.

34 *The Washington Post*, 18 September 1988 and *The Chicago Tribune*, 17 September 1987, cited in *Software Engineering Notes*, vol. 12, no. 4, October 1987, p. 14.

35 Michael Cross, 'How Fred lets the fraudsters in', *The Independent*, 30 October 1986.

36 *The Australian*, 14–15 March, 1987; *The Financial Times*, London, 24 July 1986; *Computing Australia*, 15 June 1987; and *New Scientist*, 20 November 1986.

3 Software Theft

The Growth of Software Piracy – Revenge of the
Nerds? Intellectual Property Rights and the Law –
Software Piracy and Industry Progress – Busting the
Pirates – Suggestions for Further Discussion

In November 1987, Ms Ming Jyh Hsieh, a 38 year-old product support
engineer, was fired for non-performance by her employer, the Wollongong
Group, a software company of Palo Alto, California (named, incidentally,
after a city in New South Wales). Two months later, she was caught in
the act of downloading Wollongong proprietary software into her home
personal computer. Using a 'secret' password and privileges that were
surprisingly still valid, she spent some 18 hours over several nights copying
vast amounts of her former employer's software. Noticing that someone
was logging on to its computers via modem in the middle of the night, the
Wollongong Group immediately called in the police, who placed a 'trap and
trace' device on the company's computer phone lincs in order to identify
the caller. Later, when confronted with the evidence, Ms Hsieh confessed.
She was arrested and charged with gaining illegal access to Wollongong's
computers and stealing millions of dollars worth of software.[1]

The Growth of Software Piracy

'Software' is the set of instructions which tell a computer what to do. Without software, a computer is just a useless lump of silicon, metal and plastic.
As the cost of computer hardware has declined, the importance of software
has increased: software is where the action and the money are these days.
In fact, the total world market for software is now worth in excess of $50
billion a year. Partly as a result, copying computer programs, often referred
to as 'software piracy', has become a major growth industry. In schools,
colleges and computer clubs, young computer enthusiasts run off duplicate
programs for their friends or for re-sale – just as you would make copies

of video cassette tapes or chapters of this book. Software rental agencies have mushroomed, with no questions asked about what customers do with the software once they get it home. In commerce, industry, education and even in government departments, there is mounting evidence of the mass copying of software packages, often with the collusion of management. There are few individuals who can honestly say that they have never used a program for which the developer has not been properly compensated. Software piracy is an endemic social problem which is here to stay.

According to a report issued in March 1988 by the International Trade Commission in Arlington, Virginia, American software and hardware companies lost more than $4.1 billion in sales in 1986 – most of it due to software theft. This accords with previous federal government and US Software Publishing Association estimates that software piracy was costing American software originators between $2 and $3 billion a year. With the growth in popularity of software packages, software producers have become more and more concerned about wholesale copying. For example, Lotus Inc. claims that over half of its potential sales of *1–2–3* are lost to pirates – at a cost of about $160 million every year. While MicroPro, the company behind Wordstar, estimates that two to three illegal copies of the program are made for every one it sells.[2]

A dramatic illustration of the pervasiveness of software piracy is provided by the Montreal/Macintosh case. Richard R. Brandow, a 24 year-old publisher of a Montreal computer magazine and co-worker Pierre M. Zovile created a benign virus in order to highlight the problem of software piracy. The idea was that when the internal clocks on infected Macintoshes reached 2 March 1988, the first birthday of the Mac II computer, each machine would display an innocuous 'Universal Message of Peace to All Macintosh Users'. But within two months, Brandow says, illegal copying had transferred the virus to no less than 350,000 Macs around the world. And the virus was less than benign: Marc Canter, president of a small Chicago software publisher, found that this Universal Message of Peace actually caused his computers to crash and infected disks that he supplied to software producer Aldus Corp. in Seattle. Aldus withdrew the disks, but not before some got to customers.[3]

The history of software theft in the US goes back to 1964, when Texaco was offered $5 million worth of stolen software, while in the UK there was the famous 1968 case when the airline management system BOADICEA was copied and offered for sale by employees of the developer, the British Overseas Airways Corporation. The famous Ward case in 1970 demonstrated how easy it was to steal software down a telephone line: Hugh Jeffrey Ward, a programmer working on a CAD (Computer-Aided Design) package for a Californian computer company, desperately needed a facility to print results neatly on a plotter. Knowing that a good plotter module was available in another company's computer, Ward called up the company's computer and requested a listing of the program as well as the punched cards (the method of data input in those days). The cards were unfortunately later spotted in his wastebin and Ward was caught and convicted of theft of a trade secret. He received three years on probation and a $5,000 fine while the aggrieved company got $300,000 in damages.[4]

Large-scale piracy really became common after the arrival of the personal computer and packaged software in the late 1970s. This put hardware and software into the hands of individuals at reasonable cost for the first time and enabled them to do such things as word processing, ledger accounting, business planning and mass mailing. Sales of pcs and software packages went hand in hand: as pcs proliferated, the demand for useful software soared, and as more software packages like the pioneering *VisiCalc* became available, the demand for pcs also zoomed. Software became a multi-million dollar business almost overnight as worldwide sales of software packages leapt from $250 million in 1980 to $2 billion in 1984 and to $8 billion by 1989. A major trend developed toward 'integrated' software packages that permit the user to perform several different tasks, because a number of programs are integrated together on a single storage disk. For example, Lotus's innovatory *1–2–3* enables the user to carry out spreadsheet analysis, retrieve data from a database and display graphic material without having to change discs. But because the original versions of these software packages were relatively expensive, the temptation to pirate a copy proved too much for millions of users and would-be users.

An equally serious piracy problem arose as competing software companies came out with 'look-alike' products which emulated the user-interface or the 'look and feel' of best-selling programs. This has resulted in a spate of expensive lawsuits – some of which are still current. For example, Lotus Development sued two smaller companies, Paperback Software and Mosaic Software, for copying the 'look and feel' of *1–2–3*, but at a lower price (Mosaics program was unashamedly called '*Twin*'.) In turn, Lotus itself was sued for $100 million by the Software Arts Products Corporation (SAPC), developers of the original *VisiCalc* program, who claimed that Lotus had copied many of the commands and keystrokes as well as the screen displays of *VisiCalc* in *1–2–3*. SAPC claimed that Lotus founder Mitch Kapor 'misappropriated' copyrighted and confidential aspects of the *VisiCalc* program while he was an employee of the exclusive marketing agent for *VisiCalc*. SAPC further alleged that later, as a product tester for an advanced version of *VisiCalc*, Kapor 'had access to copyrighted and confidential aspects' of the program. He 'deliberately sought to make the *1–2–3* program look and feel like *VisiCalc*'.[5]

Apple Computer sued both Microsoft and Hewlett-Packard to prevent them from using a Macintosh-style user-interface, although Apple itself had borrowed the mouse-and-icons concept from Xerox's 'Star' user-interface in the first place. Apple appeared to win a first-round court victory against Microsoft, though Microsoft attempted to put a brave face on the judgement. Some industry observers warned that a clear victory for Apple in later rounds would put Apple in a commanding position in the marketplace, but Xerox came back into the picture in December 1989 when it finally filed suit against Apple. Ashton-Tate, the third largest producer of pc software in the world, also launched suits against two smaller companies, Fox Software and Santa Cruz Operation, for violating copyright laws supposedly protecting its best-selling *dBase III* database management and development program. Announcing the suit, Ashton-Tate's chairman and chief executive, Edward Esber, said: 'The issue is simple: a company like ours spends hundreds of millions of dollars making a brand name and a family of products, and we intend to protect our rights.'[6] On the other hand, further movement down the road of protection could mean that just a handful of big companies could control the entire direction of the industry – and litigation could stifle innovation.

Meanwhile, following Micropro's suit against American Brands, the US tobacco group, for the alleged mass copying of its best-selling Wordstar word processing program in American Brands' offices, a small, bankrupt software company, Inslaw Inc. of Washington, DC, took on none other than the Federal Justice Department for the same offence – and won a landmark victory in court. Back in 1982, Inslaw landed a $10 million contract with the Justice Department to install its PROMIS case-tracking software in the 20 largest federal prosecutors' offices nationwide, plus a version for 70 smaller offices. Inslaw in the meantime spent more than $8 million enhancing PROMIS on the assumption that it would be able to renegotiate the contract to take account of the extra work done. But once the Justice Department got hold of the source code of the enhanced system, it promptly refused to negotiate new licensing fees, withheld payments of $1.8 million, terminated its contract and astonishingly went on to pirate a further 20 copies of the new PROMIS. By April, 1985, Inslaw was so short of revenue as a result of this rough justice that it was forced into bankruptcy.

But the owners, William and Nancy Hamilton, kept fighting and the case finally ended up in the US District of Columbia bankruptcy court. In February, 1988, the court handed down its decision: Inslaw was awarded $6.8 million damages, not including legal fees and 'consequential damages' for lost business opportunities, which would be determined at a later trial. Judge George Francis Bason Jr actually accused the Justice Department

of 'trickery, [...] n against Inslaw and warned
that similar [...] tment would be sternly dealt
with. Incre [...] to court because of a loophole
in the law: [...] t sue the federal government.
Inslaw wa [...] vas in the midst of Chapter 11
bankrupt [...] brought about by the actions of
a federal [...]

Reveng [...] perty Rights and the Law

The id [...] has been around since the Middle
Ages a [...] tion have evolved over subsequent
centur [...] tent Office, the World Intellectual
Prope [...] llectual property is defined as the
right [...] esults of intellectual activity in the
indu [...] tic fields. Generally speaking, copy-
righ [...] d forms of literary expression, while
pat [...] cal inventions and contract law has
cov [...] puter software is a wholly new kind
of [...] w definitional and legal problems for
so [...] ow we define ownership of this form
of [...] the rights of ownership can and should
b [...] ut-dated and confusing: we are not sure
[...] ade secrets apply or should apply to this
[...] e. And as the confusion continues, the gap
[...] eryday behaviour on the part of computer
[...] till wider.[8]
[...] Fletcher School of Law and Diplomacy,
[...] ent article, what suited the age of print and
[...] ving inadequate in the age of the computer
[...] and the distributed database. Copyright,
[...] rked relatively well in the industrial era, but
[...] ctors have eroded the effectiveness of these
[...] nisms, she says. First, the development of new
information and [...] ations technologies has blurred the boundaries
between media, and intellectual assets have become increasingly abstract
and intangible. Second, the globalization of the world economy has multi-
plied both the incentives for international violations of intellectual property
rights and the economic harm of such violations. Third, privatization and
the growing trend toward using market mechanisms to gather and dissemi-
nate information has disrupted the traditional public infrastructure for

---

Venus

Named after the Roman goddess of beauty and love.

Rotation: 243 days
Revolution: 225 days
Atmosphere: nitrogen, carbon dioxide, argon, water vapor, neon, carbon monoxide, sulfur dioxide, sulfuric acid, nitrous oxide
Temperature: 455°C (850°F)
Diameter: 12,100 km (7,520 miles)
Average distance from the sun: 108.2 million km (67,250,000 miles)
Number of moons: 0

Suggested Reading
Exploring Venus and Mercury by David Baker
Venus by Seymour Simon
Venus: Magellan Explores Our Twin Planet by Franklyn Branley

© Demco, Inc. 1995 Printed in U.S.A.
1-800-356-1200
Photo © Armaugh Planetarium 1995

sharing intellectual assets. For example, in the US, Bell Labs, federal government agencies and universities are now turning to patent rights and copyright royalties to recoup their investments in research and development. Thus, she says, 'at the very moment when information is becoming a valuable commodity, protecting the economic value of intellectual assets is proving more difficult.'[9]

The current legal position on software in the US is quite complex and it needs clarifying. The Copyright Office tentatively began accepting computer programs for registration back in 1964, but for many years the computer industry relied primarily on trade secrets to protect its software. It was not until 1980 that the Copyright Act 1976 was amended to include software in the form of the Computer Software Copyright Act 1980. Under this legislation, programs are considered copyrightable as 'literary works'. Meanwhile, the US Patent Office considered that most computer programs were collections of algorithms (mathematical formulae designed to carry out a specific task or to solve a particular problem) – which, like other mathematical equations, were excluded from patent protection. But since 1980, the US courts have steadily extended copyright protection for software – extending it, first, from embracing a program's source code to include the object code. Later, the logic and sequence of the program was also included. Moreover, the Patent Office in 1989 started granting patents for items of software, amid a growing clamour from some industry quarters for the extension of patents to more types of programs and even to algorithms.

In 1986, the Third Circuit Court of Appeals (which covers New Jersey, Pennsylvania and Delaware) found in favour of the plaintiff, Elaine Whelan, in *Jaslow v. Whelan*, declaring that copyright protection extends to structured or 'non-literal' aspects of a program, such as screen design and the commands. This set the scene for the 'look and feel' cases which were launched in the period 1987–9. Also in 1989, a federal judge in San Jose, California, resolved a five year-old battle over chip-copying between Japan's NEC and Intel Corp., by ruling that the microcode used to instruct the Intel microprocessors in question could be copyrighted, but that Intel forfeited any claim over NEC in this instance because it had failed to print the conventional copyright symbol on each chip!

At the same time, software firms are also turning to patent protection again and some are receiving it: for example, Teknowledge Inc. received patents on two new artificial intelligence products in 1986.[10] While in 1989, in a landmark decision for the industry, Quarterdeck Office Systems was awarded a patent by the US Patent Office for Desqview, a 'windows'-based multi-tasking operating environment. The patent had first been applied for in 1984 – the same year that Desqview and its Microsoft's Windows package first came on the market. Quarterdeck's persistence is seen as an attempt to get back at Microsoft and to help recoup their $6 million start-up costs. The leading office systems analyst, Mr Andrew Seybold, said the Quarterdeck decision could 'shatter' the software industry. 'This patent may have a far broader impact on the computer industry than Apple's copyright infringement suit against Microsoft and Hewlett-Packard. The Apple suit is an attempt to extend copyright protection to the nebulous area of the 'look and feel' of windows-based user interfaces. The Quarterdeck patent, on the other hand, protects the way applications run within windows, a concrete technological issue. Patent protection, much stronger than copyright protection, requires that companies making use of the technologies involved pay royalties or stop using the technology. That could affect nearly every company in the industry.'[11]

What we have, then, is a situation in the US in which three kinds of law may or may not apply to programs or even different aspects of a program. In short, the law on intellectual property as it applies to computer software is in a mess. Copyright law does not wholly protect a program, but if it did extend to 'look and feel' it could become a serious and costly obstacle to standardizing software applications. Patent law, offering a stronger form of protection, could become an even more serious barrier to the information technology industry's progress (although a suggestion that 'soft patents' – lasting perhaps ten years rather than the normal 50 years – be granted to software products seems worth pursuing). Utilizing the law on trade secrets is also in contradiction to the notion of the widest possible dissemination of innovations and would make marketing a program, for instance, virtually impossible.

Much the same sort of legal muddle exists in most other leading nations around the world, which are still struggling with their copyright laws in an attempt to take account of the new phenomenon of computer software. Back in 1985, a joint UNESCO-WIPO conference in Geneva, Switzerland, called to discuss the problem of software piracy, broke up in confusion, with the international delegates coming to no firm conclusions about how to protect programs. Since then, the UK has attempted to clarify its laws with the passing of the massive Copyright, Designs and Patents Act 1988 and Canada also extended copyright protection to software by law in 1988.[12] Australia extended copyright protection to programs as long ago as 1984, following the case of *Apple Computer v. Wombat*, in which the Australian company was accused of pirating the operating systems used in Apple's chips. But in 1986, in *Apple Computer v. Computer Edge*, the Australian High Court held that although the source code of programs was deemed to be a literary work and therefore covered by copyright, this did not extend to the object code, which was not covered. This created considerable dissatisfaction in the industry and so a new review of copyright law as it applies to software was launched by the federal Attorney-General's office in late 1988.

Meanwhile, amendments to copyright legislation to encompass computer software have been enacted in France, Italy, West Germany, Denmark, Norway, Sweden and Finland, as well as Hungary, Spain, India and Japan at the last count. Brazil leads a group of Third World nations including Thailand and South Korea who oppose US moves through GATT (the General Agreement on Tariffs and Trade) to copyright software on the grounds that this strengthens the hands of transnational computer companies and inhibits countries like Brazil from building up their own informatics industries.

Software Piracy and Industry Progress

The central dilemma facing law-makers, the IT industry and society at large is therefore how to reward innovation without stifling creativity. This is an issue which is fundamental to the whole history and the future of the industry. Without adequate legal protection, genuinely innovatory individuals and companies might wonder whether the meagre rewards for their efforts really justify the time and money expended on original research and development. On the other hand, intellectual property owners might try to stake too large a claim for their innovations in order to squelch new ideas and to get a jump ahead of their competitors. This could strengthen the hand of established large firms over small entrepreneurial firms, who have been the traditional innovators of the industry. The question is whether the developmental work put in justifies the influence innovators may gain over both users and competitors. There is a clear need to strike a balance between the interests of these three groups, as we tread the fine line between piracy and progress.[13]

Anne Branscomb argues that because IT makes the form a product takes easy to separate from the intellectual assets that go into it, copyright law, with its focus on the expression of an idea rather than on the idea itself, is inappropriate for protecting what is really valuable in the new kinds of intellectual property. This view is generally supported by Minneapolis lawyer Stuart Hemphill and British academic Paul Marett, in their contributions to the debate.[14] Branscomb suggests that a modified form of patent rights (as in 'soft patents' above), with registration procedures, monopoly time limits and rules for licensing shaped to the realities of the computer industry, may be the answer.

Deborah Johnson (Rensselaer Polytechnic Institute, New York) and John Snapper (Illinois Institute of Technology) rule out trade secrets as a means of protecting software on the grounds that it would only apply to research done under extreme security conditions. The publication of technical results would be restricted and employees would find that they cannot change jobs with ease or freely discuss their work with other researchers. This, they say, might point in the direction of patent or copyright protection. But Deborah Johnson, writing elsewhere, comes down in favour of the status quo as being broadly 'acceptable', with minor modifications to the trade secrecy laws. She specifically rejects any attempt to enact new forms of legislation to cope with software.[15]

Paul Marett of Loughborough University, UK, argues that contractual relationships rather than copyright law may prove to be more important in the future, at least in the world of electronic publishing, and that we should think in terms of developing a new field of informatics law. Pamela Samuelson, Professor of Law at the University of Pittsburgh, on the other hand, makes a powerful case for using patent law to protect innovation in the computer industry. She says that the Whelan case (which, as we saw above, favoured protecting software by copyright law) was particularly bad news for innovators and she rejects attempts to modify copyright law or to create new laws treating software as a special case. The existing system of patent law, she says, is still the best vehicle for protecting software. Samuelson also argues forcefully that the 'look and feel' of software user interfaces should not be protected by copyright law but by patent law because 'it is more consistent with legal tradition.'[16]

No doubt this important but complex debate will continue – and while it does, the aforementioned gap between the law and everyday behaviour in the real world will remain large and probably grow larger. Because copying software is so easy, it will, in the final analysis, always be primarily a matter of social attitudes and of individual consciences. In this respect, it probably won't matter what new laws are passed. As Branscomb argues, 'Although disputes about technology and intellectual property are usually cast in narrow legal terms, they are intimately related to public attitudes. Realistic legal rules depend upon a social consensus about what kind of behaviour is acceptable and what is not.'[17] It is a consensus on software theft that seems to be missing at present.

Busting the Pirates

Apart from legal remedies, various technical devices and administrative schemes have been proposed as possible solutions to the problem of software theft. The devices – sometimes called 'dongles' – take the form of programmed chips or electronic locks which are physically attached to a computer: only those in possession of the correct code or key are able to gain access to the protected program. Among the proposed schemes are either site-based or company-based licensing schemes, which would somehow channel royalties back to the program originators. Another suggestion is to popularize the concept of 'shareware' or 'honorware', by which users would be invited to send a donation to the authors named at the beginning of the program. More recently, the Copyright Clearance Center of Salem, Massachusetts, which collects royalties for magazine and book publishers when their copyrighted material is duplicated by large corporations, has suggested a similar scheme for computer software. Each time a copy of a program is made, the company or the institution would send a royalty payment back to the Center, which would collect a commission and pass the rest on to the software supplier.

Despite these suggestions and the efforts of organizations like the US Software Publishers Association and Britain's Federation Against Software Theft (FAST), many software companies have been forced to throw in the towel on software copying. In particular, those pursuing the lucrative business computing market have found that abandoning their protection codes is the best protection from competitor companies. In 1985, MicroPro International gave up all pretence of protection to its programs and Microsoft did the same with *Word*. In 1986, Software Publishing Corporation followed suit, saying: 'If you want to get into the corporate market, they won't even look at you if you're copy-protected.'[18] In the same year, Ashton-Tate decided to do likewise, claiming that new legislation around the world now strengthened the hands of software suppliers. Finally, the Washington-based Association of Data and Processing Services Organizations (ADAPSO), which also looks after the interests of the software industry, announced that it was dropping its plans to get software publishers to adopt a voluntary protection standard because it ran against current industry trends. When ADAPSO sent out 1,500 copies of its proposed standard to its members, it received only 100 replies – replies which were evenly split between support and opposition.

But the battle against international software piracy has met with more success. Taiwan, Singapore and Hong Kong were market leaders in the mid 1980s in the counterfeiting of computer software, with best-selling programs like Lotus's *1–2–3* retailing for as little as $10 in the backstreet markets of these booming Asian nations. At the time, it was suggested that the counterfeiting of books, records, audio and video cassettes and computer software was worth $1 billion a year to the Singaporean economy alone. Brazil, India, Japan, Mexico, Thailand and South Korea were also hotbeds of software piracy, according to ADAPSO.

In 1985, Taiwan – long considered the counterfeiting capital of the world – passed a new copyright law which for the first time extended legal protection to software and provided for pirates to be jailed. In 1986, IBM took on six Singaporean pirate companies itself and won a landmark victory in the Singapore courts. In the following year, international pressure – particularly from the US and the UK – finally forced Singapore to pass a new Copyright Act, which had been five years in the drafting. It, too, provided for huge fines and jail terms for software pirates. The Crown Colony of Hong Kong followed suit in 1988, with tough new legislation designed to tackle the piracy problem on Kowloon's Golden Mile. Raids by customs officers and trade department officials began soon after, although what effect they had is a matter of some conjecture. Even Italy became the target of a campaign by the US-based Business Software Association, formed by leading US software houses in 1988, which claimed that organized software piracy in Italian companies was costing the industry $500 million a year. The first lawsuit filed against Italian chemical giant Montedison claimed that 100 out of 120 personal computers inspected at their Milan HQ used illicit copies of Lotus and Ashton-Tate programs. Montedison claimed it had permission to duplicate the software.[19]

But Brazil refused to extend copyright protection to US software and in 1988 the US government imposed 100 per cent duties on $39 million worth of Brazilian goods. Thailand also appeared unwilling or unable to extend copyright protection to software and in 1989 the US government revoked special trade tariffs worth an estimated $165 million a year. This caused much consternation in Bangkok and threatened to damage US strategic interests in the South-East Asia area. The toughest nut to crack remained Japan, whose microchip and computer industries have been so successfully built up while patent, copyright and trade secret protection has been effectively denied US companies. US trade negotiators have finally got intellectual property on the agenda for high-level discussions with the Japanese government, but few expect any dramatic progress and trade friction is expected to continue.

Suggestions for Further Discussion

You may wish to think about the following, hypothetical scenario.

A computer science student, fresh out of graduate school, takes one of her completed projects and conceives of a brilliant redesign that would turn it into a revolutionary software product. She therefore sets up a small business for herself and dedicates 12 months to the redevelopment of the software, now and then taking in short commercial programming contracts to help pay the rent.

At the conclusion of the 12-month period, our computer scientist feels somewhat resentful at having sacrificed most of a year's salary in order to undertake her pet project, so she reasons that she must maximize her returns from sale of the software. Having worked hard on developing a high quality product, she believes that she should be appropriately rewarded in financial terms.

The thought of thousands of people pirating her software sends her into a state of apoplexy and she therefore devises a scheme to take vengeance upon anyone who would illicitly copy her package. Her protection feature allows each user to make one back-up copy of her discs, but any attempt to copy more than this not only corrupts the source discs, but wipes clean any hard discs or floppies accessible by the system. Having done that, an icon appears on the screen depicting a pirate with a parrot on his shoulder. The parrot squawks, 'Pieces of eight . . . pieces of eight . . . you should have paid me pieces of eight!!'

Of course the story does not end there. Dozens of individuals are caught this way and they plot their revenge as well. They do this by scouring the Arpanet and public domain bulletin boards to find any electronic mail addresses owned by our computer scientist friend. They also hack into Master Card, Visa Card and other credit-lending companies and run up enormous bills on her behalf. They deluge her with abusive electronic mail and tie up her telephone by using her own telephone billing cards to call her number incessantly. Then they doctor her electricity bills, tenant history, and credit ratings. In short, they make her life an utter misery.

Eventually, both sides to the dispute settle down to a (fairly) civilized debate about the ethical dimensions of what the other has done. Our computer scientist charges her attackers with fraud, forgery, theft and harassment. Of course, the attackers collectively do the same. The principal issue however, and perhaps the central one in any software piracy case, is the differing values placed on the software by the manufacturer/developer and the purchaser/pirate. The pirates pirate because they claim the software is ridiculously overpriced while the developer claims to have spent a whole year getting the software right and should be compensated accordingly.

The interested reader may wish to ponder the ethical issues raised by such a scenario.

Notes

1 *Palo Alto Times Tribune*, CA, 7 February 1988, cited in *Software Engineering Notes*, vol. 13, no. 2, April 1988; Katherine M. Hafner et al., 'Is your computer secure?' *Business Week*, 1 August 1988, p. 53.
2 *The Australian*, 8 March 1988 and 17 January 1989; and Anne W. Branscomb, 'Who owns creativity? Property rights in the information age', in Tom Forester

(ed.), *Computers in the Human Context* (Basil Blackwell, Oxford, and MIT Press, Cambridge, MA, 1989), reprinted from *Technology Review*, May–June 1988.

3 Katherine M. Hafner et al., 'Is your computer secure?', p. 54.

4 Hugo Cornwall, *Datatheft: Computer Fraud, Industrial Espionage and Information Crime* (Heinemann, London, 1987), pp. 127–8.

5 *The Australian*, 21 April 1987 (reprinted from *The Times*); *Business Week*, 31 August 1987, p. 21 and 22 May 1989, p. 83.

6 *The Australian*, 29 November 1988.

7 Mary Jo Foley, 'A small software firm takes on Uncle Sam – and wins', *Datamation*, 15 April 1988.

8 'Software in never-never land', *The Australian*, 17 January 1989 (reprinted from *The Economist*). For the history of copyright, see Edward W. Ploman and L. Clark Hamilton, *Copyright: Intellectual Property in the Information Age* (Routledge and Kegan Paul, London, 1980) and Judy Marcure, 'Copyright and computers', *Australian Computing*, Summer 1988 edn.

9 Anne W. Branscomb, 'Who owns creativity?' in Forester, *Computers in the Human Context*, pp. 409–10 and Pamela Samuelson, 'Is copyright law steering the right course?' *IEEE Software*, September 1988, pp. 78–86.

10 Anne W. Branscomb, 'Who owns creativity?' in Forester, *Computers in the Human Context*, p. 412.

11 Ben Brock, 'Windowing patent clouds industry', *The Australian*, 25 April 1989.

12 For a summary of the UK Act, see Barry Fox and Susan Watts, 'Whose idea is it anyway?', *New Scientist*, 5 August 1989.

13 Paula Dwyer et al., 'The battle raging over intellectual property', *Business Week*, 22 May 1989 and Judy Marcure, 'Copyright and computers'.

14 Anne W. Branscomb, 'Who owns creativity?' in Forester, *Computers in the Human Context*, p. 414; Stuart R. Hemphill, 'Copyrighting technology: are we asking the right questions?' *High Technology Business*, August 1988; Paul Marett, 'Legal Issues in Electronic Publishing', *Oxford Surveys in Information Technology*, vol. 4, 1987, pp. 1–24.

15 Deborah G. Johnson and John W. Snapper, *Ethical Issues in the Use of Computers* (Wadsworth, Belmont, CA, 1985), p. 298; Deborah G. Johnson, *Computer Ethics* (Prentice-Hall, Englewood Cliffs, NJ, 1985), p. 102.

16 Pamela Samuelson, 'Is copyright law steering the right course?' pp. 79 and 85–6; Pamela Samuelson, 'Why the look and feel of software user interfaces should not be protected by copyright law', *Communications of the ACM*, vol. 32, no. 5, May 1989, pp. 563–72.

17 Anne W. Branscomb, 'Who owns creativity?' in Forester, *Computers in the Human Context*, p. 408.

18 *Business Week*, 19 May 1986. Other information from various newspaper and wire service reports.

19 Janette Martin, 'Pursuing pirates', *Datamation*, 1 August 1989.

4 Hacking and Viruses

What is Hacking? – Why do Hackers 'Hack'? –
Hackers: Criminals or Modern-Day Robin Hoods?
– Some 'Great' Hacks – Worms, Trojan Horses and
Time Bombs – The Virus Invasion – Ethical Issues –
Suggestions for Further Discussion

On 27 April 1987, viewers of the Home Box Office (HBO) cable TV channel in the US witnessed an historically significant event, variously described as the first act of high-tech terrorism, or the world's most widely-viewed piece of electronic graffiti. On that evening, watchers of HBO's satellite transmission of 'The Falcon and the Snowman' saw their screens go blank and the following message appear:

Good Evening HBO from Captain Midnight. $12.95 a month?
No way! (Show-time/Movie Channel, Beware!)

This transmission lasted for some four minutes. It represented a protest against HBO's decision to scramble its satellite signal so that backyard dish owners were forced to buy or hire decoders in order to view HBO's programs. More significantly – and in a most impressive way – it illustrated the vulnerability of satellites and other communications services to malicious interference.

The search for and apprehension of Captain Midnight took several months and a certain amount of luck. Investigators initially reasoned that the Captain had used a commercial satellite facility to overcome HBO's intended signal, but to their dismay, they discovered that there were some 2,000 such facilities. Fortunately for them, only a much smaller number (580) used the kind of character generator that Captain Midnight used to create his text message and of these only twelve were available that night for jamming purposes. Of the remaining suitable facilities, records showed that they had all been involved in normal activities.

A breakthrough in the case did not occur until a Wisconsin tourist happened to overhear a man talking about the Captain Midnight prank while using a public telephone in Florida. The tourist reported the man's license number and this information eventually led police to the culprit – one John MacDougall, a satellite dish salesman, electronics engineer and part-time employee at the Central Florida Teleport satellite facility in Ocala. MacDougall was subsequently charged with transmitting without a license and sentenced to one year's probation and a $5,000 fine.[1]

Since the Captain Midnight episode, however, several other instances of video piracy have occurred, including an incident in November 1987 in which WGN-TV (Channel 9 in Chicago) was overridden for approximately 15 seconds. That same evening, WTTW (Channel 11 in Chicago) was also overridden by a 90-second transmission – this time by man in a Max Headroom mask smacking his exposed buttocks with a fly swatter![2]

Yet the most important aspect of the Captain Midnight 'hack' and other similar incidents is not immediately obvious. MacDougall caused mild annoyance to a large number of viewers and probably at worst, a severe case of embarrassment to HBO. Yet the mere fact that this individual was able to broadcast a particular message into the homes of thousands and to take control of a sophisticated satellite transponder demonstrates a much more significant danger. What if, instead of being an angry satellite dish salesman, MacDougall was an international terrorist and instead of interrupting a movie, he began to jam the telephone, facsimile and data communications of a number of satellites? Further, we know that satellites are directed from the ground by using radio signals to control the functioning of their small manoeuvring engines. What if MacDougall or somebody else had used these signals to move the satellite into a decaying orbit or caused it to enter the orbit of another satellite – perhaps a Soviet one – many of which carry small nuclear reactors as a power source?

Even worse, if MacDougall had been an employee of a city traffic authority, could he have used his knowledge of computer systems and traffic control to completely foul up a city's traffic lights during a peak traffic period? One doesn't need much imagination to think of the consequences of such an act for a city, say, the size of Los Angeles. Not only would the traffic snarls take days to untangle, but emergency services (Police, Fire, Ambulance etc.) would be incapacitated. Maintenance of sewage, lighting, power and telephones would probably come to a halt, and inevitably there would be fatalities and an enormous insurance bill stemming from the hundreds of wrecked or damaged cars and injured or ill people. More important, the security services would be hard pressed to deal with any additional terrorist acts such as a hijacking or the takeover of the city's water supply.[3]

What is Hacking?

In the media, incidents like the HBO prank are referred to as 'hacking'. Yet this is not an easy term to define, nor is it a recent phenomenon. According to writers such as Steven Levy, author of *Hackers: Heroes of the Computer Revolution* (Doubleday, New York, 1985), the earliest hackers were students at the Massachusetts Institute of Technology (MIT) in the late 1960s. These hackers specialized in putting together pieces of telephone circuitry and tracing the wiring and switching gear of the MIT network. Next came the phone 'phreaks' – epitomized by the famous 'Captain Crunch' (John T. Draper) – who discovered that a breakfast cereal of the same name supplied a toy whistle which generated an identical tone to one which the US telephone network used to access toll-free services. Eventually, instead of blowing the whistle into a pay phone mouthpiece, Draper and other resourceful individuals developed the 'blueboxes' – electronic tone generators which could reproduce the full series of tones that the US telephone network used in its call-routing system. With such devices, it was possible to call anywhere in the world free of charge. But unfortunately, many 'Blueboxers' and even the ingenious Captain Crunch himself were convicted of various offences and enjoyed several stints in jail.

According to Levy, hacking as we understand it – that is, involving the use of computers – only began to emerge with the development of time-shared systems. Hacking then spread quickly once VDTs allowed users to interact with a machine directly rather than through the remote mechanism of card-based batch processing. Yet even then, 'hacking' referred to a much more noble set of activities than the criminal acts that are described by the term today. Hacking was an elite art practised by small groups of extremely gifted but socially inadequate individuals. It generated its own set of folk heroes, huge rivalries, eccentricities and cult rituals. But above all, this early form of hacking was about intellectual challenge and not malicious damage. Levy portrays this period as a sort of golden era of hacking, which mainly took place at two major sites – MIT and Stanford University in California. For most hackers at this time, their chief interest lay in understanding the innards of a system down to the last chip and down to the last line of the operating system. The software they wrote was for public display, use and further development, and was their major source of self-esteem, challenge and socialization.

In Levy's view, all of this began to change once huge commercial interests moved into the software industry and flexed their legal and commercial muscles. Suddenly, software was not for public use or refinement. It had become the property of those who had paid for it to be written (and who didn't always appreciate unauthorized revisions), and once this had happened, the golden age came to an end. Intellectual challenge was not enough. Like everywhere else, there was no free lunch in the world of hacking either. Therefore, to some extent Levy indirectly blames the commercialization of software for the emergence of hacking in its criminal form. Having been introduced to the cut and thrust of the commercial world, the best and brightest may have simply taken on this different set of values – a set that has simply been augmented and made more sinister among the current crop of hackers. Then, armed with these different values and goals and with the development of nationwide networks of computers (the ARPANET being the earliest of these), hackers began to break out of the confines of their local machines and spread their interests across the US, even using links to international networks to gain access to systems on the other side of the earth.

Yet even today, it is clear that there is a wide range of definitions that are applied to the term 'hacking'. To some, to 'hack' is to roughly cause a program to work, generally in an inelegant manner. For others, a hack is a clever (generally small) program or program modification that displays unusual insight into a programming language or operating system. On the other hand, any scam or clever manipulation may also be termed a hack. For example, the famous stunt-card 'switcheroo' at the 1961 Rosebowl football game is often referred to as a great hack.[4] In this context, computer viruses – a topic we will be addressing shortly – may represent a particular kind of malicious and destructive 'hack'. Many more of us, though, tend to associate the term almost exclusively with attempts to use the telephone network to gain unauthorized access to computer systems and their data (some have preferred to call this 'cracking'). Psychologists, sociologists and others who concern themselves with the behavioural aspects involved view hacking as mere computer addiction. Those suffering from the malady are regarded as being socially inept and unable to form a peer group through any medium other than that provided by the remoteness and abstraction of computing.

In their book, *The Hacker's Dictionary*, authors Guy Steele et al. have outlined at least seven different definitions of a hacker:

1 A person who enjoys learning the details of computer systems and how to stretch their capabilities – as opposed to most users of computers, who prefer to learn only the minimum amount necessary.
2 One who programs enthusiastically, or who enjoys programming rather than just theorizing about programming.
3 A person capable of appreciating *hack value*.
4 A person who is good at programming quickly.

5 An expert on a particular program, or one who frequently does work using it or on it.
6 An expert of any kind.
7 A malicious inquisitive meddler who tries to discover information by poking around. For example, a password hacker is one who tries, possibly by deceptive or illegal means, to discover other peoples' computer passwords. A network hacker is one who tries to learn about the computer network (possibly because he or she wants to improve it or possibly because he or she wants to interfere).[5]

It is beyond the scope of this book to provide an exhaustive list of definitions of hacking and their associated behaviours. While we will attempt to primarily address those issues that most clearly pertain to ethics, this may involve us covering incidents in all of the above categories. Hence, for our purposes, hacking is any computer-related activity which is not sanctioned or approved of by an employer or owner of a system or network. We must distinguish it, however, from software piracy and computer crime, where the primary issue is the rights of information ownership and the use of computer systems to perpetrate what, in any other arena, would simply be regarded as monetary theft or fraud. To some extent, this is a rather broad and *post hoc* definition. Nevertheless, such a definition provides us with a rich load of cases and events that are very much at the heart of ethical issues in computing.

Why Do Hackers 'Hack'?

There are probably as many answers to this question as there are different forms of hacking. Clearly, some amount of intellectual challenge may be involved. Rather like solving an elaborate crossword, the guessing of passwords and inventing means of bypassing file protections poses intriguing problems that some individuals will go to enormous lengths to solve.[6] In other cases, hacking has involved acts of vengeance, usually by a disgruntled employee against a former employer. For example, in 1985, a fired employee of the Minnesota Tipboard Co. planted a 'time bomb' or 'logic bomb' in the company's computers and threatened to trigger it unless the company paid him a weekly salary of $350 while he found another job. When triggered, the time bomb would have erased sensitive information and files held on disc and threatened the company's future operation.[7] Fortunately for the company concerned, a firm of hired consultants found and successfully removed the code – while the programmer was later arrested on charges of extortion.

For others, hacking represents a lifestyle that rests upon severe social inadequacy among otherwise intellectually capable individuals – the so-called computer 'nerd' syndrome, which particularly affects male adolescents between the ages of 14 and 16. For psychologists such as Sherry Turkle of MIT, hackers are individuals who use computers as people substitutes, basically because computers don't require the kind of mutuality and complexity that human relationships tend to demand. Other researchers at Carnegie-Mellon University have provided evidence that partially supports this view: Sara Kiesler and her co-workers have investigated the social psychology of computer-mediated communication and found that this medium removes status cues (such as sitting at the head of the table), body language (nods, frowns, etc.), and provides a kind of social anonymity that changes the way people make decisions in groups. Their investigations into computer conferencing and electronic mail showed that group decision-making discussions using this medium exhibited more equal participation and a larger coverage of issues.[8] However, despite this, the limited bandwidth of the computer screen (i.e. its lack of feedback in the form of body language, etc.) often caused users to seek substitutes for it. For example, in the absence of any other (nonverbal) mechanisms to communicate their emotions, electronic mail users often substitute depictions of their face to represent how they are feeling or how their message should be interpreted. The following collection of keyboard characters are often used to represent a smile, a wink and a sad face respectively (view them sideways):

| :-) | ;-) | :-(

Hence, the form of communication that computers require, even when communicating with other human beings, may indeed be attractive to those who feel less competent in face-to-face settings where the subtleties of voice, dress, mannerisms and vocabulary are mixed in complex ways. Those who are less skilled in dealing with these sources of information may therefore retreat to more concrete and anonymous forms of interaction with a machine, while those who are limited by these communication modes attempt to extend them to incorporate more naturalistic features of communication when dealing remotely with other human beings.

In contrast to this, other commentators, such as Professor Marvin Minsky of MIT, have argued that there is nothing very special about hackers – they are simply people who have a particular obsession – and this obsession is no different from that of old-style 'radio hams' or those addicted to certain sports, hobbies, cars or indeed any other popular kind of fascination.[9] Yet this latter view ignores a very important difference between, say, an addiction to TV sports and an addiction to computers, particularly if the latter takes a malicious form. For the TV sports enthusiast, the amount of damage he or she can cause is likely to be minimal (except perhaps to their own intellectual abilities!), whereas hacking in its most malicious forms retains the potential to cause massive damage and perhaps even loss of life. The hypothetical scenarios presented in the introduction to this chapter depict some quite feasible applications of malicious hacking. Indeed, as we note several times throughout this book, it is the power that we invest in computer systems that sets them apart from conventional systems. This, allied with the remote and abstract nature of computing, provides the potential for individuals to cause massive damage with little understanding of the enormity of their acts, because the consequences are not 'fed back' to the perpetrators in any meaningful way – and especially in any form that emphasizes human costs.

Although it may contradict popular stereotypes about hackers, in fact by far the greatest amount of hacking involves very little intellectual challenge or great intellectual ability.[10] Certainly, some system penetrations or hacks display incredible ingenuity. But for the most part, hacking relies on some basic principles, an excessive amount of determination on the part of the hacker and a reliance on human fallibility. For example, when faced with a new, unpenetrated system, the commonest form of attack is to simply guess passwords because there is an amazing lack of variation in the kinds of passwords that users choose. As we have already seen, 'sex' and 'love' in the US (and 'Fred' in the UK) are very common as well as the names of pets, wives, children, the first four numbers on a computer keyboard (1234) and the first letters on the keyboard (qwerty). In addition, many systems have 'guest' accounts that are used for display purposes and these often have the log in name 'guest' with the same word used as a password as well. To assist their chances of penetrating a system, hackers will often scan the rubbish bins of computer centres looking for password clues, or they may attend computer exhibitions hoping that they will be able to look over someone's shoulder as they log on to a remote system. The details of successful or partially successful penetrations are often listed on computer 'bulletin boards' (electronic notice boards for posting and circulating information) and these allow other hackers to further penetrate a system or to co-operate in exhausting the possible mechanisms for unauthorized entry.

Most hackers use only a small suite of equipment: generally a modem, a personal computer (pc) and some communications software. The modem converts digital pulses from the computer into analogue (continuous) signals of the kind that the telephone network uses. Once on the telephone network, the pc is able to communicate with almost any machine that has a dial-in line – that is, a phone line that also has a modem connected to it. Once the hacker's modem has connected to the target machine's modem, both devices will convert the analogue phone signals back to digital ones and allow communication to proceed. Generally, the communications software that the hacker uses provides high quality emulation of a range of popular terminal types (such as DEC's VT52 or VT100) and sometimes such packages have a number of built-in features that aid the hacker. For example, some communications packages will autodial telephone numbers within a particular numeric range. This means that while the hacker sleeps, watches TV or whatever, his computer can target a particular region or suburb (where a large computer installation is believed to exist) by dialling all numbers in that region until a computer is identified. Undoubtedly, a large number of these calls will be answered by humans or facsimile machines, but every so often the carrier tone of a computer's modem will be identified and the hacker can later begin work on gaining access to that system. Furthermore, if the calls are charged to a stolen credit card number or a telephone account (such numbers are freely circulated on many hacker bulletin boards) then the hacker can make thousands of calls at no personal cost whatsoever.

Yet apart from the simple guessing of passwords, there are very few ways in which a hacker can penetrate a system from the outside – although as already mentioned, the stereotype passwords that many people use often maximizes a hacker's chances of fluking a legitimate user name and password combination. Despite this, it is well known that most system penetrations are abetted by some form of inside assistance. For example, a common trap in university computer laboratories is to leave a terminal switched on, waiting for an unwary user to log on to the system. In some cases, the terminal may still be running a program from the previous user which will simulate a log on procedure, thereby capturing the user's log on name and their password. The log on procedure will then abort with the usual failure message and – normally – the user will assume that they made an error when typing in their password and will try again. Unfortunately for this user, although the terminal appeared to be idle, in reality the program already running on it will have captured their log on details and then shut down, so that the real system log on procedure appears. Given the closeness of this sequence of events to very common log on errors (*everyone* at some stage makes mistakes in logging on) and given some amount of naivety, in most instances it is unlikely that many users would even suspect that they have been duped. Then, using the ill-gotten log on name and password, the hacker can enter the system, thereby gaining full access to the data and programs of the legitimate user.

Indeed, the need for some insider knowledge or partial access has proved to be an important part of the most spectacular break-ins that have occurred in recent years. For example, in 1986 a series of break-ins occurred at Stanford University in California. These were made possible by certain features of the UNIX operating system (one of the most popular operating systems in academic computing) as well as the laxness of the systems programmers administering these systems.[11] The weaknesses included the networking features of certain versions of UNIX and the fact that this operating system will often allow users to log on using a 'guest' account (usually with the same password, 'guest'). Once into the first system, hackers were able to impersonate other users (again, knowing a couple of the classic weaknesses of UNIX) and gain access to other machines in the network that these same users had legitimate access to. The well-publicized hack carried out by Mathias Speer in 1988, in which he penetrated dozens of computers and networks across the world, also used many of these techniques to cross from machine to machine and from network to network.

In other cases, system and network inadequacies can sometimes be exploited to obtain access. For example, a persistent hacker can sometimes grab a line with legitimate privileges after a legitimate user logs out. This can happen if the log out sequence is not yet completed and the line that the legitimate user relinquishes has not yet hung up. If the hacker happens to log on to the system in those few microseconds, it is sometimes possible for him or her to grab the line and 'job' of the legitimate user, who, more often than not, will be preparing to walk away from the terminal.[12]

For those who are interested in further details of the techniques that hackers use, a particularly clear and comprehensive guide can be found in Hugo Cornwall's book, *Hacker's Handbook III* (Century, London, 1988). Cornwall details not only a potted history of hacking in the UK, but also describes the principles of digital communication and even some of the information one needs to commit radio hacks (that is, those which involve radio transmissions and datastreams). Another 'how-to-do-it' book which has had a wide impact is Bill Landreth's *Out of the Inner Circle*. Landreth is a top system cracker who was a key figure in the legendary hacker group known as the 'inner circle'. Some press articles have reported Landreth's disappearance, amid rumours that he planned to commit suicide on his twenty-second birthday and fears that the inner circle were preparing to avenge themselves on Landreth for his breaking their code of silence.[13]

Hackers: Criminals or Modern-Day Robin Hoods?

The mass media has tended to sensationalize hacking, whilst soundly condemning it. But there are other points of view: for example, in many instances the breaching of systems can provide more effective security in future, so that other (presumably less well-intentioned) hackers are prevented from causing real harm.[14] A good illustration of this was the penetration of British Telecom's electronic mail system in 1984 by Steven Gold and Robert Schifreen, which resulted in a rude message being left in none other than the Duke of Edinburgh's account! This incident attracted enormous publicity and led directly to improved security arrangements for the whole of the Prestel system. Gold and Schifreen were therefore extremely indignant at being treated as criminals – and this illustrates once again the discrepancy between what the law considers to be criminal behaviour and how hackers perceive themselves. Although Gold and Schifreen were convicted under the Forgery Act and fined a total of £2,350, an appeal saw the charges quashed. It was argued that since the hackers caused no damage and did not defraud anyone, then they could not be held guilty of an offence.[15]

We might therefore ask ourselves whether, for the sake of balance, a truly democratic society should possess a core of technically gifted but recalcitrant people. Given that more and more information about individuals is now being stored on computers, often without our knowledge or consent, is it not reassuring that some citizens are able to penetrate these databases to find out what is going on? Thus it could be argued that hackers represent one way in which we can help avoid the creation of a more centralized, even totalitarian government. This is one scenario that hackers openly entertain. Indeed, we now know that at the time of the Chernobyl nuclear power station disaster in the Soviet Union, hackers from the Chaos Computer Club released more information to the public about developments than did the West German government itself. All of this information was gained by illegal break-ins carried out in government computer installations.

Given this background and the possibility of terrorist acts becoming more and more technologically sophisticated, perhaps we can also look to hackers as a resource to be used to foil such acts and to improve our existing security arrangements. To some extent this is already happening: in the US, convicted hackers are regularly approached by security and intelligence organizations with offers to join them in return for amelioration or suspension of sentences. Other hackers have used their notoriety to establish computer security firms and to turn their covertly gained knowledge to the benefit of commercial and public institutions.[16]

Perhaps we should simply recognize that in a fair and open society there is a tension between the capabilities of government and the capabilities of individuals and groups of concerned citizens. As the communications theorist Harold Innes stated in the the 1930s, in terms of information control, there is a constant struggle between centralizing and decentralizing forces. Clearly, total centralization of information poses significant problems for the rights of individuals and for the proper conduct of a democratic government. On the other hand, total decentralization of information resources can lead to gross inefficiencies and even the denial of services or aberrations in the quality of services provided by government. So long as this tension exists and so long as things do not become unbalanced, then we can remain reasonably assured that the society we live in and the governments we elect are fairly effective and equitable. Perhaps, with the advent of digital computers and telecommunications, hacking represents an expansion of this struggle into a different domain. Admittedly, hacking has the potential to cause enormous harm by utilizing resources that have tremendous power. Yet we should not forget that there are other, equally powerful and much older ways in which similar powers can be unleashed. Leaks to the press, espionage of all kinds and high-quality investigative journalism (such as that which uncovered Watergate and the Iran-Contra affair) have the power to break a government's control of information flow to the public, and can even destroy corporations or governments that have been shown to be guilty of unethical or criminal acts.

Perhaps therefore the hallmark of a democracy is its capacity to tolerate people of all kinds, from different ethnic backgrounds, cultural beliefs and religions, as well as those with radically opposing political views. It remains to be seen whether hacking in all its forms is banned as a criminal offence in most modern democracies or whether some forms of it will be tolerated. From an ethical perspective, does the outlawing of hacking bear any resemblance to attempts to outlaw the Nazi or Communist parties? Is it equivalent to criminalizing investigative journalism just because journalists have been known to bribe officials or to obtain information unlawfully? As always, a balance must be struck between the ethical difficulties that are attached to activities such as investigative journalism and hacking and the greater public good that may (or may not) arise from them. Indeed, to complete the analogy, we should bear in mind that a great deal of journalism is simply malicious 'muck-raking' that can damage a government or a company much more deeply than can some simple kinds of hacking. On the other hand, we need the muck-rakers: the press is the principal institution that most democracies rely upon to ensure that the people are informed and that citizens remain aware of what is being done in their name. It remains to be seen how these issues are dealt with by the criminal justice system and by the hacking community itself.

Some 'Great' Hacks

One of the most famous hackers was 'Mathias Speer' (a pseudonym), who over a two year period penetrated up to 30 computers in the US, West Germany, Japan and Canada. From his base in a university in Hanover, West Germany, Speer wandered through the networks to gain access to important sites including the Lawrence Berkeley Laboratory and various systems owned by its contractors, as well as the US Navy Data Center in Norfolk, Virginia, various army and navy bases in the US and Germany and a number of other university-owned machines. In an elaborate 'Sting' operation, Speer was caught by being enticed with dummy files that appeared to contain top secret information on the Strategic Defence Initiative ('Star Wars'). The act of downloading the files to his own system required Speer to be connected for an extended period of time and this allowed FBI officials to complete the telephone trace they had tried to set up for ten months. In some quarters, Speer has been linked with an American arms dealer who has dealt in weapons sales to Saudi Arabia and who suspiciously sent an information request to the Berkeley Laboratory on the bogus project which trapped Speer. The question is, of course, how did this person know of the fictitious project unless he had a relationship with Speer?[17]

Another famous hack was carried out by the Chaos Computer Club of Hamburg, West Germany. Among other things, this group managed to penetrate systems at the European Nuclear Research Centre (CERN) in Geneva, Switzerland and the French subsidiary of the Dutch electronics firm Phillips. It is also reported that in a six-month period Chaos used NASA's Space Physics Analysis Network (SPAN) to gain access to 175 computers throughout the world, including the West German Max Planck Institute, the West German Institute for Space Research, the Massachusetts Institute of Technology and the Paris Observatory. In 1989, a West German hacker suspected of selling Western computer secrets to the KGB was found burned to death near Gifhorn, east of Hanover. 24 year-old Karl Koch was one of eight West German hackers under investigation for allegedly supplying Soviet agents with codewords to gain access to Western defence and research computers, including Optimus, the Department of Defence's databank, NASA computers and Star Wars research computers. Three were later arrested and accused of selling secrets to the KGB. It remained unclear whether Koch's death was murder or suicide.[18]

And as we noted in chapter 2, in 1986 British hackers were allegedly breaking into the Driver and Vehicle Licensing Centre (DVLC) in Swansea, South Wales, in order to 'doctor' the records of drivers who were already disqualified or who were on the verge of it. At a price of £100 per erased offence, the profits could have been considerable.

But perhaps the most frightening aspect of system penetrations, however, is the extent to which they may go unreported. This may happen for a variety of reasons, including the eagerness of companies or corporations to avoid a loss of public confidence (which in itself could be more costly than the damage caused by the hack), the protracted nature of court cases and the hazy nature of the laws governing unauthorized intrusions into computer systems. There have even been instances of financial institutions doing deals with hackers and fraudsters, actually allowing them to keep a share of their spoils in return for information about how they accomplished their feat. For example, in 1989 the London *Sunday Times* reported the astonishing tale of six City of London banks and brokerage houses who had allegedly signed agreements with criminals offering them amnesty and money in return for their silence and the secrets of their trade. In one case, an assistant programmer is supposed to have netted £1 million for his criminal efforts. A spokesman for the Computer Industry Research Unit (CIRU), which uncovered the deals, said: 'Companies who feel vulnerable are running scared by agreeing to these immoral deals. Their selfishness is storing up serious problems for everyone else.' Police warned that employers doing such deals could be prosecuted for perverting the course of justice.[19]

Worms, Trojan Horses and Time Bombs

New terms are entering the nomenclature of computing, many of them borrowed from other domains and many of them with sinister connotations. The following definitions may assist the reader in identifying the differences and similarities among some of these terms:

Trojan Horse   A program that allows easy access to an already-penetrated system – for example, by establishing a new account with super-user privileges. This helps avoid overuse of the system manager's (super-user) account, which may show up on system statistics. It can also refer to a program that gathers the log ins and passwords of legitimate users so that those who have already penetrated a system can log in under a wider variety of accounts. Sometimes confused with a 'trap door' – which is generally a secret entry that a system designer builds into a system so that once they have left, he or she may gain access at any time without fear of discovery. The principle of the Trojan Horse relies upon successful penetration and creation of alternative entry paths.

Logic Bomb or Time Bomb   A program which is triggered to act upon detecting a certain sequence of events or after a particular period of time has elapsed. For example, a popular form of logic bomb monitors employment files and initiates system damage (such as erasure of hard discs or secret corruption of key programs) once the programmer's employment has been terminated. A simple variation on the theme is to have a logic bomb virus, that is, a virus that begins to replicate and destroy a system once triggered by a time lapse, a set of preprogrammed conditions coming into existence, or by remote control using the appropriate password.

Virus   A self-replicating program that causes damage – generally hard disk erasure or file corruption – and infects other programs, floppy or hard disks by copying itself on to them (particularly onto components of the operating system or 'boot' sectors of a disk). Viruses use a variety of strategies to avoid detection. Some are harmless, merely informing the user that their system has been infected without destroying components of the system. Most are not and identification of their creators can be virtually impossible, although some have been quite prepared to identify themselves.

Vaccine or Disinfectant   A program that searches for viruses and notifies the user that a form of virus has been detected in their system. Some are general purpose programs which search for a wide range of viruses, while others are more restricted and are only capable of identifying a particular virus type. Some are capable of eradicating the virus, but there are relatively few such programs. Other forms of virus protection include isolation of the infected system(s), use of 'non-writable' system discs so that viruses cannot copy themselves there and testing of unknown software (particularly public domain software downloaded from bulletin boards) on a minimal, isolated system.

Worm   A self-replicating program that infects idle workstations or terminals on a network. The earliest worms were exploratory programs that demonstrated the concept itself and were generally non-destructive, although they often replicated to the point when a network would collapse. The latter phenomenon was used to good effect as the basis of the science fiction book, *Shockwave Rider* by John Brunner (Ballantine, New York, 1975). Worms tend to exist in memory and are non-permanent, whereas viruses tend to reside on disc where they are permanent until eradicated. In addition, worms are network-orientated, with 'segments' of the worm inhabiting different machines and being cognizant of the existence of other segments in other nodes of the network. Worms actively seek out idle machines and retreat when machine load increases. Viruses (at present) have none of these capabilities.

Tempest   A term which refers to the electronic emissions that computers generate as they work. With the right equipment, these transmissions can be monitored, stored and analysed to help discover what the computer was doing. As would be expected, most security agencies throughout the world are interested in this phenomenon, but up to this point in time it has not been the mechanism for any known hack. But given time, who knows?

The Virus Invasion

Software viruses are the most recent computer phenomenon to hit the headlines. Indeed, hardly a day goes by without reports of new viruses or accounts of a virus attacks that have resulted in the destruction of data and the shutdown of networks.

Yet the concept of a virus is not altogether new. Its precursor – the worm – was created in the early 1980s, when computer scientists John Schoch and Jon Hupp devised a program that would spread from machine to machine, steadily occupying the idle resources of the Xerox Palo Alto Research Center's network.[20] These early worms were fairly harmless and were only released at night when network traffic was low and when the machines were unlikely to be used in any case. Whatever maliciousness was embedded in worm-type programs lay in their tendency to consume resources – particularly memory – until a system or network collapsed. Nevertheless, worms almost never caused any permanent damage – to rid a machine or network of a worm, all one had to do was to restart the machine or reboot the network.

The conceptualization and development of viruses had a longer gestation period. Other precursors to the virus included a number of experimental computer games including the game program known as 'Core Wars'.[21] This game operates by setting aside an area of machine memory (which in the earliest days of computing was often called the 'core') as a battleground for programs to compete for territory and to attempt to destroy each other. In order to understand how Core Wars works, and its relationship to the virus concept, we need to understand a little about the structure and nature of computer memory and Core Wars programs themselves.

To begin with, computer memory can be regarded as a series of pigeonholes or boxes in which an instruction, some data or another memory 'address' can be located. The following schematics represent a typical Core Wars battle:

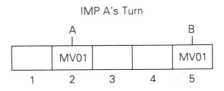

The letters 'A' and 'B' identify the location of the two combatants. The contents of address 2 in the above schematic is a machine code instruction which is in fact a Core Wars program called IMP. Address 5 also contains an IMP program – the first IMP's adversary (there are many kinds of Core Wars programs, IMP is among the simplest, but also one of the most powerful). The battle proceeds like this: it is IMP A's turn and its program is executed; MV01 (the IMP program) means 'move the contents of an address that is 0 addresses away (that is, the current address or address 2) into an address that is 1 address away' (that is, address 3). Essentially, this copies the contents of address 2 (the IMP program itself) to address 3. In other words, IMP A has replicated itself.

When this has been done and it is IMP B's turn, IMP A has copied itself to address 3 and IMP B moves to address 4 (by executing its own program). This state of affairs is represented below:

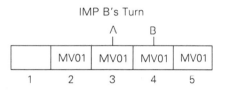

When it is IMP A's turn again, it already occupies address 3 (as well as its prior addresses), while IMP B occupies addresses 4 and 5. On IMP A's second turn (which we need not show here), it copies itself into address 4 (again by executing its MV01 instruction) which is where the current IMP B resides. Hence, by overwriting IMP B, IMP A has won this battle.

The bulk of Core Wars programs (and battles) are not this simple. Many of the more complex programs have facilities for repairing themselves, for totally relocating themselves in memory (i.e. evading enemy programs) and can even detect the approach of other programs by having 'sentinels'. What is most important about Core Wars, however, and indeed this whole genre of game programs such as the game of LIFE and Wa-Tor (both games that demonstrate evolution of 'life-forms' in a computer-generated environment) is their common notion of reproduction in a computer-based system.

Indeed, this concept of a program reproducing itself began to fascinate many people and in particular the notion that a program could spread itself beyond the boundaries of a single machine or network attracted a growing interest. The acknowledged originators of the virus concept were Fred

Cohen and Len Adleman (who actually thought of the term 'virus'). At a computer security conference sponsored by the International Federation of Information Processing (IFIP) in 1984, they publicly announced the results of a range of experiments they had conducted using viruses to infect a range of different networks and host machines.[22] Their experiments showed just how easily isolated machines and even whole networks could succumb to simple viral forms. In fact, their experiments were so successful that they were often banned from carrying out further experiments by the administrators of various systems. Yet, despite this and other public warnings of the future threat of software viruses, the first viral epidemics took much of the computing world by surprise.[23]

By far the most obvious (and common) way to virally infect a system is to piggyback a virus on to bonafide programs so that it can be transported on storage media such as tapes, floppy disks and hard disks. In addition, a virus can be transported via network links and electronic mail. So long as the virus appears to be either a legitimate program or is capable of attaching itself to legitimate programs (such as the operating system itself), then its spread to other system users and countries can almost be assured. It should be noted, though, that although most of the current crop of viruses are maliciously destructive, a number of viruses have been released that are really quite harmless – usually informing the user that the virus has only occupied a few bytes of disk space. More common viruses tend to erase the entire contents of a user's hard disk or else corrupt programs and data to the point where they are irretrievably damaged and quite useless.

Perhaps the most widely reported virus attack occurred in October 1987 when large numbers of microcomputer users throughout the United States began to report problems with their data disks. A quick inspection of the volume labels of these disks (a volume label is a user-supplied name for the disk-like 'cash flow figures') showed that they all possessed the same volume label: '© Brain'. For these reasons, the identified virus is often referred to as the 'Brain' virus or even as the 'Pakistani' virus after the author's Pakistan address which is revealed if the boot sector of the disk is inspected. Although this virus caused some data loss, procedures were soon implemented which effectively eliminated the virus. These included only using system disks that were write-protected, so that the virus could not copy itself from one system disk to another, as well as programs that identified an infected disk and rewrote the boot sector so that the virus was destroyed.[24]

Shortly before Thanksgiving in 1987 a further virus was discovered at Lehigh University in Bethlehem, Pennsylvania (and hence called the Lehigh virus). This virus appeared to be a particularly malicious one in that it totally destroyed a disk's contents once the disk had been copied four times. Unlike the Brain virus which spread when an infected disk was totally copied, the Lehigh virus appeared to be much more virulent and intelligent. Once it had infected a disk, this virus checked all other disks inserted into the machine. If they were 'bootable' (that is, they carried a copy of the operating system on them), the virus then checked if the disk was already infected and if it wasn't, it copied itself onto the new disk. Fortunately, the same kinds of countermeasures that were effective against the Brain virus were also effective against the Lehigh virus and it now appears to have been eradicated.[25]

And in yet another incident, Israeli pcs showed signs of viral infection in December 1987, when programs that had been run thousands of times without incident suddenly became too large to fit within available memory. This virus, which was disassembled by computer scientists at the Hebrew University of Jerusalem, exhibited a somewhat different *modus operandi*. It appeared to work by copying itself into memory and then attaching itself to any other program that the user might subsequently execute. The author of this virus had also been clever enough to program the virus so that it exhibited different effects over several months (almost a form of time bomb). In 1988, the virus would wait 30 minutes after the machine had been booted up, then it would slow the machine down by a factor of around five and portions of the screen would be uncontrollably scrolled. More important though, it was found that if the date was Friday the 13th (any Friday the 13th after 1987), then any program that was executed was erased from the disk. It was soon found that the virus was extremely widespread in both the Jerusalem and Haifa areas with an estimated infection base of between 10,000 and 20,000 disks. But once again, antiviral software was written to identify infected files and kill the virus, while another program was written to act as a sentinel, warning users if an attempt had been made to infect their disks.[26]

In November 1988 a 23 year-old Cornell University computer science student, Robert Morris, devised a worm program that crippled the network connecting MIT, the RAND Corporation, NASA's Ames Research Centre and other American universities. This virus was said to have spread to 6,000 machines before being detected. In June 1989 Morris was suspended from college after having been found guilty of violating the university's code of academic integrity. The FBI also carried out an investigation into this remarkable virus attack and Morris was later charged under the Computer Fraud and Abuse Act, 1986, with unauthorized access to government computers. He faced a maximum five-year prison sentence and up to $250,000 fine if convicted.[27] Meanwhile in Australia, the first person to be charged with computer trespass under the Crimes (Computers) Act

1988 appeared in court in Melbourne in August 1989. Deon Barylak, a student at Swinburne Institute of Technology, was arrested after a virus was released into computers at the college.

Conceptually speaking though, it is possible for viruses and worms to achieve much more sophisticated disruption and it is quite likely that the next 'generation' of software viruses will exhibit a quantum jump in intelligence and destructiveness. For example, it would be possible to develop a virus that only affected a particular user on a particular network. In other words, given sufficient technical expertise, instead of affecting all users, the virus would wait until a particular user ID executed an infected program. Then the virus would copy itself into the disk area of that user and begin to wreak havoc. Alternatively, viruses may have a range of effects which they carry out on a random schedule, such as slowing a system down, deleting electronic mail, 'fuzzing' the screen (which almost certainly will be attributed to a hardware problem) and encrypting files with a randomly selected encryption key (this would effectively deny users access to their own files until the key was discovered – an almost impossible task in itself). Such strategies would delay the identification of a viral infection for an extended period, since the set of 'symptoms' would be large and extremely variable.

Indeed, the next generation of viruses will probably be more selective, not only in whom they act upon, and in the acts they carry out, but also in their objectives. This raises a number of interesting questions and hypothetical scenarios. For example, could viruses be used for espionage purposes, not only infiltrating Soviet machines to delete their files, but gathering intelligence data that is mailed back (electronically) or eventually gathered as versions of the virus filter back to the West? Could viruses become the next research field for CIA-KGB competition, in much the same way that research into cryptography is currently? (Apparently, another science fiction book has encapsulated this theme – *Softwar: La Guerre Douce* by French authors Thierry Breton and Denis Beneich depicts this scenario in pre-Glasnost days.) And indeed, given the remarkable swiftness with which Western technology 'appears' on the other side of the Iron Curtain – as a result of state-sponsored industrial espionage – the ease with which such hardware could be virally infected should not be underestimated.[28]

There are some developments which also suggest that this is not mere speculation. Already, the analogy of a computer system as an organism and a virus as an infection has been extended to incorporate the development of virus-killing programs called vaccines. These programs look for virus symptoms and notify the user that their system has been infected. Some of the better vaccines actually seek out the virus and kill it by repairing infected files. Furthermore, just as we would expect to eliminate a virus by the use of quarantine procedures when dealing with infected systems and media, these procedures work equally well. But for many virus attacks the only solution – provided a vaccine doesn't work – is to erase the hard disk as well as any other media (tapes, floppy disks) that can't be guaranteed not to have come into contact with the virus (almost like burning linen and other possibly infected items!). Then, clean copies of the system and back-up disks are reloaded onto the hard disk. Until this is done, the computer should not be used for any other purpose and the trading of storage media is extremely unwise. Yet perhaps the best form of defence against viruses is to make them much more difficult to write. Some experts have argued that the way to do this is to place the operating system on a read-only disk or in ROM (read-only memory composed of chips – it cannot be altered and hence infected). Other procedures include carrying out 'parity' checks on software – basically an arithmetic calculation on a file (such as an addition) – if the calculation yields the correct result, it is unlikely that it has been tampered with; making each copy of an operating system different in its physical layout (that is, its pattern of storage on disk); and whenever using a disk for the first time, making sure that the operating system on disk matches that in memory.[29]

Because of the risks that virus attacks pose to the knowledge assets of large companies and corporations, and because of their lack of experience in dealing with them, a number of security firms have sprung up to exploit this rich commercial niche. Furthermore, the development of hardware forms of 'viruses' has fuelled the demand for such firms, particularly since the discovery of the device known as 'Big Red'. This is a small electronic gadget which is surreptitiously installed in a computer by an insider or commercial saboteur. Like software viruses, this device is parasitic in that it interfaces with the host computer's operating system and converts encrypted files into 'invisible' ones that can be easily inspected by other users, if they know where the files are and what to look for. At least 50 Big Reds have been found in the US, the UK and Australia in banking and transaction handling systems.[30]

Ethical Issues

Some of the ethical difficulties associated with hacking and viruses are already quite well known, while other more hypothetical ones have yet to emerge. With regard to hacking or system penetration, the legal position in different countries is very confusing and is sometimes contradictory. But the central issues involved in hacking remain almost universal.

When a hacker gains access to a system and 'rummages around' in a company's files without actually altering anything, what damage has he or she caused? Have they simply stolen a few thousandths of a penny's worth of electricity (as can be the case in the UK)? Indeed, if the hacker informs a company of their lax security procedures, is he creating a public benefit by performing a service that they might otherwise have to pay for? In some countries such as Canada, it is not an offence to walk into somebody's residence, then look around and leave – as long as nothing has been altered or damaged. Can a hacker's 'walk through' of a system be considered in similar terms?

Unfortunately, the legal basis of system break-ins languishes in the dark ages of real locks and doors and physical forms of information such as blueprints and contracts. Equally, the law as it applies to breaking and entering – the destruction of physical locks – and the theft of information as it exists in paper form, is a poor analogy when applied to the electronic locks that modems and password systems provide and the highly mutable forms of information that computer files represent. After all, when one 'breaks' into a system, nothing has been broken at all – hence there is no obvious intent to cause harm. When a file has been copied or selectively viewed, then what has been stolen? The information is, after all, still there. And if one happens to try out a few programs while browsing through a system, is this almost analogous to seeing someone's bicycle, riding it for a few metres and then putting it back? Again, what harm has been caused, what crime has been committed? In the eyes of many hackers, only in the most trivial sense could this be considered as unlawful use.

On the other hand, where malicious damage of information does occur (such as the destruction of patients' records in a health administration system), then clearly a form of criminal act has occurred. The problem lies in determining the extent of the damage and the degree to which the act is premeditated. Unfortunately, in a complex and perhaps poorly understood computer system, it is quite easy to cause unintentional damage, yet it is extremely difficult to determine the extent to which the act was maliciously premeditated. In addition, for those 'figuring out' a system for the first time, it is difficult to estimate the consequences of some acts or the extent to which a command sequence may alter the functionality of a system. Is this an example of ignorance of the law and is it equally unacceptable as a defence?

At present in the UK, hackers can be prosecuted under a number of different criminal and civil acts although no specific anti-hacking laws have been passed. For instance, it has now been confirmed that in the event of a hacker copying or reproducing files, the civil law provides remedies for breach of confidence and copyright law. That is, computer-based information is now considered copyright and in the event of a system penetration, the owners of this information are considered to have been damaged in terms of breach of copyright, thereby having the right to sue for damages. If a hacker destroys information, alters it or leaves electronic graffiti, then the Criminal Damage Act of 1971 can be applied, while at the very least, if he is caught, a hacker can be prosecuted under the Theft Act of 1968 on a charge of 'abstracting' electricity. But simple unauthorized access is not a crime, although it may soon be made illegal.[31]

Perhaps what is central to the ethical debate regarding break-ins, lies and other hacker behaviour, is the different conceptualizations of systems by their owners and by would-be hackers. For a system owner, the system is their property (as suggested by the above legal framework) – physical, touchable collections of central processors and disk drives – bought and paid for and maintained for the use of authorized individuals to carry out authorized functions for the company's benefit. Any unauthorized person or even a duly authorized person who uses the system for unauthorized purposes is therefore guilty of a form of unlawful use – a criminal act in the eyes of the owners. For the hacker, however, a system is an abstract resource at the end of a telephone line. It is a challenging talisman, an instrument they can borrow for a while and then return, hopefully without any damage done and without anybody being the wiser.

We enter a different arena, however, when we encounter acts of theft and wilful damage. Clearly, the theft of credit card numbers and their circulation to other hackers is indeed a criminal act as is their use to obtain free telephone calls or to charge up other goods and services. The destruction of information or its intentional alteration on a computer system can be regarded in similar terms. Yet to return to our earlier point, should we rightly regard browsing through a system a criminal act in the way that the British criminal code obviously does? Perhaps it depends upon the nature of the information and who owns it. Undoubtedly, the operators of a military installation would prosecute over any unauthorized access, even if the system was concerned with the control of the army's laundry requirements! Certainly, the government and the military have the right to deny access to certain information if they believe that it is central to the nation's defence or to its continued good government. Yet, is a laundry service central to national security or good government? Once again, we encounter a very familiar dilemma: who 'owns' this information and who should or shouldn't have access to it.

In the private sector we might even ask: 'What right does a company have to hold information on individuals and what right do they have to deny individuals access to that information? For example, many commercial institutions tap into databases which hold the credit ratings of hundreds of thousands of people. The providers of these databases have collected information from a huge range of sources and organized it so that it constitutes a history and an assessment of our trustworthiness as debtors. Who gave these companies the right to gather such information? Who gave them the right to sell it (which they do, along with subscription lists, names and addresses)? What limits are there on the consequences of this information for the quality of our lives? What rights should we have in ensuring that our particulars are correct? Now, if we imagine a hacker penetrating a system so that he can correct the records of those who have been denied correction of incorrect data, which of these entities – the database owners or the hacker – has committed the greatest ethical error (or are both equally guilty)?

Perhaps the final issue is that concerning information ownership: should information about me be owned by me? Or should I, as a database operator, own any information that I have paid to be gathered and stored? On the other hand, given that the storage of information is so pervasive and the very functioning of our modern society relies upon computer-based data storage, does the public have the right to demand absolute security in these systems? Finally, should some hackers be regarded as our unofficial investigative journalists – finding out who holds what information on whom and for what purpose; checking if corporations are indeed adhering to the data protection laws; and exposing flagrant abuses that the government cannot or will not terminate?

It would appear that there are many organizations in modern society which claim to possess rights in the gathering and maintenance of information and its application in the form of computer-based information systems. In addition, apart from the dangers of the centralization of government power and authority, the centralization of information in powerful computer systems increases their influence in running our societies and in turn acts to make us more reliant upon them, thereby increasing their influence even further. In this milieu the hacker or virus inventor represents a dangerous threat. Yet, like the corporations and institutions he acts against, he also claims certain rights in terms of information access and ownership. In monitoring these developments, perhaps we should always bear in mind that a fundamental model of a rational society is a model of conflict and consensus. Consensus does not appear without conflict (otherwise, what would be the point of it?), nor should we expect consensus to be total. Indeed, it can be argued that struggle and debate are a necessary component in the rational development of any society. In this sense, the continuing controversy that surrounds hackers and others who challenge the integrity of critical information systems, can be seen to be an extension of this same process. Given the world's present rapid rate of change, perhaps it is reassuring to note that the more things change, the more they stay the same.

Suggestions for Further Discussion

You may wish to think about the following, hypothetical scenario.

Imagine that a medical researcher who is interested in epidemiology (the study of epidemics) wishes to use a benign computer virus to help verify some of his theoretical models of how diseases spread. In fact, in the early days of computer viruses, such studies were allegedly carried out,[32] although the scenario we have constructed here is not based on this material, but merely the general circumstances which might or might not arise in such a study.

Suppose that the virus the researcher uses is of the kind that simply alerts the user to the fact that their computer has been infected and also informs them that the virus is benign and will spontaneously self-destruct or disappear in, say, a week. The 'alert' message also asks the user not to eradicate the virus (since it isn't doing any harm anyway) and to continue with the normal program-sharing and trading (illegal though it might be) that they normally engage in. The virus also asks the computer owner to write to the researcher (free of charge) to provide him with the information he needs to help study and model the epidemiological characteristics of the virus. This information, among other things, might include the location of the computer, the time the computer became infected (approximately) and the most likely source of infection. The aim of the research project is to see how fast and along what paths the virus is communicated and to determine whether this pattern of development bears any relationship to that which typical human diseases exhibit when they spread through a human population.

Now, there are some laudable aims expressed in this scenario. The researcher's ultimate aim is to more clearly understand the nature of human epidemics so that (presumably) they might be more easily brought under control. Therefore, in the end, this researcher is concerned with saving human lives. The methods used however might be thought of as unethical for a variety of reasons. To begin with, whether the virus is harmless or not, it does, nevertheless, consume resources that are not owned by the virus's creator (memory, user's time and attention, etc.). Moreover, the virus may actually rely upon the illegal software copying activities of many computer users in order to propagate itself.

Even further, although the medical researcher's aims are clearly in the medical domain, it is possible that this information could be used in applications quite outside this sphere. For example, those concerned with software piracy could use this information as some rough metric of the rate of software piracy and use it to enforce legislation of a particular sort (for example, placing a tax on all computer media to compensate software authors for the average rate of piracy that their work is likely to experience).

In addition, if these data have some bearing upon our understanding of how human epidemics develop, then other agencies, such as germ warfare establishments, may also be able to apply the data obtained to their research so that more effective forms of germ agent dispersal and disease transmission are obtained. Furthermore, in none of these applications – not even in the original epidemiological study – has the permission of the information suppliers been sought. Indeed, the computer users, almost by definition (given the nature of this project), have been 'roped in' without their consent. They may choose not to participate further, but to some extent they have already become involved without their prior, conscious and considered consent.

In many ways, this situation resembles involuntary experimentation that could occur in almost any field. How would you feel if a psychological research institute bought TV advertising time and simulated the announcement of a nuclear attack (just as Orson Welles simulated the radio coverage of an alien invasion), and then asked people to respond to them describing their reactions and feelings? In this case, too, the prior consent of individuals was not sought, although they too may have some choice about further participation. Indeed, it is most unlikely that any such experiment would ever be officially endorsed, let alone conducted by researchers in Western nations. It is clearly too unethical, not only bringing about possible psychological damage and extreme stress, but also being based on deception of the potential participants.

It is quite obvious that in the case of our hypothetical virus experiment, at least some amount of deception must be involved if the study has any chance of 'succeeding' at all. That is, unless the virus was disguised in some way or attached to another (presumably useful) program, then it is unlikely that many users would attempt to acquire it, thereby preventing their systems from becoming infected.

Furthermore, it is not difficult to see that many computer users could become suspicious of the 'real' nature of such a project. When they respond, all they are responding to is a name and an associated post-free address. The apparent aims of the project may seem noble enough, but what if this wasn't the real nature of the project? Although it may seem far fetched, in recent years a number of papers have appeared which have depicted the real possibility of computer viruses being used as a military weapon. Imagine for a moment that, say, the US military creates a virus that is attached to a very useful public domain utility program, then loads it onto thousands of discs and distributes it to bulletin boards and networks. Inevitably, the software will reach the Soviet Union either through discs being posted there or through the trade of information that is a normal component of dialogue and international relations. Of course, rather than sabotage their own networks, the American devisers of the virus have made sure that it will only be triggered by a Soviet computing environment (for example, known operating characteristics of Soviet machines, or even the presence of large numbers of text files in Russian).

Now this constitutes an act of war, but it is the kind of war that has been going on between the super-powers for more than 40 years. Among other dangerous activities, American submarines and Soviet ships and aircraft regularly play dangerous games with each other in the Arctic circle, often bringing about minor collisions and other forms of damage. For the isolated computer user faced with responding to our researcher's request, it is possible (albeit remotely) that he or she is participating in a study (by some secret security agency) that will determine if and how a campaign of viral warfare could become feasible. Indeed, the most paranoid of us could conceive of a situation where the medical research request is a clever cover and that responding is simply an unnecessary diversion. Perhaps the 'real' information is gathered by the virus anyway and accumulated as it passes from one system to the next. The 'real' project is completed when the agency begins to collect discs from isolated locations and begins its analysis of transmission rates and transmission paths, as well as forms of viral protection and defence.

Notes

1 'Conclusion of the HBO Captain Midnight saga', *Software Engineering Notes*, vol. 11, no. 5, 1986, pp. 24–5.
2 *Software Engineering Notes*, vol. 13, no. 1, 1988, p. 7.
3 'Enter the technically-competent terrorist', *The Australian*, 8 April 1986; Perry Morrison, 'Limits to technocratic consciousness: information technology and terrorism as example', *Science, Technology and Human Values*, vol. 11, no. 4, 1986, pp. 4–16.
4 Peter G. Neumann, review of Guy Steele et al., *The Hacker's Dictionary: A Guide to the World of Computer Wizards*, in *Software Engineering Notes*, vol. 9, no. 1, 1984, pp. 12–15.

5 Peter G. Neumann, ibid.
6 Stuart Gill, 'Hi-tech's hubcap thieves are in it for the buzz', *Computing Australia*, 26 October 1987, pp. 33–4.
7 *Minneapolis Star and Tribune*, 23 May 1985, p. 1A.
8 Sara Kiesler, Jane Siegel and Timothy McGuire, 'Social psychological aspects of computer-mediated communication', *American Psychologist*, vol. 39, no. 10, 1984, pp. 1123–34; Daniel Goleman, 'The electronic Rorshach', *Psychology Today*, February 1983, pp. 37–43.
9 Rosemarie Robotham, 'Putting hackers on the analyst's couch', *The Australian*, 31 January 1989, pp. 30–4.
10 'NASA hackers weren't as smart as it seems', *Computing Australia*, 13 July 1987.
11 Brian Reid, 'Lessons from the UNIX break-ins at Stanford', *Software Engineering Notes*, vol. 11, no. 5, 1986, p. 29.
12 'More on nonsecure nonlogouts', *Software Engineering Notes*, vol. 11, no. 5, 1986, p. 26.
13 Peter Lowe, 'Still no trace of high-profile hacker author', *The Australian*, 10 February 1987.
14 I. S. Herschberg and R. Paans, 'The programmer's threat: cases and causes', in J. H. Finch and E. G. Dougall (eds), *Computer Security: A Global Challenge* (Elsevier, North-Holland, 1984), pp. 409–23.
15 'Hacking away at shaky security', *The Australian*, 26 January 1988; 'Hackers found guilty after cracking duke's code', *The Australian*, 29 April 1986; 'Lords clear British hackers', *New Scientist*, 28 April 1988, p. 25; 'Hackers appeal on Prestel conviction', *Computing Australia*, 13 July 1987, p. 13.
16 Jay Peterzell, 'Spying and sabotage by computer', *Time*, 20 March 1989; Richard Caseby, 'Worried firms pay hush money to hacker thieves', *South China Morning Post*, 12 June 1989 (reprinted from *The Times*); and 'Open season for hackers', *Computing Australia*, 18 September 1989.
17 Ian Anderson, 'Hacker runs rings round military security', *New Scientist*, 28 April 1988, p. 25; also see *Time*, 2 May 1988.
18 See reports in *The Australian*, 16 September, 22 September and 6 October 1987, and 13 June 1989; and continuing coverage of the alleged KGB spies on 'Risks' and in *Software Engineering Notes*.
19 'City of London brokers buy hackers' silence', reprinted from *The Sunday Times* in *The Australian*, 6 June 1989; 'Drivers hiring hackers to erase licence records', *The Australian*, 8 April 1986.
20 J. F. Schoch and J. A. Hupp, 'The worm programs – early experiences with distributed computation', *Communications of the ACM*, vol. 25, no. 3, 1982, pp. 172–80.
21 A. K. Dewdney, 'Computer recreations', *Scientific American*, May 1984, pp. 15–19 and March 1985, pp. 14–19.
22 Fred Cohen, 'Computer viruses: theory and experiments', in Finch and Dougall, *Computer Security*, pp. 143–57.
23 Perry Morrison, 'Computer parasites: software diseases may cripple our computers', *The Futurist*, March–April 1986, vol. 20, no. 2, pp. 36–8; Lee Dembart, 'Attack of the computer virus', *Discover*, November 1984, pp. 90–2.
24 Anne E. Webster, 'University of Delaware and the Pakistani virus', *Computers and Security*, vol. 8, 1989, pp. 103–5.

25 Kenneth R. van Wyk, 'The Lehigh virus', *Computers and Security*, vol. 8, 1989, pp. 107–10.

26 Yisrael Radai, 'The Israeli PC virus', *Computers and Security*, vol. 8, 1989, pp. 111–13.

27 'Cornell virus suspect suspended for violation', *The Australian*, 6 June 1989 and 'Cornell suspends student hacker', *Computing Australia*, 12 June 1989; Peter G. Neumann, 'The Unix Internet worm and software engineering', *Software Engineering Notes*, vol. 14, no. 1, January 1989, pp. 5–6; Tony Fainberg, 'The night the network failed', *New Scientist*, March 4 1989; and 'Special section on the Internet worm' including Eugene H. Spafford, 'The Internet worm: crisis and aftermath', *Communications of the ACM*, vol. 32, no. 6, June 1989, pp. 677–710.

28 Nicholas Rothwell, 'Computer AIDS: the hitech disease that is spreading worldwide', *The Weekend Australian*, 4 June 1988; David Hebditch, Nick Anning and Linda Melvern, *Techno-Bandits* (Houghton Mifflin, Boston, 1984); and Jay Peterzell, op. cit. (n. 16).

29 Joe Dellinger, 'Virus protection strategies', *Software Engineering Notes*, vol. 13, no. 1, 1988; John McAfee, 'The virus cure', *Datamation*, 15 February 1989.

30 'What to do about computer viruses', *Fortune*, 5 December 1988, p. 16; 'Local crime team crack the riddle of Big Red', *The Australian*, 14 April 1987.

31 David Bainbridge, 'Hacking: the legal implications', *Computer Bulletin*, December, 1988, pp. 34–6; 'UK edges towards anti-hacking laws', *The Australian*, 11 July 1989 (reprinted from *The Times*).

32 A. K. Dewdney, 'Computer recreations', *Scientific American*, June 1985, pp. 12–17 and 'Computer Recreations', *Scientific American*, March 1989, pp. 90–3.

5 Unreliable Computers

Most Information Systems are Failures – Some Great
Software Disasters – Warranties and Disclaimers –
Why are Complex Systems so Unreliable? – What are
Computer Scientists Doing about it? – Suggestions
for Further Discussion

Since 1982, no less than 22 US servicemen have died in five separate
crashes of the USAF's sophisticated UH-60 Blackhawk utility helicopter.
On each occasion the machines have either spun out of control or have
simply nose-dived into the ground. Yet it was only in November 1987 after
this series of mysterious crashes had been thoroughly investigated, that Air
Force officials finally admitted that the UH-60 was inherently susceptible
to radio interference in its computer-based 'fly-by-wire' control system and
that modifications to the aircraft would be needed.[1]

Similar fly-by-wire systems to that used in the Blackhawk exist in the
European A320 Airbus as well as other modern airliners. Essentially, fly-
by-wire systems work by eliminating the mechanical linkages between the
pilots' controls and the control surfaces on the wings and tailplane (or, in
the case of helicopters, the main rotor and tail rotor). In other words, a
pilot's analogue control movements on the joystick or control column are
converted to digital pulses which in turn drive servo motors and other
power systems that move the ailerons, rudder and elevators. In effect,
pilots in these aircraft no longer have a physical link connecting their
controls with the control surfaces. Instead, onboard computers 'interpret'
control movements and relay this interpretation to the activating units.

In the case of the Blackhawk, inadequate shielding in some of the logic
modules involved in the fly-by-wire system allowed electronic 'smog' in
the form of microwave and other radio transmissions to affect the onboard
computer system. Because of this, the computer would sometimes send
spurious signals to the hydraulic system thereby bringing about an
uncontrollable nose-dive.

Most Information Systems are Failures

Although the Blackhawk scandal is an example of the extent to which we rely upon computers in the control and management of sophisticated systems, the fault identified in the UH-60 could have been easily remedied. Despite the heavy loss of life, the example itself is still a rather trivial one compared to the complex tasks and heavy responsibilities that we entrust to computer systems in many other applications. For instance, computer systems in one form or another are now indispensable in air traffic control, medicine, nuclear power stations, toxic chemical plants, spacecraft, missiles, ships, tanks and other weapons systems, as well as in the maintenance of our financial systems, stock markets and communications services. As we shall see, even in these often life-critical applications, it is apparent that the reliability of computer systems is less than we would hope. In many instances, 'system failure' is really a euphemism for disaster and/or substantial loss of life.

Computer scientist Peter Mellor defines reliability in a computer system as the probability that it will not fail during a given period of operation under given conditions. For example, measures of reliability can include the number of failures per unit of operating time and the expected length of time that a system will operate without failing. Like many computer scientists, he advocates the application of statistical principles to software quality so that, for example, it may be more acceptable to have many infrequent bugs than a small number of very frequent ones.[2] However, systems can fail not only in operation, but at various stages in their design and development.

Indeed, failures in computer system development and use are not just commonplace. More often than not they are the rule. According to one US survey, an astonishing 75 per cent of all system development undertaken is either never completed or not used even if it is completed.[3] Indeed, some writers have identified a crisis in system development which is demonstrated by the finding that 70 per cent of software projects are generally directed to maintenance after the system itself has been 'verified' and commissioned for use.[4,5]

Other figures seem to confirm this: a study in 1979 by the US government's General Accounting Office showed that of nine federal software projects which cost a total $6.8 million, projects worth $3.2 million (47 per cent of the total by value) were delivered but not used, $2 million worth were paid for but not delivered, $1.3 million worth were abandoned or reworked and just $200,000 worth were used after substantial modification. Incredibly, just one project worth less than $100,000 was used as delivered by the developer.[6] Recent reports from Logica and Price Waterhouse have also indicated that poor software quality costs the UK about $900 million per year.[7]

Systems can fail at a number of levels, from failure to meet the users' requirements, as well as massive budget blow-outs and lack of use by the system's eventual purchasers, to sheer unreliability. An extended discussion of the different types of failures and their underlying causes is beyond the scope of this book, but the interested reader can pursue these issues further in the literature available on this topic.[8] Yet even without such preparation, it is clear that much can be gained from a casual survey of some classic system failures, since many ethics-relevant issues can be found here.

For example, back in October, 1960, computers of the Ballistic Missile Early Warning System (BMEWS) at Thule initiated a nuclear alert after the rise of the moon above the horizon was interpreted as a nuclear attack.[9] In other cases involving this same system, a flock of geese was thought to be a group of inbound nuclear warheads and in June 1980, within the space of four days, a faulty multiplexer chip at NORAD *twice* scrambled B-52 bombers and simulated most of the initial characteristics of a nuclear attack.[10]

More recently, in the Persian Gulf, an American Triconderoga-class guided-missile cruiser, the *USS Vincennes*, shot down an Iranian Airbus causing the loss of 290 civilian lives.[11] As a result, much criticism was levelled at the capabilities of the Aegis fleet defence system – the constellation of radar, computers and missiles that carried out the attack. However, the record shows that the Aegis system had been soundly condemned by its critics long before it was installed on US navy ships at a cost of around $1.2 billion per unit. Both Mary Kaldor and defence journalists James Coates and Michael Kilian had pointed out that Aegis passed its capability trials by being deployed in a New Jersey cornfield.[12] Yet one would not unreasonably think that a dry agricultural plot would bear little resemblance to a naval environment with its inclement weather, rolling swells, corrosive conditions and temperature extremes.

Aegis itself is a battle management system for the co-ordinated defence of US Navy battlegroups. It is designed to track hundreds of airborne objects in a 300 km radius and to allocate sufficient weapons to simultaneously destroy up to 20 targets with its array of missiles. The system integrates phased-array radars (a quantum improvement on the rotating mechanical radars we normally visualize) with complex software that matches potential targets with a threat library, then assesses threat values and assigns weapons systems accordingly. Although Aegis is designed to deal with up to 20 targets simultaneously, its first operational test in April 1983 showed that even when presented with only three targets at a time, Aegis failed to shoot down six out of seventeen targets due to software failures.[13]

It is difficult to determine how much of the Airbus tragedy can be attributed to computer error or to human error (or a combination of both). Indeed, given present security arrangements the full story may never be known. Nevertheless, it is disturbing to note that a system such as Aegis can have such a chequered development history, be subjected to suspect testing and validation procedures, and finally figure in a major aviation mix-up resulting in huge loss of life. As many commentators have noted, if Aegis cannot discriminate between a civilian airliner and a modern fighter plane at a range of 12 miles (well within visual range!), then what chance does it have in more complex scenarios where discrimination must be much finer? More recent analyses of the Iranian Airbus incident have shown that deficiencies in the human interface of the Aegis system were significant contributory factors to the disaster. 'Replays' of the system's tapes show that the A-320 was indeed on schedule and on course but the manner in which the system displayed information was inadequate in the context of a time-critical, highly charged combat decision.[14]

Military case studies provide rich sources of information on computer unreliability, yet system failures can occur in all areas of society and involve most aspects of our lives. We should further bear in mind that although a large number of such failures are caused or exacerbated by human operator error, a significant number are almost wholly due to poor design, sloppy implementation and inadequate testing and verification procedures. (However, some failures can be benevolent: for example, when a teenager in the UK recently requested £30 from an ATM of the Halifax Building Society at Horsham, West Sussex, he received a £2,600 payout instead!)[15]

More often than not, when civilian computer systems fail, they cause widespread hardship and inconvenience. For example, on Saturday 6 August 1988 during one of the busiest days of the year, Heathrow airport was due to handle some 830 takeoffs and landings – but the air traffic control system failed. Despite the employment of some 70 full-time specialists to keep the computer running and to update its software, in the 12 months to April 1988 there were five similar software failures.[16] And of course Heathrow's situation is certainly not unique: its computers use a traffic control system known as the National Airspace Package, which consists of around a million lines of program code that took approximately 1,600 worker-years to write and 500 worker-years to develop. Yet despite this massive amount of effort which was made more complicated by the system's conversion from US air traffic control requirements to British ones, it is evident that the system's performance is far from satisfactory.

Perhaps an even more potentially dangerous failure occurred on 23 August 1987, when the National Air Traffic Services' Oceanic Centre at Prestwick in Scotland found that their Flight Processing System – the computer which controls the bulk of trans-Atlantic flights – had 'crashed'. It was the ninth serious breakdown of the system which had experienced minor failures every other day since its commission earlier in the year. The new computer system is totally electronic and does not make provision for the printed cardboard strips that controllers like to use as a manual backup procedure. The system crashed at 11.30 am and by mid-afternoon Heathrow, Paris, Frankfurt, Zurich and other major European airports had begun to run out of parking space for delayed aircraft, many with passengers on board. The Oceanic controllers were forced to telephone nearby air traffic control centres to discover which airliners had been handed over to which facilities and to find out which aircraft were still supposedly under their control. A senior controller was reported as saying: 'They wonder why we have so little confidence in our top management when they give us tools like this – aeroplanes have to have duplicated or even triplicated systems as back-up, but the same safety rules clearly do not apply to our equipment. These continual failures are the basic ingredients of a mid-air disaster.'[17]

Other system failures, although perhaps less threatening to human life, illustrate the extent to which the very lifeblood of our economies – cash and capital – have become controlled by complex systems that border on the limits of our understanding. A good illustration is what happened on the morning of Thursday, 20 November 1985, when more than 32,000 government securities transactions were waiting to be processed at the Bank of New York. At 10 am, the bank's computer systems began to corrupt these transactions by over-writing records. As a consequence, it was impossible for the bank to determine which customers should be charged for which securities and for what amount. Meanwhile, the New York Federal Reserve Bank continued to deliver securities to the Bank of New York and to debit its cash account. At the close of business that day, the bank was $32 billion overdrawn with the Federal Reserve – and despite half-successful efforts to patch up the program, by 1.30 am the next day the Bank of New York was still overdrawn by some $23.4 billion. Frantically, the bank borrowed to help cover its deficit, using its total asset base as collateral. By late Friday morning, the software had been fixed and processing restarted. However, this fiasco cost the bank $5 million in interest for its overnight loans - and it also shattered dealer confidence. As has been noted by Hopcroft and Krafft,[18] it was fortunate that an error of this sort did not coincide with the October 1987 Wall Street Crash, since the drain on the Federal Reserve and the effect on investor confidence could have been even more disastrous.

To illustrate the fact that even a nation's best minds can be defeated by computer-based system failures, the *San Francisco Chronicle* of 13 September 1988 reported that the $115 million Stanford Linear Collider (a huge device for studying elementary particle physics) had to be shut down after several months of work had failed to get it running properly. Basically, the problem was that despite the efforts of 100 scientists and technicians, the system itself was so complex that it proved impossible to keep enough of its components or computers working long enough to get any results. Meanwhile, the USSR has also suffered from software snafus in space. In 1988, the Phobos I spacecraft was lost after Soviet ground controllers reprogrammed the craft by beaming up a 20–30 page message. Unfortunately, the program contained an error that caused the vehicle to point its solar panels in the wrong direction – away from the sun – and eventually the spacecraft lost power and was abandoned.

Some Great Software Disasters

If one has a black sense of humour, then case studies of software problems can be a definite source of amusement – such as the inertial guidance system of the F-16 fighter which, in simulation, caused it to become inverted whenever the aircraft crossed the equator – or the loss of the 12th F/A-18 prototype when its software refused its pilot the control authority he needed to recover from a spin. In another military incident, an F/A-18 attempted to launch a wing-tip mounted missile, but although the weapons system ignited the missile correctly, it closed the restraining clamp on the wing-tip before the missile had generated sufficient thrust to move. Thus the pilot found an extra 3,000 lb of thrust on one wing-tip and was about to eject after dropping 20,000 feet when control was finally recovered.[19] Another amusing incident involved former President Reagan's E-4B aircraft (a modified 747) which is alleged to have closed thousands of remotely controlled garage doors in California whenever it operated from March Air Force Base, about ten miles south of San Bernadino. It is said that the volume of broad spectrum electronic transmissions that the jumbo emitted effectively jammed garage door receivers in a wide area around the base, thereby preventing them from opening.[20]

It would be a mistake to assume that computer failures only occur in super-sophisticated military or aerospace applications. As digital technology infiltrates almost all aspects of our lives – even the humble automobile – our involvement in mystifying technological failure becomes more common. The case of the Audi 5000 is a case in point. At least 250 incidents involving this car – including two deaths – have cast suspicion upon its computer-controlled systems. Essentially, the problem appears to lie in the 'idle stabilizer' which is responsible for ensuring a minimum fuel flow to the engine when the brakes are applied. In one case, a boy was opening a garage door for his mother when she applied the brake and shifted the automatic transmission into forward gear. The car then accelerated rapidly, punching the boy through the garage door and crushing him against the rear wall. The rate of acceleration was so great that a large skid mark was left behind and even after impact, the wheels continued to spin at high speed. Despite Audi's dismissal of the problem, a group of owners allegedly were able to demonstrate that the accelerator pedal actually moved downward when the car was placed into gear. Yet in March 1989 a US National Highway Traffic Safety Administration (NHTSA) report ruled out mechanical defects as the cause of sudden acceleration in Audis and other cars. The NHTSA said that the most likely cause was drivers' stepping on the gas pedal instead of the brakes. However, some safety experts disagreed with the report's findings and Audi increased its reserve for US liability claims to $105 million.

In other well-known foul-ups, the loss of the Mariner 18 space probe was found to be due to a one-line error in a crucial program, while the Gemini V capsule splashed down 100 miles off target because the programmers who wrote the inertial guidance system failed to take into account the rotation of the earth around the sun. The US Navy has also admitted that during an exercise off San Francisco, a computer glitch caused one of a guided-missile frigate's 3-inch guns to fire a shell in the opposite direction from that which was intended. The shell missed a merchant ship by about nine miles.[21]

In 1980, a man undergoing microwave arthritis therapy was killed when the therapy reprogrammed his pacemaker, while it has also been reported that another man was severely affected when his pacemaker was reprogrammed by interference from an anti-theft device in a store. He subsequently died as a result of the trauma.[22] In other computer-related medical incidents, an infusion pump for insulin had a software problem which caused insulin or dextrose to be delivered at incorrect rates; a reprogrammable pacemaker 'locked up' in a doctor's office while it was being reset by an external programming device – though, luckily, the patient was revived; a patient monitoring system was recalled after it was discovered that it incorrectly matched patients' names and data;[23] and in a widely-publicized case it was revealed that the malfunction of two computerized 'Therac 25' X-ray machines over a period of several months killed one person, burned others and left yet others with partial paralysis.[24] The malfunctions occurred in 1985 and 1986 at the East Texas Cancer Center in Tyler, Texas and at the Kennestone Regional Oncology Center in Marietta, Galveston. A subtle software error caused some body areas to receive between 17,000 and 25,000 rads, when research has shown that doses as low as 1,000 rads when delivered to the whole body can be fatal. Typical therapeutic doses to small areas of the body range from between 4,000 and 6,000 rads delivered in 20 or 30 treatments over a month or more.

Not only can software inadequacies have a detrimental effect on the health of individuals, it may eventually be demonstrated that one particular software problem will affect the future health and lifestyle of every person on earth – because of limitations in the programs on board NASA observation satellites used during the 1970s and 1980s. Surprising as it may seem, these programs actually rejected the ozone readings they were registering at the time – because they were so low, they were regarded as spurious. In other words, deviations from established, normal levels were so extreme that they were assumed to be errors. It was only when British scientists using ground-based instruments reported that a decline in ozone levels was occurring that NASA scientists reprocessed data going back to 1979 and confirmed the British findings.[25] It may eventually be the case that our treatment and handling of the ozone layer problem, and its ultimate effects on the planet, would have been substantially better had the NASA systems been able to provide us with warnings a decade earlier.

Perhaps this is too gloomy a prospect to contemplate for long, but even at the individual level there are blatant cases of computer foul-ups which have severely reduced the quality of life of the persons affected. For example, in an editorial that appeared in the *Los Angeles Times* of 24 May 1986, an individual by the name of Foreman Brown provided a testimonial that was both amusing and horrifying:

I first became aware of my death last May when my checks began to bounce. Never having experienced bouncing checks before, and knowing that I had quite a respectable balance at the bank, I was both shocked and angry. When I examined the returned checks and found, stamped over my signature on each of them, in red ink, 'Deceased', I was mystified. Then, when one of the recipients of my checks, a utility company, demanded that I appear in person, cash in hand, plus $10 for their trouble – *their* trouble – I was shocked, angry and mystified. I wondered just how they expected us deceased to acquiesce.

Eventually, Brown went to the bank to inquire but received little in the way of explanation except that it was somehow 'the computer's fault'. The next month his social security payment was not credited to his account. It appeared that the problem with the bank had affected the social security system as well. Even after it appeared that the mess had been sorted out, Brown reported that his physician was unable to bill Medicare because Medicare's computers indicated that the service was performed six months after the patient had deceased.

This is an example of the way in which an individuals' rights and privacy can be violated and how extensive our reliance on computer systems really is. However, it is also a very useful illustration of how 'tightly coupled' or dependent our systems are – a bank's mistake feeds into a social security network and eventually into medical insurance systems. Even more noteworthy, however, is how resistant these systems are to correction and how persistent problems remain even after they have been identified. Although it is unclear in the Brown case whether the root of the error lay in inadequate software or in operator error, the simple fact that a number of sophisticated systems did not independently verify the date, location and/or cause of the alleged death indicates that their design and/or operational procedures were grossly inadequate.

Warranties and Disclaimers

Given the incidence of faulty software and system failure in general, it is perhaps not surprising that software developers rarely provide their clients or purchasers with warranties of any substance. Indeed, if one compared this situation with that of almost any other form of purchased goods, then it is difficult not to be amused and perhaps even incredulous. While refrigerators, cars, washing machines and computer hardware are sold with worthwhile guarantees of quality and workmanship, the same cannot be said of software. The following disclaimers provide a clear picture of the faith (or lack of) that software developers can have in the products that they produce and market:

Cosmotronic Software Unlimited Inc. does not warrant that the functions contained in the program will meet your requirements or that the operation of the program will be uninterrupted or error-free.

However, Cosmotronic Software Unlimited Inc. warrants the diskette(s) on which the program is furnished to be of black color and square shape under normal use for a period of ninety (90) days from the date of purchase.

Note: In no event will Cosmotronic Software Unlimited Inc. or its distributors and their dealers be liable to you for any damages, including any lost profit, lost savings, lost patience or other incidental or consequential damage.

We don't claim Interactive EasyFlow is good for anything – if you think it is, great, but it's up to you to decide. If Interactive EasyFlow doesn't work: tough. If you lose a million because Interactive EasyFlow messes up, it's you that's out of the million, not us. If you don't like this disclaimer: tough. We reserve the right to do the absolute minimum provided by law, up to and including nothing.

This is basically the same disclaimer that comes with all software packages, but ours is in plain English and theirs is in legalese.

We didn't really want to include a disclaimer at all, but our lawyers insisted. We tried to ignore them, but they threatened us with the shark attack at which point we relented.[26]

Another extraordinary aspect of software marketing is the fact that it is the user who generally pays for software updates. This is especially the case with operating systems and large packages for mainframe machines. In other words, even if the product is faulty or needs amendment, the user pays the software supplier to provide more correct versions.

Why are Complex Systems so Unreliable?

The issue of computer unreliability and its disastrous consequences begs several questions, most of which have ethical aspects to them. Some of these questions are: Why can't we build computer systems with the same inherent reliability that we find in other designed artifacts such as bridges and buildings? Why isn't software guaranteed in the same way that other purchased goods are? Why does so much shoddy software exist and how can so much of it appear in important systems? Should we entrust responsibility for the conduct of nuclear war, the control of massive energy sources and even national (and international) economies to computer systems that are less than totally reliable?

The answers to such questions highlight the present plight of computer professionals and the realistic role they may be expected to play in the development of reliable computer systems. In other words, the ethical dimensions of computer reliability are to some extent bound up with the nature of computers and software and the complexity of such systems. To a large degree, the behaviour of existing complex systems is at the outer edge of our intellectual understanding, so that our ability to know or predict all the possible states (including error states) that a system might take is severely restricted.

A quick calculation provides some powerful support for this assertion. For example, suppose that a system is designed to monitor 100 binary signals in order to determine the performance of a particular industrial complex – say, a nuclear power station. This amount of monitoring is certainly not excessive given the huge numbers of valves, pressure pumps and switches that must be used to keep the behaviour of such systems within tolerable limits. Given these 100 different signal sources, then there are 2^{100} or 1.27×10^{30} possible combinations of signal inputs. Now, the path that such a program follows is utterly dependent upon the combinations of signals it receives in any given time period (signal values might be read or updated, say, every few milliseconds). That is, if a particular combination of signals is registered, then a particular part of the program will be executed, while other, different parts of the program may be executed for other input patterns. Given the large number of such subroutines in a program of this scale, then there may be at least 10,000 (10^4) possible paths through it. This means that the system can exist in at least 1.27×10^{34} possible 'states', any one of which could cause the software to fail or return information that is wrong.

Now, if one wanted to test such a program empirically to identify incorrect states and then to correct them, and if one could do this automatically at a rate of say 100 per second (which is, incidentally, far beyond present capabilities), then the software testers would need some 4×10^{24} years exhaustively to test the array of possible states that this piece of software might conceivably take. Unfortunately, such a figure is many times the life of the universe.[27] Furthermore, some of these states will involve error recovery subroutines – modules that have been designed to identify errors and overcome them – and for testing, these are generally triggered by modifying the program to simulate an error state. However, these modifications in themselves can create new bugs. Indeed, Adams has estimated that 15 to 20 per cent of attempts to remove program errors actually tend to introduce one or more new errors.[28]

To rub even more salt into the wound, it is now accepted that for programs with between 100,000 and 2 million lines of code the chances of introducing a severe error during the correction of original errors is so large that only a small fraction of the original errors should be corrected. In other words, it is sometimes better to be aware of an error and to work around it by informing users of particular circumstances that will trigger it, rather than to take a chance of creating other, worse, bugs by tampering with the program.[29] As a result, honest programmers generally admit that for non-trivial software it is impossible for them to write a program which they can guarantee to be bug-free. And this is even truer of sophisticated software such as compilers and operating systems.

So what does all this imply? Because of these realities, are programmers unobligated in the event of a substantial system failure? If such a system (say a robot) kills someone, is the programmer a murderer? If a patient dies on an operating table because software running the life support equipment fails, is the programmer guilty of manslaughter or malpractice? Is he or she excused if they provide a disclaimer or inform the surgeon of potential configurations that could cause problems? Or is the programmer guilty simply because they provided a system that (both theoretically and practically) could not be guaranteed for application in a life-critical situation? After all, if a manufacturer of heart pacemakers knowingly supplied defective equipment, surely they would be required to answer in court!

These issues involve the area of software engineering, which is, if you like, computer science's attempt to answer the problem of reliability by developing new intellectual tools for the design and development of software. At this stage, too, it is probably helpful if we abandon the distinction between hardware and software since, in many instances, the line dividing them is already very grey. Software becomes hardware when it is burned into Read Only Memories (ROMS) and is 'firmware' when it is encoded as Electronically Erasable ROMS. Moreover, although the interaction of problems at the physical level of hardware (voltage spikes, short circuits, cracked joints, poor connections, overheating etc.) combine with those at the abstract level of software to produce problems that are greater (and more interesting) than the sum of either of these parts, it is essentially the abstract nature of software and the intellectual problems we have in dealing with it that provides us with most difficulty.

What are Computer Scientists Doing about it?

We have been particularly scathing in our criticisms of the capabilities of software engineers and the systems they create. It would be unfair of us, however, if we did not represent their side of the story and the peculiar circumstances they find themselves in when designing the abstract artifacts that computer systems actually *are*.

It would also be irresponsible if we did not take account of the environments that software engineers must work in. A noteworthy case in this regard is the apparent persecution of Sylvia Robins, who began work on the space shuttle program as a software engineer shortly after the Challenger disaster. This involved working with UNISYS and Rockwell on the software for the onboard flight management system –

an experience which has since caused her to sue these companies for \$5.2 million in damages for wrongful dismissal and harassment. Essentially, Ms Robins claims that the software controlling the shuttle was never properly checked, and indeed was untestable, with modifications not properly verified and not even documented. Her efforts to remedy this lapse led to levels of intimidation and harassment that eventually brought about her physical collapse and dismissal from her position. The Robins case illustrates that software engineers can often fall prey to the pressures of a commercial environment which may force them to skimp in applying rigorous methods to their software. Yet, as we shall see, these same methods have severe limitations as well, many of which stem from the nature of digital computers and binary logic itself.

Essentially, digital computers are discrete state devices – that is, they use digital (binary) representations of data (in memory, on tape or on disk or other media) and instructions (i.e. a program) – so that a computer program can effectively 'exist' in literally millions or even billions of different states. Thus, every change in a variable's value (and some programs contain thousands of variables with thousands of possible values) effectively alters the system's state. Every input or output, disk access, print request, modem connection, or calculation (indeed, anything that the system can engage in) alters the state in which the system exists. Multiply all of these and other relevant factors (time of day, load on system, combination of jobs in progress, etc.) by each other and you have effectively calculated the number of possible states that the system can be 'in'. Our earlier example illustrated the difficulty of exhaustively testing the correctness of all such states, even for programs of modest size. For most complex systems it is impractical to list all of the possible variables that may cause a state change; and even if it were possible to calculate, the number describing the total set of states would generally be so large that it would be on the verge of meaningless.

The problem with finite state machines such as digital computers is that each of these states represents a potential error point. Unlike an analogue system such as a simple thermostat or bi-metallic strip, these states are discrete – you are either in a particular state or you are in another state. Analogue systems in contrast have an infinite number of 'states' – they are in fact continuous – in that, say, a bi-metallic strip used in a thermostat can take on an infinite number of positions within a certain range, just as a ruler has an infinite number of points. The real difference, however, is that while the continuous movement of the bi-metallic strip is unlikely to fail catastrophically, our discrete state machine on the other hand can fail in a catastrophic manner because the execution of each state depends on the previous state being 'correct' or achieving the computational goal that the programmer hopes to achieve. If the previous state is not correct or even prevents the next instruction from being executed, then the program will malfunction. If the program stops or behaves erratically, then this is referred to as a discontinuity – a departure from what was otherwise predictable behaviour (and the mathematics that describes digital computers is referred to as discontinuous mathematics).

In general, analogue systems like thermostats or, say, a tuning knob on a radio, tend to have few or no discontinuities. In other words, it is unlikely that you will ever encounter a situation whereby they will be working perfectly and then reach a point where they behave aberrantly or fail totally. Analogue systems do not depend upon the correctness of the previous state, indeed states really have little direct relationship to their functioning. They can best be described by continuous functions or curves and these curves have a great deal of predictability embedded within them. For example, we can follow the performance curve of an analogue device and predict how it will function at particular levels. Essentially this is how we construct buildings – we know the properties of steel and other materials since they, too, can be mostly described by continuous functions. Steel, for example, will take increasing loads and exhibit stress in an extremely predictable way until it reaches the point at which it fails. These mathematical tools help us to make very accurate predictions about the behaviour of analogue systems and, what is more, we can build a 'fudge factor' or safety margin into our computations and predictions so that the resultant design is 'over-engineered' for robustness.

With large discrete state systems, however, and indeed even in quite simple ones, this is not the case. A simple analogue system such as a thermostat may not function correctly – it may change too quickly or too slowly for example – but it would be rare for it to fail totally – apart from very obvious faults such as a loss of power or breakage of a component. A computer program performing the same function, however, could quite easily fail in a catastrophic manner and in a surprisingly large variety of ways. In such a system, in order to actually measure temperature values, a device known as an analogue-to-digital converter would convert the room's temperature value at a particular time into a numeric value. This numeric value would then be compared to the required temperature and depending upon whether the actual temperature value was high or low or about right, an instruction would be sent to the heating unit to turn on, turn off or remain as it is. In achieving this, a large number of states will be 'executed' according to the algorithm or procedure that the programmer has devised to achieve the task and each state represents a potential point at which the program could simply stop or begin to behave unpredictably. Finding the particular state which caused such a problem can take some time, simply because of the sheer number of them. The conditions that existed at the time of the problem (which is essentially the error state) have to be replicated so that the error can manifest itself again and be identified.

Our discussion up to this point may appear to paint a rather grim picture of digital computation, yet a moment's thought should convince us that its weakness is also its source of strength. With digital representation, we can represent almost anything from, say, a real-time graphic simulation of aircraft flight to a 3-D map of Mars. Indeed, it is conceivable that we could take a photograph of deep space, digitize it, apply some mathematical formula that would convert its digital form into an appropriate range of musical notes, and play the resultant music – or we could even use the data to drive a laser beam in the production of a hologram. This is the essence of digital computation – the ability to represent abstract or physical qualities and to manipulate them in powerful ways. It is also the reason why we are able to understand and manipulate theories and environments beyond our immediate perception, or which are so abstract that they can have no physical analogues. For these reasons, despite the obvious difficulties we have in building reliable, complex systems, digital computation cannot be discarded, even if it were possible for us to physically run the world without machines of this kind. Indeed, much of software engineering in its most modern forms concerns itself with methods and techniques for making software more reliable, useful and trustworthy. Most of this work can be grouped around a number of rubrics.

The first area of 'structured programming' stems from criticisms of the 'spaghetti-like' code that programmers tended to produce using the earliest high-level languages such as FORTRAN and Cobol. More recent languages, by the very nature of their design, impose structure and modularity as well as information 'hiding', so that individual programmers on a large project need not concentrate on minute details that are more properly the concern of the project manager or those overseeing the production of the software. This drive to produce more powerful, usable programming languages still continues, but some critics such as David Parnas are doubtful that it will produce the order of magnitude improvements that are needed in software engineering if reliable programs are to be regularly produced.

A second research domain lies in the area of 'program verification and derivation'. This field is concerned with mathematical techniques for proving programs correct once they have been written (verification) or showing programs to be correct in the process of building them (derivation). Unfortunately, these techniques are not yet able to handle programs of even modest size, let alone those demanded by most commercial applications or by megaprojects such as SDI. Furthermore, even the most correct of programs can still be shown to be unsatisfactory or even useless if it fails to meet the needs of the individual user or organization. No mathematical technique can tell us if we have encapsulated the users' needs adequately or indeed if we have probed deeply enough to discover what they are.

Another partial answer to the problems of software engineering lies in the development of 'programming environments'. These are essentially operating systems and collections of software tools that aid programmers by providing flexible and powerful ways of managing much of the complexity of software development. Hence environments such as UNIX provide powerful facilities for managing different program versions, updating all files affected by a modification, sophisticated bug identification, etc. Yet again, although these environments are a significant advance in handling the drudgery and complexity of software development, they, too, do not approach the magnitude of the improvements that are required if software is to meet the standards of reliability that we have come to expect in other areas of engineering.

Lastly, the 'human management' aspects of software development have also been tackled and a large variety of methodologies and project management practices have come into vogue. The assumptions underlying these methodologies are that by appropriately managing and controlling the software development process in its human-organizational forms (specifying client need, prototyping, documentation, further client consultation, testing and debugging, etc.) a higher quality product can be delivered more reliably.[30]

In conclusion, we are forced to acknowledge that the construction of software is a complex and difficult process and that existing techniques do not provide software of assured quality and reliability. This is especially the case with large, complex systems to which we entrust major responsibilities and sometimes awesome energies. Furthermore, given the evidence that we have presented here, it is clear that several ethical questions emerge: when software engineers are asked to build complex systems, should they be more honest about their limitations? If, as with SDI, it is possible that a system cannot be made to work at all (see appendix A), should computer professionals accept funding for its research and development? If it is theoretically impossible to demonstrate the correctness of a program and the program causes catastrophic loss, is the programmer immune from an ethical obligation? What is the ethical status of existing warranties and disclaimers?

These are the kinds of questions that all of us, computer professionals and lay persons alike, need to address in considering the proper role of computers in our lives and the responsibilities and obligations that should be imparted to those whom we employ to construct them.

Suggestions for Further Discussion

You may wish to think about the following, hypothetical scenario.

Consider the case of a group of civil engineers who are involved in a major construction project. Their duties include liaison with the architects and builders, especially by way of providing advice on appropriate structural materials for different parts of the building. The major tool they use to provide this advice is a program that calculates stress analyses using CAD/CAM-produced plans and a small expert system that contains expertise on the physical properties of building materials such as different kinds of steel, ducting, concrete and insulation.

Now, suppose that the stress analysis system has a bug that produces arithmetic errors in some calculations. (The reader might note that a rather famous bug in IBM systems had pretty much this same property.) Imagine that the engineers do not notice the odd values produced by the system and that, unfortunately, these incorrect calculations are used as a basis to build the new building. Indeed, suppose that it is impossible for the engineering team to check the calculations by other means simply because they are too complex, too numerous and the project deadlines won't allow it in any case.

Furthermore, suppose that the expert system contained in the package contains incorrect information or facts. Specifically, the steel being used in parts of the building is an alloy that has very good corrosion properties but at the cost of a slightly diminished ability to bear loads compared to more conventional metals. Unfortunately, the expert from whom the expert system was constructed did not fully understand the difference in load-bearing ability with this particular alloy and hence this factor is not taken into consideration in calculating the stresses to which the building will be subjected. In selling the package to engineers and architects, the developers of the system have promoted it as being the safest in the world.

Half-way through the construction process, the building is unable to support the loads being placed upon it and a crane on the uppermost floor crashes through several floors killing a number of workers in the process. An analysis of the disaster shows that the arithmetic bug and the misunderstanding of the structural properties of the steel essentially interacted to bring about the failure. That is, had more conventional materials been used, then the errors in the calculations would not have been of any consequence, but when combined with the weaker structural properties of the steel used, the calculations were totally inappropriate.

In these circumstances, who has the greater ethical responsibility for the accident? The engineers who failed to recognize stress values that were incorrect? The developers and commercial backers who demanded such a tight schedule that checking the stress calculations was an impossibility? The software developers who supplied a faulty product? The so-called expert whose knowledge of the properties of building materials was simply inadequate?

In considering these questions, one might want to consider the kinds of defence that each of these individuals or groups might have.

The engineers might argue that checking the calculations was simply impractical given the deadline. The developers might argue that they have a responsibility to their shareholders and their investment. They were assured by the architects, engineers and designers that automation of the design/engineering process would save time and cut costs. It's not their fault that this new technology did not make the grade.

The software developers might argue that the arithmetic bug would have been of little consequence had more conventional construction materials been used. In any case, 'everyone knows' that all software has bugs and that no complex system can be said to be entirely error-free. The users of the system should have been aware of this fact. Therefore the software company blames the engineers for not attempting to check at least some of the calculations since this would have revealed the presence of an error.

Ultimately though, they blame the construction materials expert they consulted. His job was to provide them with the facts and rules that needed to be encapsulated into the expert system contained in the stress analysis package. If this person's knowledge of building materials and their structural properties had been better then the errors of arithmetic would have been inconsequential. As it was, in combination with the calculation errors, this slip in understanding precipitated the disaster. Hence, the expert provided inadequate knowledge and it was this that caused the accident.

For his part, the materials expert claims that all human knowledge is inadequate and incomplete. Moreover, much of any expert's knowledge and rule-based behaviour is actually contradictory. Furthermore, he argues that no one individual can be expected to know or to keep pace totally with such a fast-moving and complex area of study. The software company should have realized this and incorporated knowledge gained from other sources. It should also have built more checks and controls into the software.

The software company argue that they are not in the business of building perfect systems, since this is both practically and theoretically impossible for the scale of systems they market. No amount of further knowledge, no amount of further checks and validations can guarantee that the software is correct. These procedures may help, but they are not a sufficient condition in themselves for providing perfect systems. Users must reconcile themselves to the real world where systems *do fail*, despite the best of efforts, methodologies and procedures. But this situation is only exacerbated by users who place blind faith in their technology, developers who abbreviate the design and engineering process, and consultants who are unrealistic in representing the state and accuracy of the knowledge they possess.

For classroom discussion, the instructor may wish to assign roles to selected individuals and act out a role play based on this material. Alternatively, students may be asked to summarize the major arguments of the key protagonists and participate in a structured debate.

Notes

1 B. Cooper and D. Newkirk, Risks to the Public from Computer Systems, ARPANET electronic news group, November, 1987.
2 Peter Mellor, 'Can You count on computers?', *New Scientist*, 11 February 1989.
3 G. R. Gladden, 'Stop the lifecycle, I want to get off ', *Software Engineering Notes*, vol. 7, no. 2, 1982, pp. 35–9.
4 E. Sibley, 'The evolution of approaches to information systems design methodologies', in T. W. Olle, H. Sol and A. Verrijn-Stuart (eds), *Information Systems Design Methodologies: Improving the Practice* (North Holland, Amsterdam, 1986), pp. 1–17; see also J. A. Bubenko, *Information Systems Methodologies – A Research View* (SYSLAB Report no. 40, The Systems Development and Artificial Intelligence Laboratory, University of Stockholm, Sweden, 1986); as well as James Martin, *The Information System Manifesto* (Prentice-Hall, Englewood Cliffs, NJ, 1985).
5 R. G. Canning, 'Getting the requirements right', *EDP Analyzer*, vol. 15, no. 7, 1977, pp. 1–14; B. P. Lientz and E. B. Swanson, *Software Maintenance Management* (Addison-Wesley, Reading, MA, 1980).
6 US Government Accounting Office Report FGMSD-80–4, 1979 as cited in *Software Engineering Notes*, vol. 10, no. 5, 1985, p. 6.
7 Roger Woolnough, 'Britain scrutinizes software quality', *Electronic Engineering Times*, 13 June 1988, p. 19.
8 K. Lyytinen and R. Hirschheim, 'Information systems failures – a survey and classification of the empirical literature', *Oxford Surveys in Information Technology*, vol. 4, 1987, pp. 257–309; Alan Borning, 'Computer system reliability and nuclear war', *Communications of the ACM*, vol. 30, no. 2, February 1987, pp. 112–31; Jonathan Jacky, 'Programmed for disaster: software errors that imperil lives', *The Sciences*, September/October 1989. See also Charles Perrow, *Normal Accidents* (Basic Books, New York, 1984); as well as Peter Checkland, *Systems Thinking, Systems Practice* (John Wiley and Sons, Chichester, 1981).
9 See Perry Morrison, 'An absence of malice: computers and armageddon', *Prometheus*, vol. 2, no. 2, 1984, pp. 190–200.

10 See Perry Morrison, ibid. as well as A. Chayes and J. Wiesner, *Underestimates and Overexpectations in ABM: An Evaluation of the Decision to Deploy an Anti-Ballistic Missile* (Harper and Row, New York, 1969), pp. 122–3.

11 See *The Guardian Weekly*, 17 July 1988; *Sydney Morning Herald*, 4 August 1988, pp. 1 and 11.

12 James Coates and Michael Kilian, *Heavy Losses: The Dangerous Decline of American Defense* (Penguin, New York, 1986).

13 Admiral James Watkins, Chief of Naval Operations and Vice-Admiral Robert Walters, Deputy Chief of Naval Operations, Department of Defense Authorizations for Appropriations for Fiscal Year 1985. Hearings before the Senate Committee on Armed Services, pp. 4337–79.

14 As reported in *Software Engineering Notes*, October 1988, p. 3. See also *Software Engineering Notes*, vol. 14, no. 1, January 1989, pp. 6–8 and ongoing discussion on 'Risks' e.g. 30 May 1989 and 4 September 1989.

15 Chris Trainor, 'ATM gives away "free" money', *The Australian*, 3 January 1989.

16 John Lamb, 'Computer crashes and the stranded traveller – air traffic control in Britain', *New Scientist*, 8 September 1988, p. 65.

17 D. Black, *The Independent*, 24 September 1987, also reported by D. Kranzberg, *Software Engineering Notes*, vol. 12, no. 4, 1987, pp. 2–3.

18 J. E. Hopcroft, and D. B. Krafft, 'Toward better computer science', *IEEE Spectrum*, December 1987, pp. 58–60.

19 M. Shaw, 'A sampler of system problems and failures attributable to software', compiled from a variety of sources in *Software Engineering Notes* (no other publication details available).

20 *Software Engineering Notes*, vol. 11, no. 2, 1986, p. 7.

21 *Electronic Design*, 15 September 1983.

22 *Software Engineering Notes*, vol. 10, no. 2, 1985, p. 6; *Software Engineering Notes*, vol. 1, no. 1, 1986, p. 9.

23 H. Bassen, J. Silberberg, F. Houston, W. Knight, C. Christman and M. Greberman, 'Computerized medical devices: usage trends, problems and safety technology', in *Proceedings of the 7th Annual Conference of IEEE Engineering in Medicine and Biology Society*, 27–30 September, 1985, Chicago, pp. 180–5.

24 Richard Saltos, *Boston Globe*, 20 June 1986, p. 1 and Jacky, op. cit. (n. 8).

25 *New York Times* Science Times Section, 29 July 1986, p. C1.

26 As reported in *Software Engineering Notes*, vol. 12, no. 3, 1987, p. 15.

27 Tony Wray, 'The everyday risks of playing safe', *New Scientist*, 8 September 1988, pp. 61–4.

28 E. N. Adams, 'Optimizing preventing service of software products', *IBM Journal of Research and Development*, vol. 28, no. 1, 1984, p. 8.

29 David Parnas, 'The Parnas papers', *Computers and Society*, vol. 14, no. 9, 1985, pp. 27–36; David L. Parnas, 'Software aspects of strategic defense systems', *American Scientist*, vol. 73, no. 5, September–October 1985, pp. 432–40.

30 David Parnas, 'The Parnas papers'; Brenton R. Schlender, 'How to break the software logjam', *Fortune*, 25 September 1989.

6 The Invasion of Privacy

Database Disasters – Privacy Legislation – Big
Brother is Watching You – The Surveillance Society
– Just When You Thought No One was Listening –
Computers and Elections – Suggestions for Further
Discussion

On Friday 9 November 1979, three young Frenchmen filled their car with petrol at a service station in Etampes, a small town near Paris. The owner of the service station noticed that the licence plate was patched together with pieces of tape and became suspicious, especially after the cheque they offered had a scrawled signature on its face. He took a note of the licence number and contacted police after the men had left. A routine interrogation of their database revealed to police that the car had been stolen and a patrol car was dispatched to intercept. The police caught up with the young men who had stopped at traffic lights. Two officers in plain clothes jumped out of the patrol car, one holding a machine gun, the other a .357 magnum revolver. The only uniformed officer remained in the car. Although the precise sequence of the subsequent events is still not clear, it is known that the officer with the magnum revolver opened fire on the trio. A bullet pierced the windscreen and hit one of the young men just under the nose. The other two men were then informed that their assailants were police (not gangsters) and they were handcuffed while an ambulance came to assist their injured friend.

Later investigations placed the whole matter in a quite different light. One of the three men had purchased the car, quite legally, ten days before. It was true that the car had once been stolen, but that was in 1976 and it had been recovered by the insurance company which then sold it to the firm from which the man later legally bought it. The primary cause of this incident therefore was a failure to update the computer file covering the vehicle so that changes in status and ownership were accurately represented. Unfortunately, at the time of interrogation, police records still labelled the vehicle as stolen and police reacted as if they were dealing with potentially dangerous criminals.[1]

This example shows the impact that databases and computer-based information of all kinds can have on the quality of our lives. It also demonstrates the considerable faith we place in computer-based records – a faith that may be unjustified – and shows some of the dangers for individuals when such records are inadequate for the purposes for which they were designed. We shall encounter a number of such incidents in this chapter, but what we must bear in mind from the outset is that the hallmark of any truly democratic society is a balance of power between limits that are acceptable to the majority of its citizens. This is much easier to say than to achieve, since conflicts exist between the needs and expectations of the individual and the obligations and roles of the organizations and agencies that serve key functions in any complex, technological society. Therefore, this chapter is really about balance and how it is (and isn't) maintained in the kind of society that the Western democracies have constructed. It is through this lens that the fundamental ethical issues associated with privacy, surveillance and democracy will be viewed.

Database Disasters

Although the following cases were isolated incidents, they are nevertheless starkly illustrative of the way things can go wrong with computer-based record keeping and surveillance.

Houston schoolteacher Darlene Alexander believed that she had a respectable credit record – that is until she applied for a $75,000 mortgage and the lender informed her that she had accumulated too much debt to be considered. Her records showed outstanding accounts for American Express, MasterCard and Visa, and a $22,800 loan for a Chevrolet Camaro. None of the accounts were really hers – and she owned outright a 1983 Datsun. Ms Alexander had become a victim of the so-called 'credit doctors' – people who steal good credit histories and then sell them to those who have accumulated atrocious credit histories. An impostor had opened accounts in her name and had taken out loans, the net result being that Ms Alexander is now stuck with a poor lending history and has little chance of gaining credit for a home purchase or other important purposes.

In many ways the *modus operandi* of credit doctors is very similar to that of the most malicious kinds of hackers. Generally, credit doctors work by bribing credit agency employees to reveal the passwords to their systems. Then, logging in with a personal computer, they search for someone with the same name as their client – someone who also happens to have a good credit history. Having found this, the credit doctor copies the information associated with this person (including the all-important social security number) and supplies it to their client. Hey Presto! The client now has instant, easy credit. But what makes credit doctoring even more attractive is that generally the offence will not be discovered until the real owner of the identity happens to make an inquiry – mostly as a result of too much debt being accumulated. But by that time the credit doctor will have already supplied them with another illicitly gained line of credit.[2]

In another interesting incident, American Express contacted one of its members because of concern that he may not be able to pay his account. American Express had actually accessed this person's current account to discover that the member had less money than they were owed, causing the company to 'deactivate' his card. However, it appears that the fine print of the American Express application form reserves the right to access members' accounts in order to determine if the member has the capacity to actually pay. Some might argue that we vilify used cars dealers for less then this![3]

A further example of a database dust-up severely affected the life of Michael DuCross, a Canadian-born Indian living in Huntington Beach, California. At around 9.00 pm on 24 March 1980, DuCross drove to a local supermarket and was stopped by a police patrol car after he had made an illegal left-hand turn. The policeman took down DuCross's name and driving licence number and asked for a check of identity using his two-way radio. The request went to Sacramento, the state's capital and then was sent 3,000 miles east to the FBI's National Crime Information Center in Washington. These records indicated that DuCross was wanted by the Federal government for going AWOL from the Marine Corps at Christmas, 1969. Based on that information and despite his protestations of innocence, DuCross was taken to the brig at Camp Pendleton, California. *Five months later*, the charges were dropped after it was discovered that DuCross had never gone AWOL – he had left the Marine Corps voluntarily in 1969 under a special discharge program for resident aliens. Again, the faith placed in the accuracy of computer-based records appears to have been totally misplaced: the victim, Michael DuCross, lost five months of his life because of blatant database mismanagement.[4]

Another example of misplaced trust in the adequacy of computer-based records is provided by the experience of a US citizen whose wallet was stolen by a criminal who subsequently adopted his identity. The thief was later involved in a robbery involving murder and through the circumstances of the case, his adopted identity became known to the Los Angeles Police Department. This information was duly stored in their database and when the legitimate owner of the identity was stopped for a routine traffic violation, the computer indicated that he was a prime murder suspect and he was immediately arrested. As might be expected, he spent a few days in jail until the full details were revealed. Now, at first sight this incident might be regarded as a tolerable error. However, even after the confusion of identities had been discovered, this individual was arrested *five times in fourteen months* on the basis of the same incorrect data records. After extensive frustration, he managed to obtain a letter from the local chief of police indicating that he was *not* a real murder suspect and that the database records were wrong. Yet, although the letter was sufficient for his local area, experience soon showed that it held little weight when he travelled in other states. Only after a protracted court battle was the record finally expunged.[5]

Of course the vast majority of database errors are not as devastating as this – mostly they just produce hardship and frustration. Yet the frequency with which such hardship and frustration occurs is increasing, given the rapid penetration of database services into more domestic areas of our lives. For example, in 1977, Harvey Saltz, a former Los Angeles district attorney, formed UD Registry Inc., which provides landlords with information about prospective tenants. Saltz's company takes information from legal suits filed by landlords against tenants and 1,900 landlords (at the last count) pay him an annual fee to identify potential tenants who have been sued by landlords in the past.

On the face of it, this seems like a reasonable precaution for landlords to take. However, anyone who has ever attempted to find rented accommodation and been puzzled by rejection could gain some insight from the case of Barbara Ward, a resident of Los Angeles. In 1972, she rented an apartment and found that it was infested with cockroaches and rodents. When her landlord refused to deal with the infestation, Ward gave him 30 days notice and he countered with an eviction notice. Ward went to court with documentary evidence in the form of county health records, but the landlord failed to show. The case was dropped, but a few years later, Ward was refused accommodation by several landlords because her listing in Harvey Saltz's UD Registry computer showed that she had once been served with an eviction notice. Unfortunately for Ward, she was not aware of UD Registry's existence, let alone the fact that it had generated and was perpetuating incomplete information about her tenancy history.[6]

Perhaps the most extensive case study in the public domain on the effects of surveillance can be found in *The File*, by Peter Kimball, a former professor of journalism at Columbia University.[7] When released under the Freedom of Information Act, Kimball's personal file at the FBI revealed that for more than 30 years he had been classified as an undesirable citizen and a communist sympathizer – one who was 'too clever' to be found holding a party card. This classification resulted from the combination and embellishment of two incidents early in his life. The first occurred when he applied for a government position shortly after his release from the Marine Corps at the end of World War II. One of the referees he nominated had very briefly questioned his political views, but that same referee made no mention of communism or of any other school or flavour of political thought. The second event was his rejection of the government position after it had been offered, so that he could take a more promising position with a leading American newspaper. In his book, Kimball shows how, over a 30-year period, these events and subsequent inquiries to elucidate the reasons for his rejection of the position, were combined and magnified to the extent that his file received the attention of J. Edgar Hoover and his later applications for senior government posts, academic appointments and even passports, were substantially affected.

Kimball's book provides an interesting account of an individual's protracted and ultimately futile struggle with bureaucratic indifference and inertia. In particular, it details how the quizzical comment of an elderly right-wing referee could be snowballed into a massive document proclaiming Kimball to be a 'dangerous national security risk of doubtful loyalty to the US government and institutions'. Subsequent discussions with those individuals who were allegedly interviewed by the FBI revealed that there was deliberate distortion or suppression of individuals' testimonials and other evidence, in order to preserve the file's early and presumably unalterable theme. More importantly, Kimball had never been made aware that such allegations were being made against him, let alone been given the opportunity to publicly defend himself.

Although the Kimball case relates to the days when record keeping was based on physical rather than computer-based files, its implications are made perhaps even more sinister given the ease with which widespread computer-based surveillance and high technology intelligence gathering can be carried out. Furthermore, although there is very little doubt that the technological capabilities to gather awesome amounts of personal information has increased exponentially in recent decades, there is even less doubt that the abilities of humans to judge the worth and validity of such *data* (as compared to information) has not improved at all.

This, therefore, is one of the greatest dangers associated with the application of technology to covert intelligence and population surveillance: although the apparent accuracy and sophistication of the new technologies lends an aura of accuracy and correctness to the data gathered, ultimately human beings have to make judgements based on it, and this in itself is based upon prejudices, prior assumptions and personal interpretations. We cannot ask machines to identify conspiracy, even if they actually could gather data and store it with unerring accuracy (which they don't). These judgements are human judgements: is a reader of communist literature a communist (or simply a scholar?); is an observer of military aircraft an enthusiast or a low-level espionage threat? Of course, given what we understand about the unreliability of computer systems in other contexts, the problems of data accuracy, completeness and relevance merely compound the difficulties attached to the storage and processing of personal information by the application of computer systems.

Privacy Legislation

Most countries have come to terms with the need to treat information as property, as evidenced by the array of patent and copyright protection laws now in existence. The extension of legal powers to cover personal information is also occurring, especially now that the number of private organizations or companies holding such information is growing exponentially.

In the UK, the Data Protection Act of 1984 provides individuals with a number of safeguards against abuse of personal information contained in databases. Individuals are able to apply for a copy of all data stored on computer which relates to them. They can also insist on that information being corrected if it is wrong or out of date. The Act even makes provision for compensation for financial loss or physical injury which occurs as a result of data which is inaccurate, lost, destroyed or disclosed without authority. However, there are exceptions which are outside the scope of the Act, including manually held as opposed to electronically stored records and any records held for the purposes of national security, or for preventing or detecting crime or for prosecuting offenders or for tax collection. Others exceptions include files relating to judicial appointments and medical records that a doctor may feel could seriously damage a patient's health if disclosed.

Of course, no amount of legislation can be of real use unless it has some penalties attached: the legal teeth of the Act therefore lies with the Data Protection Registrar – the individual responsible for the maintenance of the register of data collectors and processors. Under the provisions of the Act, if an individual or organization is involved in the routine processing of personal data, then it is a criminal offence for the data handlers not to register themselves along with relevant details of the kind of data they maintain and the purposes to which it is put. It is also a criminal offence for a company or individual data user to use that data in any way not stated in the register entry. Furthermore, if there is a breach of the Act or its principles, then citizens can complain to the Registrar or pursue a claim in the courts. In such circumstances, the Registrar may either try for a 'mediated' solution or else use his or her powers to issue enforcement notices. These notices require data users to take specified action to comply with the law and failure to do so is regarded as a criminal act. The Registrar is also empowered to issue a notice removing a user from the register, thereby preventing them from legally processing their data. Of course, as would be expected, there is an appeal procedure which can be invoked against all such judgements.[8]

Much of the thrust behind the implementation of the Data Protection Act in the UK came, not from a desire to protect individuals, but from the need for the UK to conform to European Community (EC) guidelines on databases and data flows. Failure to comply could have been a major stumbling block to trade.[9] However, there were other influences and precursors to these developments. For instance, European countries had been strongly influenced by two publications: the first of these, *Guidelines on the Protection and Privacy of Transborder Flows of Personal Data*, published by the OECD in 1980, was adopted by all 24 OECD member countries; second, the Council of Europe's *Convention for the Protection of Individuals with Regard to Automatic Processing of Personal Data*, which came into effect on 1 October 1985, was signed by 18 countries and ratified by a further seven, including the UK. Although the OECD *Guidelines* have no legal force attached to them, the European Convention is legally binding upon member states who have ratified it.

The data privacy principles set out in the *Guidelines* are:

- The collection and limitation principle. Data can only be obtained by lawful means and with the data subject's knowledge or consent.
- The data quality principle. A data collector may only collect data relevant to their purposes and such data must be kept up-to-date, accurate and complete.
- The purpose specification principle. At the time of collection, the purposes to which the data will be applied must be disclosed to the data subject and the data shall not be used for purposes beyond this.
- The use limitation principle. The data is not to be disclosed by the collector to outsiders without the consent of the data subject unless the law otherwise requires it.
- The security safeguards principle. Data collectors must take reasonable precautions against loss, destruction or unauthorized use, modification or disclosure.
- The openness principle. The data subject should be able to determine the whereabouts, use and purpose of personal data relating to them.
- The individual participation principle. The data subject has the right

to inspect any data concerning him as well as the right to challenge the accuracy of such data and have it rectified or erased by the collector.

- The accountability principle. The data collector is accountable to the data subject in complying with the above principles.

Although the UK Data Protection Act is in accord with the above principles and on the face of it appears admirably responsible in terms of the protection of individuals, some damaging accounts of its practicalities have recently emerged. For example, the journalist Duncan Campbell recounts his efforts to actually utilize the protective mechanisms contained in the Act.[10] With the aim of obtaining details of his record on the Police National Computer (PNC), he began by searching for a copy of the Data Protection Register – a list of all computer systems registered under the UK Data Protection Act. Although a copy is supposed to be located in every public library, Campbell found that most libraries had never heard of it. Finally, having found a copy, the librarian concerned was extremely reluctant to let him even see it. With some perseverance, however, Campbell managed to find out which systems comprised the PNC network and lodged queries with each of these five systems – at a cost of £10 per request. Furthermore, the request forms required several personal (and apparently irrelevant) questions to be answered and replies only appeared after 40 days – the maximum delay permissible under the legislation.

On a more optimistic note, there is some evidence to suggest that the impact of the *Guidelines* and the European *Convention* has actually filtered down to private corporations. For example, IBM and the Bank of America have developed and published rules that conform to these principles.[11] In Australia, however, the situation is somewhat different: a major report on privacy by the Australian Law Reform Commission in 1983 indicated that major constitutional difficulties might hinder the passage of comprehensive legislation for data protection. The major reason for this is the division between the federal sphere and the individual Australian states. That is, although the federal government may enact appropriate legislation, its influence will be restricted to the federal public sector. The individual states will be responsible for drafting their own legislation and although at least two states – New South Wales and Queensland – have done so, they do not provide direct mechanisms for investigation and prosecution. Complaints about alleged violations are simply received and reported to the relevant state minister. Furthermore the relationships between these collections of legislation and the various copyright, patent and trade secrets laws have yet to be clarified, as well as the complicated muddle of court decisions and precedents and both state and federal acts of parliament.

Big Brother is Watching You

For many civil liberties' campaigners, the US National Security Agency (NSA) is the very epitome of what we have most to fear in terms of the invasion of individuals' privacy and the covert control of peoples' lives. The responsibilities and limitations of the NSA have never been clearly defined by the US Congress and since its establishment by President Truman in 1952, it has operated solely on the basis of a series of White House directives. This agency has a budget that is some five to six times that of the CIA and is reputed to have the most sophisticated and awesome computing capability of any single existing organization – enough to intercept and analyse perhaps 70 per cent of all telephone, telex, data and radio transmissions generated on earth. In 1971, the agency decided it needed a high-temperature incinerator to dispose of the masses of printouts and secret documents that it generated every day in the course of its activities. The specification required that the unit be capable of destroying at least six tons an hour and not less than 36 tons in any eight-hour shift, such is the size and extent of the agency's activities.[12,13]

Of course, the NSA was not created in some political or social vacuum. Like a number of other intelligence agencies in the United States, it emerged as a response to perceived threats and social circumstances that alarmed governments of the day. For example, during the Kennedy administration, far-reaching efforts were initiated to keep track of civil rights' activists such as Martin Luther King, members of Congress such as Abner Mikva and members of civil liberties' organizations like the American Civil Liberties Union, the American Friends Services Committee and the National Association for the Advancement of Colored Peoples (NAACP). During the Johnson administration, concern about race riots, civil rights demonstrations and anti-war protests prompted the President to order the army to increase its surveillance activities, thereby creating files on about 100,000 individuals and a vast number of organizations. Richard Nixon was accused of having violated the law by obtaining the computerized tax files of his political enemies – but he was unsuccessful in his attempts to require all television sets sold in the United States to be equipped with a device that would allow them to turned on from a central location![14]

In 1967, the FBI established the National Crime Information Center to maintain computer-based files on missing persons, warrants, stolen property, securities, criminal histories and registered property (guns, vehicles, etc.). With an annual operating budget of approximately $6 million, NCIC houses some 8 million individual dossiers (that is, on one in every 30 Americans) and this is expected to grow to encompass records on 90 per cent of all US residents with arrest records – or as many as 35 million people, approximately 40 per cent of the US labour force. About 64,000 federal, state and local police agencies have authority to access NCIC data via one of the 17,000 terminals now linked to the Center.[15]

Once more, this illustrates the classic tug-of-war between the perceived role of the state in preserving law and order and its own national security, versus the rights of individuals to fundamental democratic freedoms. A good example of the instability of this democratic tightrope is the NSA's involvement with the establishment of encryption standards. Encryption – or more properly cryptography – is the science of codes and code-breaking. Because of the sensitivity of many financial transactions and other data communications, encryption is becoming an increasingly favoured precaution. With encryption, even if a transmission is tapped or illicitly recorded, decoding the message is so computationally demanding that only the most skilled of individuals with the best of computing facilities could hope to achieve it within a reasonable period of time.

During the establishment of the Data Encryption Standard (DES) – a set of universally acceptable conventions for encryption – the NSA lobbied strongly inside ANSI (the US representative within the International Standards Organization (ISO)) to have the DES disapproved. The most popular interpretation of this act is that wide standardization of encryption and its concomitant routine use would make it substantially more difficult for the NSA to monitor overseas voice and data communications. Similarly, in the early 1980s several major banks and financial institutions in the US met to determine characteristics of encryption keys (the number sequences used to decode encrypted messages) that were of prodigious length (some 50–100 digits long). Once more, the NSA successfully exerted enormous pressure on these bodies to drop the proposal and again for very obvious practical reasons. The facts are that encryption keys of this length would have possibly meant that messages would have taken 3–4 days to break using the existing facilities of the NSA and obviously this would have placed the agency in extreme difficulties if it wished to monitor such transactions. Even worse, it would have become a nightmare for the organization if such practices caught on and became commonplace.[16,17]

Despite these alarming developments, we must also bear in mind that in many circumstances the need for surveillance appears patently obvious and totally warranted. For example, in the war against drugs and terrorism, the application of sophisticated technology would appear to be an appropriate and much-needed source of countermeasures. In accordance with this, the US Defense Advanced Research Projects Agency (DARPA) is now involved in a multi-million dollar program to apply artificial intelligence and parallel processing techniques to the detection and elimination of drug-related criminal activities. These initiatives will involve tracking currency, cargo shipments and telephone usage so that subtle, but tell-tale, patterns are revealed to investigating authorities. By tracing serial numbers of cash and monitoring the movements of container shipments, DARPA also hopes that almost real-time control and detection of narcotics activities can be provided.[18]

Yet while almost all of us would want to see the drug trade and its social destructiveness ended, we might not appreciate such technologies being applied to our everyday lives – and this is the practical implication behind such moves. After all, what distinguishes your telephone from that used by a drug dealer? What differentiates your bank account from the slush fund of a narcotics racket? Given these problems, several pertinent questions come to mind. Are the costs to privacy greater than the benefits of squeezing drug trafficking out of existence? Is the damage visible on the streets preferable to the kind of invisible, secret damage that surveillance could bring to society and its freedoms? Might we expect that the drug rackets – just like the oldest profession – can never be eliminated? Instead, their collective response might be to counter with high technology foils of their own – scramblers, encryption devices, etc. After all, drug syndicates already use some of the best and most sophisticated equipment – a brand-new wrecked aircraft or two is a negligible business cost, given the incredible profits that can be made from narcotics trading. Furthermore, with huge amounts of money on offer, what defence can high technology offer to the ancient art of bribery and corruption? What point is there in creating elaborate technological surveillance systems if their locks, keys and blueprints have already been sold? And if this is the most we can hope for from high technology in combating the drug problem, why should we accept the destruction of privacy that its possibly ineffectual application may bring?

In another instance of the rationality of the NSA pursuing its perceived role, a recent report suggests that the National Computer Security Center (a division of the NSA) contacted researchers at Purdue University, Indiana, asking them to remove information from campus computers showing the internal workings of Robert Morris's worm program (see chapter 4 on hacking and viruses). Ostensibly, the NCSC's concerns stemmed from the belief that not all sites had corrected the security problems that the worm program relied upon and exploited. Computer security experts, however, have said that the NSA was more concerned with the dissemination of such techniques and their potential exploitation in system break-ins.[19]

Yet the role of the NSA in attempting to restrict the flow of information (of all kinds) goes much deeper than this. In 1984 President Reagan signed an executive order for the NSA – National Security Decision Directive 145 – that describes information contained in databases as part of a mosaic in which individual pieces are innocuous, but which, when aggregated, allows a more complete picture to appear. This notion of an information mosaic has had far-reaching consequences that are only now beginning to be felt. Perhaps the most cited example of the mosaic concept is the publication of the blueprint of the H-Bomb in a 1979 edition of *The Progressive* magazine. All the information contained in the article was gleaned from unclassified data scattered throughout various scientific journals. Under the influence of the mosaic concept and as part of this initiative, the former director of the NSA, Admiral John Poindexter, moved to restrict unclassified information affecting not only national security but also 'other government interests' including 'government or government-derived economic, human, financial, industrial, agricultural, technological and law-enforcement information.' Because of its calls for 'a comprehensive and co-ordinated approach' to restricting foreign access to all telecommunications and automated information systems, Poindexter's directive prompted fears that US intelligence agencies would monitor virtually all computerized databases and information exchanges in the United States. The White House withdrew the notice in March 1987 under pressure from Congress, but the underlying policy as set out in NSDD 145 is still in place.[20,21]

The Surveillance Society

As we suggested in our chapter on hacking and viruses, a useful model of democratic societies is one which depicts their functioning as a constant dialogue involving two basic processes – conflict and consensus. Indeed, anyone who has ever witnessed a natural disaster and observed the ease with which law and order and 'normal' civilization can break down, can strongly testify to the fact that society is a finely balanced construction of obligations and expectations that is negotiated within the bounds of these processes. Clearly, this balance is frighteningly easy to tip (in any direction) and one of the most important 'weights' we must consider concerns the rights and obligations of the individual versus the rights and obligations of the group. In particular, we must be concerned with those groups who hold enormous power and influence over the effective management of society – our governments, judiciaries, police, security agencies and so on.

Rather like a delicate tightrope act, we can expect that the powers accorded to these groups will teeter and sway to some extent, but hopefully the processes of public debate, information released by the press and that released by informants or ethically troubled members of such groups ('whistle-blowers') can help to preserve a rough semblance of balance, both in terms of increasing and diminishing the power they are accorded. We should also bear in mind that 'overbalancing' (in all directions) of the democratic balancing act, emerges not simply from blatant attempts to marshal greater power (although this can happen, too), but more often from attempts to fulfill a particular role and to maximize effectiveness in that role. That is, organizations and groups of all kinds possess a rationality that is attuned to their objectives. The police, for example, see their role as the prevention of crime and the apprehension of law-breakers. The maximization of this function is of supreme interest to them and the costs associated with invasion of privacy, wrongful arrest, forced confessions and even fabrication of evidence, can often be considered to be acceptable so long as the primary role of the police in the prevention and apprehension of criminal elements is achieved. Hence, like most organizations faced with a demanding organizational mission, their rationality is concentrated upon fulfillment of this mission or role, perhaps with serious disregard to the costs that may accrue in consequence. This is not to say that the individuals who comprise such organizations (not just the police) do not have misgivings about the methods used. But collectively, for any large organization an organizational rationality prevails which is maintained by peer pressure, selection, socialization and training of an organization's recruits, as well as by reward structures and overt and covert penalties for failure to demonstrate loyalty.

Again, we need to question whether our democratic tightrope act is not becoming dangerously unbalanced when we learn of the already mentioned incidents and the statistics on surveillance. For example, the US Office of Technology Assessment (OTA) has recently found that of 142 domestic federal agencies surveyed, 35 already used or planned to use electronic surveillance methods including concealed microphones. The OTA also found that 36 of these agencies (not counting those in intelligence) used a total of 85 computerized record systems for investigative purposes and maintained 288 million files on 114 million people. In addition, OTA found that 35 agencies in Justice, Treasury and Defense departments already used or planned to use:

- Closed-circuit television (29 agencies)
- Night vision systems (22)
- Miniature transmitters (21)

- Telephone taps, recorders and pen registers (these show the telephone number dialled) (14)
- Electronic beepers and sensors (15)
- Computer usage monitoring (6)
- Electronic mail monitoring (6)
- Cellular radio intercepts (5)
- Satellite interceptions (4)

As for the 85 computer-based record systems, none of the operators provided statistics requested by the OTA on record completeness or accuracy. (Note that the OTA study did not include the CIA, NSA or Defence Intelligence Agency.)[22]

Just When You Thought No One was Listening

It is a mistake to believe that the only threat to privacy lies in the databases of super-secret intelligence agencies, police or other authorities. Developments in surveillance technologies are also available to those with sufficient need and sufficient funds to purchase them. For example, microphone transmitters these days are almost the size of a pin head and can be embedded almost anywhere. Some do not need wires to transmit – they send out microwave signals that can be read by equipment outside the building. They can be turned on and off by remote control, or set to be activated by heat, radiation, the vibrations of a voice, body movement or pressure. A bug located in a chair, for example, can be programmed to turn itself on whenever someone sits down. Bugs can also be hidden in typewriters and computer keyboards, picking up and transmitting the electronic signals given off by each key – effectively allowing the eavesdropper to watch as the message is keyed in.

One way to make bugs harder to detect is to design them so that they transmit along frequencies that are very close to those used by standard radio or TV broadcasts. Another method is called 'frequency hopping'. With this technique, the bug transmits using a preset sequence of frequencies – often for only a few milliseconds on each frequency – and a 'frequency agile' receiver also attuned to this sequence, picks up the transmissions in a perfectly synchronized fashion. Yet the hardest bugs to detect are those that do not transmit through the air. Instead, they transmit using any available metallic medium: a power cable, an air-conditioning vent or even metallic paint. A listening post somewhere outside the building then 'plugs in' and monitors whatever the bug relays. Finally, the 'Hollywood' countermeasure we all know – turning on the shower, radio and taps to provide a noisy background to defeat bugs – is a thing of the past. Sophisticated electronic filters can now remove almost all extraneous noise and produce a clear, untainted voice signal.

More exotic methods of surveillance allow eavesdroppers to monitor computers as they work. The electromagnetic transmissions emitted by chips and CRTs – a phenomenon known as 'tempest' – can be recorded some distance away from the machine for later analysis. The only known precaution against this kind of interception (and the exploitation of tempest itself is still in its infancy) is the use of specially designed and prohibitively expensive shielding. Another exotic surveillance technique uses laser beams that are aimed against a window or any surface that can vibrate slightly from the impact of sound waves. The laser beam is affected by the minute vibrations caused by voices and these can be decoded by appropriate ancillary equipment.[23]

However, we don't need to look for industrial espionage, cloak-and-dagger experts and switched-on private eyes in order to find evidence of high-technology surveillance. Although we might immediately associate surveillance with bugging devices and sophisticated electronics, it appears that our own employers, with the very computer systems we are familiar with, are involved in surveillance of their own employees. At Pacific South West Airlines offices in San Diego and Reno, the main computer records exactly how long each of their 400 reservation clerks spends on every call and how much time passes before they pick up their next one. Workers earn negative points for such infractions as repeatedly spending more than the average 109 seconds handling a call and taking more than 12 minutes in bathroom trips beyond the total one hour allocation they have for lunch and coffee breaks. If employees accrue more than 37 points in any single year, they can lose their jobs. One employee of 14 years' standing, Judy Alexander, took disability leave after compiling 24 demerit points and complaining that 'I'm a nervous wreck. The stress is incredible.' PSA defends the system by arguing that it's a productivity booster and that it's no more severe than the monitoring that occurs in other airlines.[24]

As part of this general defence, supporters of computer monitoring argue that it is also used to provide incentives for employees and effectively rewards individuals for true merit and effort. They also point out that what is being measured is factual and hard, and that workers tend to favour such systems – they've seen too many cases of the wrong people being promoted for the wrong reasons. With the facts that the computer gathers, diligent workers can legitimately argue a case for better pay and conditions and this case does not rely upon personal opinions or personalities. Furthermore, these systems can help eliminate rampant waste – employees calling long-distance for private purposes, a team carrying the load for an unproductive team member, identifying the theft of materials by matching the stock used with the amount processed by line workers (and discovering discrepancies). Finally, monitoring on a computer network can assist in troubleshooting and fine-tuning of a system,[25] as well as streamlining job design and fairly apportioning workloads.

However, there is also the danger of turning workers into better-paid battery hens – denying them job satisfaction and eliminating the human element from their work. For example, although reservation clerks may be given an incentive to process more calls when they are being monitored, it may also eliminate any human spontaneity or friendliness in their communication. Surely this is as big a factor in return business as prompt and efficient handling? Similarly, workers may become sufficiently aggravated to devise ways to beat the system – as workers in one particular factory did by leaving their machine tools running while they had their coffee breaks. Unfortunately for them, the computer detected differences in the amount of power used and managers twigged the scam. However, the point surely is that such adversarial circumstances are best avoided and that a constant contest between the employees and the system is, in the long run, mutually disadvantageous.

Once again it seems, we are faced with a question of balance between the rights and expectations of the individual versus the obligations and objectives of the group – the group this time being our employers. Clearly, profits are important to the continued functioning of capitalist societies and profit itself is dependent upon competitiveness. However, just how far we are willing to proceed in the pursuit of competitiveness and profitability is a matter of judgement. For example, the use of cheap child labour was once regarded as a sensible business strategy, but now our ethical sense and labour protection laws prohibit this practice. It remains to be seen in which direction our ethical intuitions will take us in determining the nature of future employment – whether we can all expect to be monitored in the interest of profit and accountability, or whether we shall see a renewed interest in designing jobs for people.

In addition, we need to ask what kind of precedent computer-based monitoring of employees will set for other invasive practices. For example, similar arguments can be marshalled for compulsory drug-testing of key personnel such as pilots, train drivers, plant operators and so on.[26] If these people have the potential to kill thousands by accident, then do we not have the right to ensure that they are in a fit state to work? On the other hand, why not also monitor the alcohol purchases of convicted drunk drivers? And after that . . .? Perhaps this is the most contentious aspect of any form of computer-based monitoring: it is not so much the harm it may currently be causing, but what it represents – a yawning Pandora's box of things to come. More on computer monitoring in chapter 8.

Computers and Elections

Another application of computers which has important implications for the functioning of a democratic society is their use in the planning and conduct of free elections. Along with other critics, Eva Waskell, an independent science writer and former computer programmer, has spoken out against the unregulated use of computerized vote counting systems in America. Waskell's interests stemmed from her study of several lawsuits pending against Computer Election Systems Inc. (CES) of California – the leading provider of voting software and hardware in the US. Losing candidates in three state elections have sued CES, claiming that its equipment produced inaccurate or fraudulent results. Among other findings, Waskell's investigations revealed that only one person outside CES (a consultant for one of the plaintiffs) had ever examined the software to check its validity!

The most popular form of computerized balloting involves pushing a stylus through a punch-card that has been inserted into a special book identifying the candidates. Usually, when the polls have closed, the punch-cards from all the precincts are taken to a central location and counted using a mainframe computer with software supplied by CES or a competitor.

As a result of her investigations, Waskell identified four main problems with such a system:

1 The centralized counting system takes control away from precinct poll workers who would otherwise provide an additional level of control. Furthermore, centralization makes rigging an election easier – a single computer operator can be bribed rather than the dozens or hundreds of poll workers involved in ordinary elections.
2 Technical skills are now involved in the vote-counting process and this alienates most of the poll workers from the results. An air of mystery surrounds the computer, and in at least one state, workers 'rubber stamped' the results without examining them.
3 There are no standards for election software and so anyone can write a vote counting program. Often, State Boards of Election fail to consult outside computer experts, and when they do, they've been known to ignore them, as happened in the case of two professors from Carnegie-Mellon University.
4 Vendor's software is considered by them to be proprietary and as a consequence, over the last 20 years almost no independent experts have examined such programs. Given what we know about software unreliability in other contexts, it is surprising to say the least that we

entrust such an important function to software that is virtually in-house and insufficiently validated.

However, at least one independent consultant has been able to study CES's programs and found the following range of technical errors:

- Problems with the punch-card code and characters being nonstandard.
- Memory was constantly redefined and the same memory locations were re-used for different vote counts.
- Total lack of program structure.
- The code was potentially self-modifying (it altered itself).
- Calls were made to an undocumented, unknown subroutine.
- The program required heavy interaction with the operator who had the opportunity to modify areas of memory and therefore the count itself.
- The program permitted the operator to turn off error logging and audit trails.
- Knowledgeable voters could include a card that changed the program's processing of results.
- The program did not correctly count 'cross-over' votes which are a valid feature of some elections.

A report to the Illinois Board of Elections in September 1985 revealed that 28 per cent of the voting systems tested before elections contained errors. Recently, CES and two of its competitors – Thornber and Governmental Data – were taken over by another firm trading under the name of 'Cronus'. This merger effectively gave Cronus somewhere between 60 and 80 per cent of market share in voting systems – but of perhaps greater concern is that Cronus is financially linked with Tyler Corp, whose chief executive, Fred Meyer, is the Republican Chairman of Dallas County, Texas.[27]

Other problems with computerized voting emerged on 13 September 1988 when a computer entry error apparently increased the vote count of the incumbent Lieutenant Governor of Delaware, S. B. Woo. The correct number of votes in one district was 28 but the operator keyed in 2828 by mistake. Later reports confirmed that the error had been made but that another candidate, Sam Beard, was the recipient of the extra votes and not Mr Woo.[28]

More recently, Roy Saltman has written extensively about the problems of computer-based vote counting and concludes that 'election administrators [cannot] demonstrate that the results they have certified are correct', and 'The data provided are insufficient to demonstrate the correctness of results reported.'[29] In other evidence, Saltman has argued that 'Investigators have shown that the computer programs used are sloppily designed . . . although I don't feel that that would be significant if one could show that the programs were not tampered with, and that procedures were sufficiently protected in order to demonstrate that the results were highly accurate.' Saltman also suggests that 'Audit trails that document election results, as well as general practices to assure accuracy, integrity and security, can be considerably improved.'[30] Others have questioned the procedures that match computer-generated tallies against counts from precinct boxes.[31]

Given this, perhaps we should ask why vote-tallying systems have not undergone the rigid testing and validation that we expect of other systems. Part of the answer to this is that the ballot process is a secretive procedure in which, for the purposes of a poll's validity, the link between the vote and the voter is removed. Hence, unlike other systems where records can be checked by its users, it is difficult to determine the accuracy of voting systems without seriously jeopardizing the anonymity of the electoral process.[32] A number of commentators have proposed guidelines for the construction and operation of computer-based vote tallying. These include eliminating software by placing the programs in chips (hence the programs cannot be deliberately or unwittingly altered), extensive pre-election testing, establishment of national standards, levels of redundancy, cross-checking with different hardware and manually counted samples.[33]

But perhaps the major point of this discussion is to ask whether the computerization of elections places them at risk through fraud or rigging. Given the history of intelligence agencies and civil rights abuses in the US, should we not expect that such organizations would be interested in interfering in key elections, especially in the case of a candidate whose policies are a threat to their operation? And as computerized voting spreads to other countries, might this not represent a perfect opportunity to guarantee that governments friendly to the US are returned with comfortable margins? Certainly, it is matter of historical fact that the CIA has been guilty of worse offences elsewhere.

Therefore, we need to ponder the larger issue of what the application of computing to social processes actually means for the rights and freedoms of ordinary citizens. How can we ensure that our lives are not a litany of database errors? How can we ensure the proper functioning of a democratic society, control of criminal elements and yet still maintain a society relatively free of surveillance? How can we provide jobs with the participative, trusted and profitable involvement of workers without resorting to high levels of invasive performance monitoring? Lastly, unless we have the capacity as a society to elect to office those whom we collectively endorse, how can we achieve any of the foregoing social goals? Perhaps the final answer is that nothing in life can be guaranteed, but that the first step toward the resolution of any problem is to be aware of it. All else follows from this, and that, at least in part, is one of the aims of this book.

Suggestions for Further Discussion

You may wish to think about the following, hypothetical scenario.

It is 1999 and the spread of the AIDS virus has continued along its predicted path of exponential growth, almost unchecked by educational campaigns, safe sex and the identification of high-risk groups. Like most clinical tests, the test for the HIV virus is not error-proof and misdiagnosis does occur, however small the odds against it.

Unfortunately for you, double-testing of blood from a blood bank does not identify it as being infected and as a result of transfusion with this blood, you now carry HIV antibodies – that is, you are antibody positive and are expected, eventually, to display the symptoms of the full-blown AIDS syndrome. Of course, the AIDS virus is totally unlike any other epidemic in one very important sense – it takes several years for individuals to die. Most other major epidemic diseases such as smallpox, cholera and so on kill people very quickly and hence quarantining of people is usually both short term and a very effective epidemiological control; people either survive the short quarantine period and are prevented from infecting others during the infectious period, or they die. Simple. However, with AIDS, the prospect of actually quarantining people for periods of up to ten years while they progress through the stages of the disease appears to be unacceptable and hence infected individuals must live within society and suffer varying degrees of fear, discrimination, rejection and alienation.

Into this scenario comes the government, which has begun conducting compulsory AIDS testing programs to help predict the course of the epidemic and to determine the impact of various initiatives. Test results are said to be totally confidential and in order to prevent avoidance of the test, social security numbers, tax returns and databases of all kinds are used to track down individuals and to present them (forcibly if necessary) for testing. Of course, as a law-abiding citizen you present yourself. You are diagnosed as antibody positive and the outcome is logged onto a government database system. However, you are confident that because the outcome of the test is confidential, you will be able to lead a fairly normal life, you follow safe sex practices to protect others and you hope that in the time that you have left a cure or at least better treatments will be found.

With the growth of AIDS as one of the more common terminal diseases, however, an increasing number of people have been lying to insurance companies about their infection, and upon reaching a terminal stage, kill themselves in car accidents and other apparently non-suicidal forms of ending it all. In this way, victims' families are securing massive insurance payouts and the insurance companies are feeling the pinch. However, in the interests of individuals' rights, the government absolutely prohibits insurance companies from demanding an AIDS test on an insurance applicant. It is sufficient that the government knows who is infected and the public release of such information is considered socially destabilizing.

Nevertheless, insurance companies are still desperate to discover such information so that they can offer competitive premiums without such a high degree of risk. There are two options open to them: somehow gain access to government files or else obtain the same information through alternative sources. Like insurance companies everywhere, the US companies hate risk and choose to do both. Through the tried and trusted method of bribery through a third party, some of this information is obtained. The remainder is gained by indirect means. Medical insurance companies note the kinds of treatments that patients receive and by looking for patterns in these ailments, quickly determine the chances that particular policy holders and applicants might actually have AIDS. This information is sold to other insurance companies as well.

Furthermore, in order to secure lower premiums for their businesses, employers are encouraged to monitor workers' usage of sick leave, any gossip about sexual preferences and any drug usage. This, too, is added to the information 'mosaic' gathered by the insurance companies. Lastly, landlords and other employers are eager to obtain access to these records as well. In the case of landlords, they don't want to provide accommodation for an AIDS victim because, given the hysteria over AIDS, they may never be able to rent their premises again. In the case of employers, they don't want to invest heavily in training and providing a career structure for an individual if they are likely to die before that investment is recouped. After all, no amount of money can retain a key employee if that person is already dead! Furthermore, being an AIDS victim makes a person susceptible to blackmail and that too cannot be tolerated for employees trusted with heavy responsibilities and financial powers.

What kind of quality of life do you think you can expect from this point on? Remember that federal and state employees of all kinds might have access to information about you, from police and ambulance personnel to doctors, lawyers, parole officers and tax officials. Could their services or actions be modified as a result? And if similar information was available to anyone sufficiently interested to interrogate insurance databases (for a fee, of course) then what does this imply for the kind of life that you are likely to lead? Do you have a right to privacy in this regard or does the public have the right to know of a potential threat in its midst? Does computer-based storage of this information increase the risk of individual threats at the price of providing governments and health authorities with the information they need to combat the spread of AIDS? Over to you . . .

Notes

1 Jacques Vallee, *The Network Revolution: Confessions of a Computer Scientist* (And/Or Press, Berkeley, CA, 1982).
2 Larry Reibstein and Lisa Drew, 'Clean credit for sale: a growing illegal racket', *Newsweek*, 12 September 1988, p. 49.
3 Sundar Iyengar, 'American Express is watching . . .', *Forum on Risks to the Public in Computer Systems*, 4 May 1986, vol. 8, no. 66. See also Jeffrey Rothfeder et al., 'Is nothing private?' *Business Week*, 4 September 1989.
4 David Burnham, 'Tales of a computer state', *The Nation*, April 1983.
5 D. Dyer, 'The human element', *Forum on Risks to the Public in Computer Systems*, 16 October 1985, vol. 1, no. 22.
6 David Burnham, 'Tales of a computer state'.
7 Peter Kimball, *The File* (Harcourt Brace Jovanovitch, San Diego, CA, 1983).
8 Francis Gibb, 'Data act sheds first light on "secret" personal files', *The Australian*, 3 November 1987.
9 Greg Tucker, 'Europe grasps nettle of data privacy protection legislation', *Computing Australia*, 19 September 1988, pp. 24–9.
10 Duncan Campbell, 'On and off the record', *Personal Computer World*, October 1988, p. 146. See also *Personal Computing Weekly*, 9/15 February 1989.
11 Francis Gibb, 'Data act sheds first light on "secret" personal files'.
12 Perry Morrison, 'Limits to technocratic consciousness: information technology and terrorism as example', *Science, Technology and Human Values*, 1986, vol. 11, no. 4, pp. 4–16.
13 David Burnham, *The Rise of the Computer State* (Random House, New York, 1983).
14 Morrison, 'Limits to technocratic consciousness'.
15 Charles Bruno, 'The electronic cops', *Datamation*, 15 June 1984, pp. 115–24. For a more up-to-date account of the NCIC see Evelyn Richards, 'Proposed FBI crime computer system raises questions on accuracy, privacy – report warns of potential risk data bank poses to civil liberties', *Washington Post*, 13 February 1989.
16 Curtis Jackson, 'NSA and encryption algorithms', *Forum on Risks to the Public in Computer Systems*, 2 March 1986, vol. 2, no. 20.
17 Dave Platt, 'Data encryption standard', *Forum on Risks to the Public in Computer Systems*, 28 February 1986, vol. 2, no. 17.
18 Gary H. Anthes, 'DARPA program to battle war on drugs, terrorism', *Federal Computer Week*, 24 April 1989, vol. 3, no. 17, pp. 1 and 53; Gary T. Marx, *Undercover: Police Surveillance in America* (University of California Press, Berkeley, CA, 1988).
19 Jonathon Markoff, 'US is moving to restrict access to facts about computer virus', *The New York Times*, 11 November 1988, p. 12.

20 John Shattuck and Muriel Morrisey Spence, 'The dangers of information control', in Tom Forester (ed.), *Computers in the Human Context* (Basil Blackwell, Oxford, and MIT Press, Cambridge, MA, 1989), reprinted from *Technology Review*, April 1988, pp. 63–73.
21 Bryan Boswell, 'US military seeks control of data', *The Australian*, 22 March 1988.
22 Lee Byrd, 'Americans' privacy exposed by new technology, Congress told', *ARPANET Telecom Digest*, vol. 5, no. 155, 24 October 1985. See also *Criminal Justice, New Technologies and the Constitution* (OTA, US Congress, Washington, DC, 1988) and David H. Flaherty, 'The emergence of surveillance societies in the western world: toward the year 2000', *Government Information Quarterly*, vol. 5, no. 4, 1988, pp. 377–87.
23 Gary T. Marx and Sanford Sherizen, 'Monitoring on the job', in Tom Forester (ed.), *Computers in the Human Context* (Basil Blackwell, Oxford, and MIT Press, Cambridge, MA, 1989), reprinted from *Technology Review*, November–December 1986; and George J. Church, 'The art of high-tech snooping', *Time*, 20 April 1987, pp. 19–21.
24 Stephen Koepp, 'The boss that never blinks', *Time*, 28 July 1986, pp. 38–9.
25 Geoffrey S. Goodfellow, 'Electronic surveillance', *Forum on Risks to the Public in Computer Systems*, 16 October 1985, vol. 1, no. 22.
26 Katie Hafner and Susan Garland, 'Privacy', *Business Week*, 28 March 1988, pp. 49–53.
27 As summarized by Ron Newman, 'Computerized voting: no standards and a lot of questions', *Forum on Risks to the Public in Computer Systems*, 14 April 1986, vol. 2, no. 42; 'US elections rigged: experts', *The Australian*, 30 July 1985, p. 23.
28 Gary Chapman, 'Computer error in vote tallying', *Software Engineering Notes*, October 1988, p. 8.
29 Roy G. Saltman, 'Accuracy, integrity and security in computerized vote-tallying', *Communications of the ACM*, vol. 31, no. 10, 1988, pp. 1184–91; Roy G. Saltman, *Effective Use of Computing Technology in Vote-Tallying* (Institute for Computer Sciences and Technology, National Bureau of Standards, Gathersburg, MD, no date); Lance J. Hoffman, *Making Every Vote Count: Security and Reliability of Computerized Vote-Counting Systems* (Department of Electrical Engineering and Computer Science, George Washington University, Washington, DC, no date).
30 Roy G. Saltman, op. cit. (1988).
31 Jeff Mogul, 'Computerized voting', *Forum on Risks to the Public from Computer Systems*, 5 March 1986, vol. 2, no. 23. See also *Software Engineering Notes*, vol. 14, no. 1, January 1989, pp. 19–21 and 'Risks', 4 September 1989.
32 Karen A. Frenkel, 'Computers and elections', *Communications of the ACM*, vol. 31, no. 10, 1988, pp. 1176–83.
33 Peter G. Neumann, 'Comments on the New Yorker article', *Forum on Risks to the Public in Computer Systems*, 3 November 1988, vol. 7, no. 70; Saltman, op. cit. (1988); Suleiman K. Kassicieh, Glen H. Kawaguchi and Len Malcyznski, 'Security, integrity and public acceptance of electronic voting: managing elections in the 1990s', *Journal of Systems Management*, December 1988, pp. 6–10 and 39.

7 AI and Expert Systems

What is AI? – What is Intelligence? – Expert Systems
– Legal Problems – Newer Developments – Ethical
Issues: is AI a Proper Goal? – Conclusion: the Limits
of Hype – Suggestions for Further Discussion

In 1986 a Nevada woman, Ms Julie Engle, underwent routine surgery in hospital. The operation was completed without complication. However, soon afterwards Ms Engle was given pain relief by a computerized dispensing machine. Unfortunately, the system mistakenly instructed hospital staff to pump more than 500 mg of pain relieving drugs into Ms Engle's body and less than half an hour after the successful completion of the operation, she was in a coma. Five days later, she was pronounced brain dead. Ms Engle had been secretary to Salt Lake City lawyer Mr Vibert Kesler, who immediately launched a damages suit against the hospital concerned for incorrect and irresponsible use of a medical expert system.[1]

If this kind of tragedy can occur with a comparatively simple application of 'artificial intelligence' (AI), imagine what might happen with some of the more complex applications planned for AI and 'expert systems'. For example, the FBI is developing 'Big Floyd', an expert system designed to catch drug smugglers and to target *potential* terrorists and other possible miscreants. The US Treasury Department wants to identify money-laundering banks, the Environmental Protection Agency wants to catch polluters, the IRS wants to find tax cheats, the Secret Service wants to target potential assassins and the FBI's National Center for the Analysis of Violent Crimes is keen to identify potential serial killers, arsonists and rapists. The application of expert systems is looked upon by all these agencies as one way in which their aims can be achieved by using the vast amount of personal, financial and census data now contained in various American databases.[2]

What is AI?

Definitions of 'artificial intelligence' or AI vary quite considerably and more often than not tend to emphasize the peculiar (and sometimes pecuniary) interests of the expert or researcher offering the definition.

111

Briefly though, AI consists of two branches of research: one branch which attempts to shed light on the nature of human intelligence by simulating it, or components of it, with the eventual aim of totally replicating it (or even surpassing it); and another branch which attempts to build 'expert' systems that exhibit 'intelligent' behaviour regardless of its resemblance to *human* intelligence. The latter school is particularly concerned with the construction of 'intelligent' tools for assisting human beings in complex tasks such as oil exploration, medical diagnosis, chemical analysis and fault-identification in machinery. Other activities that fall under these two branches of endeavour include attempts to build systems with visual perception, systems that understand natural language, systems that demonstrate machine-learning capacities, systems that can manipulate objects (e.g., robotics), systems that can provide intelligent tuition and systems that play games.

Artificial intelligence emerged as an academic discipline at a Dartmouth College, Massachusetts, conference in 1956. The term itself was invented by John McCarthy, the developer of one of AI's most popular programming languages – LISP. Much of the earliest work in AI was concerned with the construction of programs to play games in an intelligent fashion. Indeed, programs have now been constructed that can beat more than 99 per cent of all human players in games such as noughts and crosses, draughts and especially chess.

It is chess which has highlighted some of the major differences in the way that humans and machines solve demanding 'intellectual' tasks – and it is chess that has also fuelled criticism of other forms of problem-solving using artificial intelligence. For example, while computers are forced to consider all possible moves from a given position, humans appear to be able to take a chess pattern and rapidly identify a handful of powerful moves. In other words, computers solve chess problems by the application of brute computational power (and even then, the total combination of moves is beyond them – 10^{120} possible combinations), while humans are able to exclude millions of disadvantageous moves at a glance.

It appears that this ability depends very much upon experience in the recognition of meaningful chess patterns. In a classic experiment, one of the high priests of AI, Herbert Simon, showed that meaningful chess positions were much more easily remembered by chess experts than by novices, but that when positions were essentially random, no differences in recall existed between novices and experts.[3] From this, we can conclude that at least part of human expertise in chess lies in the ability to take a meaningful chess position (one that resembles known patterns of offence and defence) and focus on the few lines of development that are likely to improve the position. Computers, on the other hand, are unable at present to adopt this approach and must tediously calculate the worth of each possible sequence of future moves.

Part of the reason why humans are able to do this and indeed, why they behave so intelligently across such a multitude of tasks and situations, is that they have actively experienced the world and have accumulated a great deal of background or 'common-sense' knowledge that assists them. For example, in navigating around a room, it is obvious that I know an enormous number of things about the physical properties of the world: doors, walls and objects are solid and cannot be walked through, although doorways can if open; I know about gravity and objects falling if I knock them; I have enormously powerful perception that gives me depth and distance cues under great variations in lighting, including an understanding of the nature of glass; I know what purposes stairs fulfil and why they are designed the way they are, as well as the hazards associated with using them. Clearly, for a constant environment, this kind of knowledge can be provided for a computer, as shown by MIT's Terry Winograd in his block world known as SHRDLU – an environment of blocks, pyramids and other shapes that can be manipulated by a computer on command.[4] The real difference however, is that the knowledge I use to navigate a room represents only a minuscule fragment of the knowledge I have of the world in all of its physical, social, cultural, historical, political, economic and scientific forms. In Winograd's block world, the smallest changes in the environment required extensive changes to the program, yet, in general, ordinary human beings deal with the world in a totally fluent, adaptable, and quite amazing manner when compared to the most adaptable and 'intelligent' of man-made machines.

One answer to this problem – namely the common-sense knowledge that we have and that computers don't – has been to construct systems that attempt to learn from experience. Yet this, too, has met with disappointing levels of success.[5] We do not know in advance just what a program needs to possess in terms of knowledge if it is to demonstrate real intelligence. Further, allowing a computer to interact with the world in order to acquire such knowledge often seems to fall foul of the sheer size of the knowledge that needs to be accumulated, as well as the difficulties of storing it in an appropriate form for it to be used again. Even more fundamentally, we don't understand what 'learning' is (since much of learning also involves discarding unnecessary information – that is, forgetting), let alone what kinds of knowledge should be learned and how it should be structured.

Given a moment's thought, the existence of these difficulties makes a great deal of sense. As infants, human beings spend several years acquiring the kind of experiential knowledge they need in order to interact physically with the world and to manipulate it (and themselves) in an intelligent manner. Furthermore, it appears that, to some extent, we are 'wired up' to develop in this way. That is, we are constructed in a fashion that predisposes us to learn language and develop intellectually, via years of experience. For example, children have an innate ability to acquire language – indeed it is quite easy for children to learn several languages before puberty. Yet once this point is reached, it becomes extremely difficult for individuals to acquire multiple languages (as any adult language learner can attest!).

In addition, the evidence from cases of feral children (those raised by wild animals such as wolves) shows that without exposure to language in these pre-pubescent years, individuals are incapable of developing human language at all. It is almost as if the human body regards puberty as the turning point to adulthood before which everything we need to survive (intellectually and perhaps even physically) should have been developed. After that point, the system loses its flexibility and 'locks up' taking the young adult through life with whatever intellectual capacities they have or have not developed. It therefore remains a moot point whether researchers in AI can ever simulate this kind of experiential acquisition of knowledge, especially given the advantages that humans obviously have in their evolved predisposition to intellectual development.

What is Intelligence?

The lessons learned from these efforts have also raised interesting questions about the very nature of human intelligence and indeed, exactly where the dividing line between intelligent and unintelligent behaviour lies (or even if such a line exists). Several critics of AI, for example, have claimed that the brute computational approach to chess playing outlined above could hardly be called intelligent. On the other hand, proponents of AI argue that the criterion of intelligence is constantly (and unfairly) redrawn by critics as soon as that criterion has been reached.[6] For example, at one stage arithmetical ability was regarded as a hallmark of intelligence, yet now that computers can calculate millions of times faster than any human who has ever lived, this is no longer regarded as a requirement of intelligence. Similarly, chess playing was once regarded as a demanding intellectual activity, yet now that computers can easily defeat the vast majority of chess players (though not all), this, too, seems to be losing its status as a litmus test of intelligence.

This begs the question of exactly what intelligence is and whether or not it can exist in non-human forms. After all, if at least one branch of AI aims to create intelligence (human or not) in a computational form, then surely a necessary first step is to define the parameters of that goal. Again, critics have argued that AI is simply a form of modern alchemy that is based on the latest metaphor of the mind, or at least its physical manifestation as the brain. In the days of Descartes, the brain was thought to be composed of hydraulic lines and pistons (then, the most powerful of technologies); while later it was regarded as a telephone exchange (again, the most sophisticated of technologies of the time); and now that the computer has gained supremacy as the ultimate technology of our age, not unexpectedly the brain is regarded as an information processing engine – a computer with non-silicon circuits. Thus critics of AI believe that the brain and hence the mind itself is unlikely to be understood in computational terms, since there is little evidence that AI is based on anything other than the most recent technological metaphor of mind. For them, whatever achievements have occurred in AI are pathetic parodies compared with the richness, power and fluency of the intelligence that every average human being displays in the course of their daily life.

Despite this, many AI researchers are adamant that human intelligence is a symbol-manipulating activity that can be simulated *in toto* or at least in part by computational means. In other words, as intelligent beings, we have internal symbols or processes that have external referents and associated meanings and by manipulating those symbols in rule-governed ways, we come to exhibit meaningful behaviour in a dynamic environment. Yet one of the most powerful of arguments against this view is John Searle's so-called 'Chinese room' scenario.[7]

Searle, a philosopher and long-time sceptic of the claims for artificial intelligence, proposes the following thought experiment: suppose that a man is inside a room which has a gap under the door and through this gap he receives sheets of paper from someone outside. No other form of communication is possible. The sheets of paper have Chinese symbols written on them and the task before this individual is to translate those symbols into some other language such as English. To do this, he simply looks up a table on the wall and writes down the equivalent of the Chinese symbol in the required language. He then passes these under the door to the person waiting outside.

Now Searle's claim is that although the man in the room has manipulated symbols such that Chinese language has been translated into English language, in no sense could the man be said to 'understand' Chinese. He has simply followed rules in order to change one particular input format into a desired output format – and this is essentially what digital computers do (note: Searle rightly ignores the difficulties associated with actually achieving such a performance level; this is assumed for the sake of the argument). Hence, any claim that rule-governed symbol manipulation can allow a computer to understand language, or more broadly, exhibit 'intelligence,' is totally without foundation. Humans may manipulate symbols, but in communicating or demonstrating intelligence in other ways they must be doing other things as well. It is these other things that AI has not come to grips with.

Another approach to identifying just what intelligence is, and therefore how we might approach the re-creation of it, was proposed in the 1950s by one of the founding fathers of computing – Alan Turing. 'Turing's test', as it has been termed, has appeared in corrupted and in incorrect forms in numerous places. We have therefore chosen to use the original representation of the test as proposed by Turing himself: to begin with, imagine a game between three players, A, B and C. A and B sit together in a room, unseen by C who converses with them via typewritten messages (modern forms of this scenario could include VDTs). A is a man and B is a woman, but C's sex is immaterial. C has to identify which of his interlocutors is A and which is B. In addition, A's role is to confuse C and B's role is to minimize C's confusion. The question that Turing asks is: what will happen when a machine takes the place of A in this game? The suggestion made by Turing is that any machine capable of taking A's place without C knowing it must have a strong claim to intelligence. By simplifying the scenario somewhat, many others have generally inferred that any machine that can convince a human that it, too, is human must be capable of thinking.

Yet Turing's test is not without ambiguity. For example, it has been claimed by some that both Joseph Weizenbaum's program, ELIZA,[8] which simulates a Rogerian psychotherapist's conversation, and Kenneth Colby's PARRY program,[9] which simulates a paranoid schizophrenic, are able to satisfy the Turing test. Hence it appears that the extent to which machines are able to simulate human conversational intelligence is subject to a very human and subjective process – judgement.

Of course, both Searle's and Turing's tests do not provide a great deal of assistance in determining just what intelligence is and therefore how it may (or may not) be recreated in either human or non-human forms. Searle's argument goes some distance in this direction, however, by arguing that intelligence is essentially the property of human brains. To get to this point, Searle argues the following: the man in the Chinese room is following instructions just as a computer does – indeed, the instructions constitute a program – and like any computer program, these instructions will yield identical results regardless of the physical mechanisms used to execute them. That is, we could replace the man with a complex system of pattern-matching video cameras, or with an electromechanical device that ran templates over the symbols until one matched, then returned the relevant English translation. In principle, we could construct a computer out of beer cans (yes, it would work!) and the Chinese translation program could be made to execute on such a machine.

This principle is one of the very foundations of AI – that programs are formal representations and are therefore executable on any form of computational equipment. Furthermore, since AI proponents argue that the brain is simply a form of computational device, then the program that executes within the brain (the product of which is our mind) must be able to be executed on other forms of computational machinery – such as digital computers. Therefore, in order to replicate the mind, all we need do is discover the nature of the program that executes within the brain – we can then run it on a digital computer and replicate a mind. However, Searle's scenario is a strong criticism of this principle – a principle which essentially disregards the physical architecture on which a program executes. In his view, our mental states are an outcome of the physiology of the brain: the mind is not a program that can be executed on any computer whether it be composed of beer cans, silicon or neurons – instead, our mind emerges as a result of the particular neurophysiological properties of our brain.

Now that is not as ridiculous as it may sound. Searle is not saying that our intelligence cannot be recreated. Indeed, a common but incorrect representation of Searle's argument claims that he believes that only brains or organic mechanisms can become conscious. This 'carbon chauvinism', as it has been called, is not true of Searle's approach, but it is true that any mechanism which is 'causally equivalent' to the brain (that is, in the way that it 'produces' thinking) would be capable of producing comparable mental states. In other words, as systems theorists would have it, thinking or the mind itself is an emergent property of the brain as a physical organ in action.[10] A good analogy is to argue that whirlpools, steam, ice, raindrops, snowflakes and sleet are phenomena which emerge from (or are caused by) the physical properties and characteristics of the water molecule. Similarly, Searle might argue, minds emerge from the peculiar structural, electrophysiological and chemical qualities and processes of the human brain. By extrapolation, we might also infer that other animals may also have minds or at least possess mental states which are a by-product of their own peculiar neurophysiological characteristics.

Lastly, simply because for many commentators language is the hallmark of intelligence, we need to devote some further attention at this point to the enormous difficulties it poses for efforts to understand it computationally. Again, as with our ability to navigate around a room, it is fairly evident that in understanding language we bring to bear an enormous amount of experience in hearing it, producing it in a variety of forms and developing it formally through our education systems. Hence when I utter the sentence, 'I can't bear it any longer', we immediately understand the *context* – one knows from experience that I'm not talking about a large, hairy and sometimes dangerous mammal, nor am I talking about the fruitfulness of a tree or the load-carrying capacity of a steel girder.

Such multiple meanings could, of course, be encoded in computational form (although this would be tedious and difficult), but there are other forms of language that remain intractable for computers. For example, if I said 'I have never failed any student in second-year mathematics', the implication is, of course, that I have taught such a course and that I have done so for some considerable length of time. Also, if I were to say, 'I can't sit for the examination. My doctor has provided me with a medical certificate', the implications are that my illness *prevents* me from sitting the examination, that the medical certificate is a form of evidence for this claim and that possibly some alternative assessment arrangements may be made or that the absence of an exam mark will be considered in the context of my illness.

Yet for a computer, the second sentence, 'My doctor has provided me with a medical certificate', might just as well be 'I like eating chocolate' – the inferences we draw are based upon our immense background and commonsensical understanding of the world. As a further example, the sentences 'The porridge is ready to eat' and 'The tiger is ready to eat' are syntactically identical but semantically disparate – in order to understand these, too, one needs considerable background information about what tigers and porridge are and the whole host of properties that we know they do and don't possess. Obviously, one conjures up thoughts of breakfast and the other thoughts of predation.[11] Unfortunately, as yet, computers do not have the necessary experiential context to understand such sentences, although there is hope that in the future some mechanism might allow us to represent efficiently such knowledge (massive and inconsistent though it might be) or allow them to gain it in a similar experientially (learned) manner to the way humans acquire it.

As a criticism of this approach, however, it is clear that – at least for human language – so much of it is dependent upon its anthropocentric basis – that is, the complex experience we have of being human and interacting with the world from inside a human body and within a human society and culture.[12] For example, when I say, 'He was heavy hearted', I don't mean that he has an inability to support his own heart, or that his heart is made of lead. Even a human who had never heard of this expression could probably decipher its meaning, having experienced the physiological or at least physical symptoms that depression or sadness brings. Similarly, 'An iron fist inside a velvet glove' requires an understanding of what a fist represents (anger, repression, violence . . .)

as well as the physical (and metaphorical) properties of velvet (softness to the touch, delicate nature . . .).

Now this is not to say that some restricted subsets of language with identified meanings in fixed contexts (e.g., legal, economic) cannot be understood by machines – quite the opposite. But it does imply that what we term 'natural language' is natural to us as humans and is determined to a very large extent by the nature of human beings as physical and physiological, social and emotional entities. It also implies that without a similar physiological and experiential basis,[13] computational efforts to understand language by application of syntax and grammar alone cannot approach the experience of language as it exists for humans.

Expert Systems

In essence, expert systems are programs which encapsulate an expert's, or several experts' knowledge of a particular domain in a computer-processable form. From this 'knowledge base', inferences may then be drawn which may equal or (hopefully) exceed the quality of similar inferences made by human experts. Other definitions of an expert system that have been offered at different times include: 'An expert system is a computer system that uses a representation of human expertise in a specialist domain in order to perform functions similar to those normally performed by a human expert in that domain' and 'An expert system is a computer system that operates by applying an inference mechanism to a body of specialist expertise represented in the form of "knowledge".'[14]

Such systems have been applied to many problem areas – for example, the analysis of chemical compounds (DENDRAL),[15] the diagnosis and treatment of infectious diseases (MYCIN),[16] the configuration of computer systems for shipment (XCON),[17] as well as identifying likely areas for mineral exploration and mining (PROSPECTOR).[18] Yet in some senses, expert systems have been around for many years in one form or another as sophisticated programs – the difference being that the knowledge base encapsulated in an expert system is not just the programmer's, but the structured understanding of acknowledged experts in a particular problem domain. Indeed, for the most part, expert systems are collections of rules that have been 'extracted' from an expert by a 'knowledge engineer' and they very often, although not exclusively, take the form of IF . . . THEN statements. For example, suppose that we wanted to construct an expert system for fault diagnosis of jet engines (and such systems do exist), then some of the rules we might identify could include:

IF the engine stalled in flight,
AND the aircraft's wing was at a high or excessive angle of attack
at low speed,
AND the engine subsequently restarted at a normal angle of
attack,
THEN the engine may have suffered a compressor stall due to
inadequate airflow into the engine, caused by the aircraft being
close to stalling.

Similarly, in the case of a medical diagnostic system like MYCIN:

IF the infection requiring therapy is meningitis,
AND the type of infection is fungal,
AND organisms were not seen on the stain of the culture,
AND the patient is not a compromised host,
AND the patient has been in a region where coccidiomycoses are
endemic,
AND the race of the patient is black or Asian or Indian,
AND the cryptococcal antigen in the csf was not positive,
THEN there is suggestive evidence that the cryptococcus is not one
of the organisms which might be causing the infection.[19]

Of course, IF . . . THEN type rules are not the only form in which
knowledge can be stored in an expert system's knowledge base. Other
forms include semantic networks, frames and predicate logic, yet the
essential nature of expert systems in applying deductive (and often
inductive) methods to a body of knowledge remains unchanged. We
should also note that the real benefit of expert systems occurs in
applications of much greater complexity than this and that many such
systems are able to supply the appropriate intervention, therapy or
repair procedures for the particular case in hand. In order to achieve
this, expert systems not only use a knowledge base and an 'inference
engine' to operate on that knowledge, but they also usually provide an
explanatory interface that justifies their conclusions – by explaining the
system's line of reasoning with relevant probabilities for each of the
conclusions it draws. Furthermore, much of the hard work involved in
constructing an expert system is not so much at the programming level
(although that can be difficult enough in itself), but in the extraction
of rules from human experts by the knowledge engineer. Very often,
experts do not consciously *know* the rules they use and the knowledge engineer has to be skilled in identifying a rule component when
it appears in an expert's explanation. Furthermore, experts' rules and
knowledge often conflict, not only across experts but even in the same

expert. Therefore, resolving such clashes is also part of the knowledge engineer's task.

Given the growth in development and use of expert systems – particularly now that 'shells' (software environments) for building such systems are quite common, perhaps it is appropriate to ask some questions about expert systems and their relationship to AI.

For example, are expert systems intelligent? Are they part of artificial intelligence in any meaningful sense? Clearly, expert systems are part of that branch of AI that is concerned with the construction of intelligent tools, regardless of whether that 'intelligence' resembles human intelligence or not. Perhaps then we should simply regard expert systems as 'smart' tools, not possessing intelligence in any real sense (although again, being cognizant of whether or not we are simply redefining the criteria for intelligence), but simply assisting in the performance of tasks that humans find difficult and take many years in acquiring sufficient expertise to solve. If this is the case, then perhaps their inclusion under the label 'AI' is a misnomer which is inappropriately applied to what effectively represents just another arm of computer science or information systems. We need to contrast this claim with that made by people such as Donald Michie of the University of Edinburgh, Scotland, who argues that expert systems can actually provide syntheses of knowledge bases that represent new forms of knowledge that do not have any human analogue (for example, in the categorization of multiple heart arrhythmias that humans find difficult to diagnose).[20] If this is so, then perhaps expert systems do constitute a form of intelligence. Yet again, we need to judge whether such new knowledge forms are in any way different from mathematical transformations applied to satellite weather data (which show different features of the climate) or chemical stains applied to cell cultures, which again yield new features or phenomena.

Legal Problems

According to a recent report, at least half the US corporations listed in the *Fortune 500* are currently developing expert systems either for their internal use or for commercial sale. This would seem to suggest that many of America's major companies have considerable faith in the future of expert systems. But despite this apparent confidence, there are substantial legal problems with expert systems in the US. These need to be resolved before we are likely to see their more widespread application. For example, the Medical Software Consortium, a St Louis supplier of medical software, baulked at becoming involved in a joint NASA–US Army project to develop an autonomous intensive care stretcher with expert diagnostic capabilities. For them, the potential for lawsuits was simply too daunting – and this is becoming a common perception given the eight-fold increase in product liability cases that has occurred between 1974 and 1986, when 13,595 such cases were filed.[21] Moreover, it seems that no particular company wants to be the test case for an expert system product liability case (who would?) and everyone in the industry is concerned about how such a case would affect product liability insurance costs.

According to some sources, there are cases where government agencies have applied the same measures to software that they use to help regulate human experts. In 1986, for example, the Internal Revenue Service allegedly began treating software used to generate income tax returns in the same way that it deals with humans involved in tax preparation: if such a program makes a mistake, then it's liable.[22] However, this raises a major problem that is not resolved by such rulings – namely, just *who* is liable (since a system obviously cannot be). To help anwer this question and to examine its complexities, we will cite a scenario and the associated interpretation by one expert in the area, Richard M. Lucash.

Suppose that a chemical company, Chemcorp, obtains an expert system from a manufacturer, Syscorp. The purpose of the system is to control a process at one of Chemcorp's plants. Imagine that part of the system's task is to control the temperature of this process and that a defect in the system causes the plant to explode, thereby damaging the plant, causing injuries to workers and bystanders and financial losses to Chemcorp due to shipping delays. In accordance with general practice in the software industry, Syscorp will have signed a contract with Chemcorp, specifying that the system would have to meet certain performance standards as well as Syscorp's obligations if such standards were not met. These obligations might include repair of the system within the warranty period and reimbursement of financial loss. However, most such contracts place a specified limit on the software company's liability and so in this scenario, Chemcorp would have to bear some proportion of the costs resulting from the malfunction. Furthermore, Syscorp would be relieved of liability if the cause of the fault could be traced to Chemcorp or some other party – for example, in the case where the system was not used as directed.

Moreover, Syscorp's contracts with other suppliers or contractors (say, chip or software companies) could further affect attribution of liability. In general, most of the elements of this chain, from designers to suppliers and subcontractors, would carry some form of insurance to protect themselves. *Hence, for those parties who have contractual arrangements among themselves, attribution of liability is an ordered process and in this sense expert systems and any other form of computer system are no different.* However, for those parties who are not linked by contractual arrangements, such as those bystanders injured in Chemco's explosion and who now seek compensation, a different set of procedures applies – those pertaining to negligence and defective production.

It needs to be pointed out that *negligence* in the legal framework we are discussing is somewhat different from *malpractice*. Negligence means a failure to act as a reasonable person would under the same circumstances, whereas malpractice is a failure to demonstrate the minimum level of competence required by a *profession*. Judgements of malpractice in the US turn on the extent to which an event could be foreseen, whether the work was primarily for the benefit of the client (and not other unknown parties who could be affected by it) and whether or not extending the professional's liability to the situation in hand would discourage others from entering the profession.

As Lucash argues, perhaps the most interesting case that has general implications for all expert systems is where a professional uses an expert system containing the codified knowledge of another professional. For example, imagine that a doctor uses an expert system and as a result of the system's faulty knowledge, the patient dies. In these circumstances, clearly the doctor who supplied the knowledge could foresee that it would be used by other doctors – yet at the same time, an attribution of liability here could effectively discourage any doctor from helping to construct such expert systems. In these circumstances, Lucash suggests that experts require software companies to indemnify them against liability for errors or other inadequacies in the knowledge they supply. Certainly, the doctor using this system could be liable, especially if it was discovered that he failed to exercise a professional judgement, or if he used the system contrary to manufacturer's instructions. As a point of interest, though, a doctor may also be liable if he failed to use such a system should it be available, especially if it can be demonstrated that it would have improved patient care.

Given the above framework, clearly it is senseless to attribute liability to a system, although there are legal mechanisms in the US by which product 'liability' can be invoked. The doctrine of 'strict liability' requires that one who sells a product in a defective condition – that is, unreasonably dangerous to the user – is subject to liability for the physical harm caused to the ultimate user. Injured parties can thereby claim compensation from the manufacturer or any other party in the chain of distribution. This removes the need to demonstrate that the manufacturer or distributors acted negligently. Only the defect which rendered the product unreasonably dangerous need be demonstrated.

However, this doctrine is problematical when applied to expert systems.

First, the doctrine only applies to *physical harm* to persons or property. Some applications of expert systems will not involve this (e.g, a faulty prospecting program). Second, the doctrine does not apply to services (where expert systems have enormous application) – only to products. This is basically because professional services are subsumed under the malpractice provisions outlined above. And when a combination of goods and services are provided (as with many expert systems), a court must look to whether the primary purpose of the transaction was to provide a product or a service. Applying these rules to a computer system, it appears that strict liability would not be imposed when the injured party is not a user of the system, because that user was primarily obtaining a service. Hence, in our example of the medical expert system above, the patient was obtaining a service and when the patient's next-of-kin sues the doctor for malpractice may wish to seek compensation from the manufacturer through product liability, but this would probably be disallowed since this again is usually limited to cases where the injured party is a consumer only.[23]

Thus although the application of existing legal doctrine is of extreme importance to expert systems, the applicability of such legal frameworks is not without problems. Yet given the nature of the legal system and its foundation on precedent, it is unlikely that such inconsistencies and ambiguities will be resolved before the first test cases have worked their way through a tangled web of litigation and counter-claims. Like everyone else, though, we can only speculate as to what these might be and what their outcomes will determine.

Newer Developments

Despite these serious legal problems, expert systems are in fact one of the more successful technologies to emerge from recent research into artificial intelligence. Others have tended to be mostly smoke and mirrors. The Japanese Fifth Generation Project, for example, launched with great fanfare back in 1981, aimed to advance significantly the development of AI and parallel processing by 1991. More specifically, it was expected to create systems that could understand natural language and speech, interpret the visual world, tap large databases and solve complex problems by the application of inductive and deductive inference. Experts disagree as to the exact state of play with the Fifth Generation Project – and indeed about the nature and aims of the project in the first place – but most accept that progress has been disappointing and no really major breakthroughs have yet been announced by Tokyo. Its main effect has been to galvanize Western governments into action – leading directly to the establishment of the MCC consortium in the US and the Esprit project in Europe, for instance.[24]

A more promising line of research included under the rubric of 'connectionism' aims to create intelligent machines by building 'neural networks'. These consist of thousands of processing units, each analogous to a neuron in the brain, which are interconnected by links that are in turn analogous to the synaptic connection between neurons.[25] Each link has a 'weight' or a connection strength and a system's knowledge is encoded in link weights and in the interconnection pattern of the system. Some units serve as input units and others as 'hidden units' (they are connected to other units and thus cannot be 'seen' from either the input or the output channels). Such networks have demonstrated the ability to *learn* by being given particular inputs and associating them with desired outputs. Furthermore, neural nets can exhibit *associative recall* in that they are able to produce a complete pattern of output once they are given a fraction of a particular pattern's input. A final interesting property of this technology is the extent to which it is *fault tolerant* (in something like the way the brain continues to function despite daily cell deaths and developmental decline).

To date, most neural nets have been simulated using very large Von Neumann architecture machines, but such simulations have been very slow in execution. There is hope, however, that with the development of massively parallel machines, neural networks will improve dramatically. David Waltz has estimated that if the present thousandfold increase in computing power every ten years continues, then, aided by connectionist models, a computer with the processing power of the human brain could be built for around $20 million (at today's prices) by the year 2012. In addition, if the decline in the cost of memory continues at its present rate (around a factor of ten every five years) then a machine with the connectionist memory capacity of the brain might be constructed for a cost of about $20 million (at today's prices) by the year 2017.[26] However, other writers such Jacob Schwartz have been at pains to point out the enormous differences between what is known about the functioning of the brain and what we can reasonably expect from extrapolating existing developments in connectionism.[27] Although many researchers are optimistic that connectionist models may help diminish this gap, the issue remains an empirical question.

More recently, in a rather dramatic turn-around from his earlier work, Terry Winograd (and Fernando Flores) have mounted a grave challenge to the idea that machines will ever understand natural language and have even questioned the fundamental principles underlying AI.[28] Their argument is highly philosophical, claiming that most of the past and present discourse in artificial intelligence is based upon a misinterpretation of human cognition and language. They say that the 'rationalist' tradition in Western science and technology assumes that reality has an objective existence which is independent of the observer. In this view, cognitive processes are involved in mapping this reality – by manipulating mental representations of it we create consciousness or at least exhibit thought. Winograd and Flores invoke phenomenologists such as Martin Heidegger and the biologist of perception, Humberto Maturana, to argue that cognition does not so much represent reality as much as a dynamic interaction with it to determine what is perceived and how it is understood.

For example, if a stick is illuminated from one side with white light and from another with red light, one shadow appears red and the other green, even though there is no light that normally falls within the range of the spectrum normally associated with green. In other words, they argue, our internal pattern of retinal states *determines* our perception (rather than the other way around), often with little correspondence to external reality. If we extend this to neuronal states, then cognition is essentially a series of perturbations (by the environment) of the nervous system and the range of possible perturbations (i.e. the range of events that can possibly alter our cognition) and their effect are determined by an evolutionary or (in the case of learning) an historical process of interaction and selection. That is, in the case of the perception of green described above, we have evolved to perceive green in these circumstances of reality and our cognitive interaction with it does not involve a direct mapping – a one-to-one correspondence – between what is out there and its representation in our minds.

Winograd and Flores argue that our cognition of colour, for example, involves a 'structural coupling' between our cognitive capacities to perceive colour and the environment itself. In other words, the nervous system cannot be seen as a passive filter of reality, but as a generator of phenomena which may have little correspondence to the external world. Instead, patterns of stimulation cause 'perturbations' in our nervous system – a nervous system that has adapted and learned to accept such perturbations (while rejecting others) for the purposes of survival and species development. Perhaps, to put it crudely and simply, Winograd and Flores believe that our cognition is *constructed* from (selected aspects of) reality, and that, in turn, evolution and historical interaction with the world determines how we perceive it and deal with it.

Now this complex argument is not easy to understand or deal with, but it does identify and reinforce some of the major difficulties that AI has and will continue to experience. For example, it suggests that language is a constructed phenomenon, bound up in the nature of human experience and of interaction with the world. This is a point that many AI thinkers would agree with. It also suggests that for computers to become intelligent in the way that humans are (or to assume intelligence in any form) they need to develop interactively with the environment, just as human beings do. This, presumably, would allow them to develop their own 'structural coupling' and cognitive mechanisms for dealing with the world in the constructivist sense that human beings do. Clearly though, just how this can be achieved, or whether it can ever be achieved, remains an open question. Nor is it yet clear how such claims stand in relation to the arguments of Searle – that a mind has causal mechanisms that determine it and that computer programs (as they currently exist) do not have such properties. Despite all of this, it is clear that Winograd and Flores have proposed a radical conceptualization of cognition that runs counter to the 'symbol manipulation' hypothesis endorsed by most mainstream AI researchers. It remains to be seen what status it will be accorded in the light of future theoretical and practical developments.

Ethical Issues: is AI a Proper Goal?

The promotion of 'artificial intelligence' and 'expert systems' provides a rich source of ethical dilemmas for computer professionals and users. For example, given the extent to which AI has been funded from military sources, should we question the entire ethical basis of such a discipline? Or, because so much research of all kinds is funded by the military, is AI simply guilty of being more successful in this regard? We also need to be very careful about the credence that is placed on claims made by the 'artificial intelligentsia' as they go about promoting their subject. So many of their utterances over the years have proved to be just so much hype, hot air and bulldust that most AI watchers have learned to take AI predictions about future developments in the area with several large measures of salt.

But even their more practical and seemingly down-to-earth proposals have disturbing ethical aspects. Is it not dangerous, for example, to support, as Donald Michie does, the use of expert systems to make judicial judgements, administer our cities for us and perhaps even replace our governments? Indeed, Michie has been known to state that such systems would have to be taught how to lie, since that is precisely how real (and presumably good?) administrators work – you just can't tell *everyone* the truth simply because they ask for it (or so the argument runs). Indeed, Michie and Rory Johnston seriously believe that expert systems will solve our problems of unemployment, pollution, crime, war, overpopulation and terrorism.[29] What faith should we place in such claims? Are they just another technocrat's folly, never to see the light of day? Or should we take a long, hard look at the Maginot line and its role in the Second World War?

Furthermore, what is the real value of claims by AI enthusiasts that we need to provide Third World countries with expert systems for medical diagnosis, agricultural advice and geological analysis because these countries lack substantial human expertise in such areas?[30] Is this yet another technofix that attempts to fix the symptoms without addressing the causes? Perhaps we could argue (as many scholars have) that the reasons for these inadequacies can be traced to exploitation by the developed world (through irresponsible loan practices, trade cartels, cash crop economies perpetuated by Western involvement, etc.) and that the appropriate strategy for Third World countries is to eliminate these problems rather than attempt to 'bootstrap' economies by technological means. After all, what use is an expert system in a country that doesn't have a regular power supply, the parts or people to maintain it, nor the expertise to tailor it to local conditions and local needs. Of what benefit is expert system advice that improves, say, agricultural output, if that output merely help pays off a foreign debt – a debt that was incurred buying weapons for a civil war brought about by colonial powers deciding that disparate racial groups should become a country? What purpose is there to an agricultural surplus that goes into the pockets of a political elite – an elite maintained by one or other power bloc which happens to need bases or a strategic buffer zone? From such an analysis, perhaps we are inevitably led to the conclusion that the most appropriate line of attack for solving the problems of these countries lies at a nontechnological level rather than through a computerized technological fix.

Now these issues might seem a long way from our home territory of AI and expert systems, and to a large extent they apply to almost any technology, but the point is that those whom we have termed the 'artificial intelligentsia' appear to exercise enormous influence and certainly command considerable resources. If they and their disciplines represent yet another technological talisman for resolving historically intractable problems, then perhaps there is a need for all of us to point out the human dimensions of the kinds of problems addressed above. Perhaps, too, we should bear in mind that many distinguished experts in particular fields regularly make fools of themselves by transgressing the boundaries of what they understand.

At another level, we might also question the ethics of other proposed applications of AI. For example, the fascination that Joseph Weizenbaum's conversational ELIZA and DOCTOR programs generated has led to a number of suggestions that AI be used to assist in the 'counselling' of emotionally disturbed individuals. Given the present state of the art in

AI, this proposal is mildly ridiculous and appears even more so when one considers the theoretical and philosophical impediments we have already outlined to machines even understanding natural human language. Perhaps of even greater importance, though, is not just whether AI itself is a *possible* goal, but whether AI is a *proper* goal of human endeavour.

For example, one might argue that the counselling of emotionally disturbed people demands that the counsellor have some insight into the nature of emotion and sentiment, not just at an abstract, symbol-manipulating level, but as a fellow human being who can empathize with the emotions of the individual concerned.[31] Certainly, MIT's professor of computer science, Joseph Weizenbaum, has had a considerable amount to say about such questions. In his book, *Computer Power and Human Reason: From Judgement to Calculation*, Weizenbaum outlines some potential goals in AI that he believes are simply immoral. For example, the wiring up of sensors to the visual cortex of blind people is something that he regards as morally obscene. Similar ventures include plans to hook up a machine to the corpus callosum (the main nerve trunk between the brain's hemispheres) of a person so that the machine could monitor nerve fibre traffic and 'learn' from it.[32] Critics like Weizenbaum may find such suggestions to be morally repulsive, but on the other hand somewhat similar experimental work has provided enormous benefits for some afflicted individuals. For example, the replacement of the human cochlea with a 'bionic ear' has been pioneered by Australian researchers and has undoubtedly saved some people from the prospect of life-long deafness.

But there are still other ways in which AI could be seen to be an improper goal for society – in the kinds of developments imagined by science fiction writers such as Isaac Asimov.[33] Perhaps the most fundamental question of all is: do we really *need* to replace humans by intelligent machines? Do demands for productivity require that clever computers of some description replace thousands of workers – say, by replacing typists with scanning machines that recognize different handwriting? The counter-argument may be best represented by an anecdote: a union leader looking over a quarry site bemoans the fate of his workers. He approaches the quarry owner and says, 'If it wasn't for those steam shovels, we'd be employing 500 men with shovels.' To which the owner replies, 'And if it wasn't for your 500 men with shovels, we'd be employing 10,000 men with thimbles.' Perhaps the message of this anecdote is not just that technological change demands changes in the nature of work, but that work can also be dangerous, dirty and simply degrading to human beings. In that case, perhaps the design of work for human beings in conjunction with intelligent technology is what we require. Beyond that, the job-reducing potential of technology needs to be managed more effectively by the provision of training programs, incentive schemes and appropriate government policies.

Quite apart from its consequences for employment, there is also an argument that AI is demeaning to human beings simply because it degrades the human condition itself. For example, it has been proposed by experts in robotics that 'the specifically human characteristics of emotion, free will, moral responsibility, creativity and ethical awareness can be accommodated by the doctrine of robotic man'.[34] Historically, most cultures have come to regard human beings as apart from animals, the supreme pinnacle of creation or evolution. Humanists in particular have felt uncomfortable with the notion of consciousness as a mechanical process, or indeed as any process which can be decomposed, understood and recreated. For them, this denies human beings their mystery, or the possibility of an essence or soul that exists beyond the physical plane.

On the other hand, AI proponents such as Margaret Boden argue that this reaction arises simply because we have such a limited (and perhaps demeaning!) view of machines, that stems from nineteenth-century images of clockwork and gears. She argues that such preconceptions do not encompass the potential richness and subtlety that machines can possess.[35] Yet J. David Bolter in his book, *Turing's Man*, argues that the metaphor of the computer leads us to view humanity in finite terms as opposed to the infinite view of human consciousness popular during medieval and renaissance periods.

Returning to our original line of argument, there may be at least one way in which AI could be unambiguously (in our minds anyway) considered an improper goal for society – that is because of its funding base and clear links with the military establishments of both the US and the UK. For example, through funding from the US Defense Advanced Research Projects Agency (DARPA), artificial intelligence researchers have now embarked upon a huge spending spree to develop key weapons or weapons-related systems that form part of the Strategic Computing Initiative (SCI). These systems include an intelligent 'pilot's assistant' that can assist a fighter pilot under the stress of high 'g' manoeuvres to plan target approaches and exits, evasive action and monitor threats in a hostile aerial environment. Similarly, researchers have begun to develop prototypes of autonomous reconnaissance vehicles that would head out into enemy territory, evade enemy attacks and transmit tactical information back to a computerized HQ. Researchers are also investigating how to build expert systems that could assist generals to make correct decisions in the face of the enormous complexity, conflicting reports and speed that characterizes modern conflicts.[37]

Again, we must ask, is it ethically responsible – in other words, is it a *proper* goal – for us to expend enormous amounts of money on such projects? In particular, given the incredible difficulty we have in getting machines to do even the most basic of 'intelligent' acts, what are the chances that such programs can possibly succeed? And if they cannot succeed, then surely they must be seen as an improper and totally wasteful enterprise. For example, it is still extremely difficult to get computers to 'see' and deal intelligently with invariant objects that exist in a fixed environment such as in a factory. In comparison, the problems in getting a machine to recognize objects in a *dynamic* environment (where, for example, a tank may take on 20 or 30 different forms) with camouflage, rain and poor visibility, and different seasons (which change foliage patterns and landscapes, e.g. with snow) simply boggle the imagination. Photograph interpreters, for example, often find it difficult to interpret the prints they receive from reconnaissance cameras on aircraft.

Now, given that human beings are extremely adept at interpreting their visual world (and have had millions of years of practice), do we really believe that a 20-tonne 'intelligent' monster blundering around a forest can run into tank and aircraft mockups and distinguish them from the real thing? Of course, the visual input could be relayed to remote humans for interpretation, but this rather destroys any claims for intelligence (and perhaps further funding). Furthermore, such vehicles are supposed to conduct their activities in a hostile environment. Therefore they must make their decisions in real time – they can't sit there for hours calculating whether the obstacle in front of them is an anti-tank trap, a natural culvert or an old latrine trench. If they do, someone will destroy them. And here we come to the bottom line – how could such machines be cost effective in any sense whatsoever? Incorporating millions of dollars of computing machinery into an armoured shell with tracks and sensors to many people seems tantamount to saying, 'Here is a lot of money . . . please destroy it for us.' Again, if such projects face such enormous practical difficulties, should they be funded at all? There is little doubt among many commentators that without the constant military funding that it has received over the last 30 years or so, AI would almost certainly be just a quaint academic curiosity which few people would have heard of and even fewer were interested in studying.[38]

We have earlier provided in this book an extended discussion of computer unreliability and its ethical consequences. Interested readers are also encouraged to pursue the issue by reading the Appendix on the 'Star Wars' Strategic Defence Initiative. The problems of unreliability encountered with conventional computer systems do not diminish in those that are said to possess artificial intelligence. If anything, because of the complexity of these systems, their unreliability tends to be worse.

Therefore we need to ask once more: is it a proper goal to develop systems that attempt practically impossible tasks and which, even if commercially 'released', may be subject to levels of even greater unreliability than those we already experience in the course of our everyday lives?

Conclusion: the Limits of Hype

In an address to the Operations Research Society of America, on 14 November 1957, the Nobel Prize laureate Herbert Simon stated: 'Within ten years [i.e. by 1967] a digital computer will be the world's chess champion, unless the rules bar it from competition.' He went on to state that 'Within ten years, a digital computer will discover and prove an important mathematical theorem and within ten years a digital computer will write music that will be accepted by critics as possessing considerable aesthetic value.' Futurologists such as I. J. Good and Ed Frenkin of MIT's project MAC have also claimed that within a few short years we will have ultra-intelligent machines able to reprogram themselves and become hundreds of times cleverer than people.[39]

By 1970, Marvin Minsky of MIT was willing to be more specific: 'In from three to eight years we will have a machine with the general intelligence of a human being', he said.[40] More recently, Hans Moravec from Carnegie-Mellon University publicly stated that 'In an astonishingly short time, scientists will be able to transfer the contents of a person's mind into a powerful computer, and in the process make him, or at least his living essence, virtually immortal.' Even more astonishing, Professor Moravec went on to say: 'Natural evolution is finished. The human race is no longer procreating, but designing its successors.'[41]

Now there is little doubt that other disciplines have also been guilty of exaggeration, but it is difficult to see how any of these could possibly rival the kinds of hyper-inflated claims and grandiose predictions that regularly tumble from the mouths of AI aficionados. Quite simply there are obvious monetary advantages to be gained from maintaining a wall of pro-AI propaganda. Or as one of the most noted of AI gadflies, Harvey P. Newquist III, put it: 'In the late 70s and early 80s, everyone with a PhD in LISP programming from MIT, Carnegie-Mellon or Stanford formed a company, and there was enough venture capital floating around at that time to fund everyone with a business plan longer than an index card.' Hard-line critics such as the Dreyfus brothers have regularly ridiculed the inflated claims made by AI exponents.[42] They would argue that part of the motivation for AI hyperbole lies in the large monetary incentives that AI researchers have placed before them, not only in terms of large research grants that buy machines and research assistants (plus lots of prestige, conferences in exotic places and international lecture tours) but also in terms of private companies developing 'intelligent' software products.

There is nothing wrong with attempting great feats (where would Silicon Valley be if everyone took the opposing view?), but in the face of monstrous theoretical and applied difficulties one would expect that AI enthusiasts would be a little more cautious and conservative in their predictions. Of course, many so-called AI companies provide useful goods and services in robotics, vision systems and even expert systems, but for a great many their claims just do not live up to the reality.[43]

In a review of the Dreyfus brothers' book, *Mind Over Machine*, sociologist and social critic Theodore Roszak joined in the attack against AI with the following devastating summary: 'Defenders of AI are apt to dismiss the Dreyfus' critique as old hat. It may be. But AI is also old hat, still repeating the same unfounded claims, working with many of the same discredited assumptions after failing again and again to perform as advertised. AI's record of barefaced public deception is unparalleled in the annals of academic study.'[44] Roszak goes on to say, in the context of AI's potential application to Star Wars and other complex systems, that we should be mindful of the Dreyfus' characterization of AI as 'snake oil', a 'money grab' and a 'genuine stupidity'. For these critics, informing the public about the seamy side of AI is an obligation that may possibly prevent the dangerous application of an immature and overrated lucky dip of technologies.

Suggestions for Further Discussion

You may wish to think about the following, hypothetical scenario.

It is 1999. Among its many other problems, the United States is wracked with intolerable levels of criminal activity and violence. Much of this is the aftermath of crack – the cheap cocaine derivative that has now been on the streets for many years. However, there are other chronic contributory factors, including high levels of unemployment for a large percentage of the black community, slum conditions, inadequate education for the poor and a health system that operates on a cash basis only.

Among America's most pressing problems is a situation that threatens to make a mockery of the Bill of Rights and the United States' claim to being a great democracy. This problem lies in the numbers of persons who are incarcerated and awaiting trial. These individuals, although technically innocent until proven guilty, are nevertheless spending periods in jail of up to a year before appearing before a court. The sheer number of cases being dealt with by the criminal justice system has become impossible to handle: as a result, periods of remand have become quite ridiculous with innocent citizens being deprived of long periods of their lives without compensation.

Moreover, as a result of these extended periods of incarceration, more and more are emerging from jail as AIDS carriers without having a history of high-risk activity. Although often found innocent, they have nevertheless been given a kind of life sentence by the penal system.

To help solve this problem, the Federal government authorizes dramatic changes to court procedures in all states in order to accelerate the rate at which cases are heard and resolved. One of these changes includes the development and application of an expert system for determining the length of sentence in the event of a conviction. The system includes the entire history of US court cases, their findings and associated sentences, as well as the laws in the individual states.

In essence, once a guilty verdict has been returned by a jury, the system immediately determines the maximum and minimum sentences prescribed for the crime under the relevant state's laws. It then consults what its designers have termed its internal 'conscience'. Here, the system pattern-matches as closely as possible the characteristics of the crime with a database of 'benchmark' cases for which 100 independent judges have provided sentences after having read the details of the case. Once the crime has been 'matched' and the mean sentence calculated from its conscience, the standard deviation of these sentences is calculated (in other words, a measure of the variability of the recommended sentences is found). A statistical test is performed to determine if the mean sentence arrived at by the conscience is actually lower than the maximum sentence and if it is, then this mean sentence is imposed.

Is there anything wrong with this system in an ethical sense? After all, it does prevent a judge from taking a day or two before imposing sentence and therefore it must help the throughput of cases. This in itself must assist those who are still awaiting trial. Furthermore, under this system, sentences are determined by a much larger cross-section of judges than most courts would allow. Surely this remote judicial forum would be much more fair and balanced than one which allows an aged judge with indigestion to vent his discomfort by imposing the maximum sentence?

However, imagine now that of those 100 judges who were consulted in order to provide the 'conscience' of the system, no less than five of them are borderline psychotics who have been known to impose maximum sentences for crimes that particularly disturb their already disturbed psyches. For other, equally serious crimes which do not offend their toilet training, they have been known to systematically impose rather trivial sentences – the minimum allowable by law. Furthermore, at least another five of these same 100 judges are on the verge of senility – too revered to be fired or have their judgement questioned, but effectively incompetent to have a jury before them.

Now, this means that at least 10 per cent of the program's conscience is either psychotically unbalanced or simply mentally incompetent. Given the average age of senior judges, these figures are probably not unrealistic. Yet that still leaves (we hope) about 90 per cent of the conscience based upon the reasoning of sound, experienced individuals and perhaps we should be satisfied with that. Indeed, even if only 90 per cent of these people are reasonably competent, if appropriate numbers of females and those from various ethnic backgrounds and religions are included, then this should be a much fairer judicial forum than the one-person-lottery we currently experience.

However, if this system were a centralized one with courtrooms all over the country consulting it as required, then it is clear that what we effectively have is a standardized system for dispensing sentences. But do we also have a system with standardized defects? Will all flashers invariably offend the psychotic judges and receive maximum or at least longer sentences, whereas in our present system, through sheer luck-of-the-draw, they may have been treated more leniently?

Obviously, some percentage of the population who commit crimes that enrage the small number of psychotic judges on the panel will always be unfairly treated, even if only marginally, although the margin might be quite large if all of the unsystematic seniles also happen to coincide in returning a hefty sentence. Perhaps this is no different from our present circumstances – after all, clearly some ethnic groups and sections of society are over-represented in our jails and like all human beings, individual judges are as susceptible to prejudice as anyone else.

Therefore, if both systems are biased in some form, then are we simply replacing one inadequate system by another? Is it better to allow chance to determine some aspects of the judicial forum? Or is it better to allow (perhaps small, perhaps large) biases to be dispensed in a more standardized fashion?

Moreover, we might argue that merely sampling 100 judges simply replicates the status quo, which as we noted above is clearly not without bias. Perhaps even a 1000 judges would not be sufficient to provide what we might call a 'fair' system. Where do we find an adequate number of black female judges or others from deprived origins? Where do we get sufficient judges who can relate in any way to the circumstances that impoverished, addicted or abused people find themselves in? Clearly we could go to excessive lengths to provide a perfect system – reformed alcoholic judges or drug addicts to try cases involving substance abusers, Vietnam veterans to judge other Vietnam veterans, and so on.

Certainly the present system doesn't provide this level of 'fairness' (and perhaps it shouldn't be expected to), but perhaps it does provide the human context in which trials actually occur. Remote evaluation of case notes does not provide this context and certainly one could argue that no amount of fine pattern-matching can come close to understanding the idiosyncracies and human texture that distinguishes almost any case from any other.

Hence we come to several rather fundamental questions, beginning with: what are the ethical dimensions of such a scenario? Is a faster, less faulty machine-administered system of justice better than a slower, more faulty human-administered one? Should justice be administered by individuals who are permitted to experience the nuances of a real case, or by the recorded judgements of individuals who remotely consider case details and rely upon group stability to guarantee fairness? In any case, would our anticipated system simply replicate the status quo, which we may already assume to be unjust? Or inevitably, are we forced to mete out justice in the best way we can – faulty or not, biased or not, human or not?

It is at this point that we ask what we should have probably asked ourselves at the outset – what is this system designed to achieve? Or in essence, what is the problem we hope to solve? Are we attempting to achieve a better system of justice? If that's the case then we had better ask ourselves what we think justice really is. We might be surprised to find that even on this rather fundamental point, not much agreement can be easily found.

Is the problem simply what we originally specified – that the judicial process is too slow to cope? Or is there more to the problem than this? Is the problem really that for too many people, their lives are so empty or squalid that they resort to substance abuse in order to make their lives that much more bearable? Is it that as a society we have failed to provide the social conditions necessary for people to hope and to raise their horizon beyond the next meal, the next day or the next fix? Perhaps these are the problems we should really be attempting to solve and if that is the case, then our expert system is simply an attempt to solve a superficial manifestation of them.

The contemporary literature in the philosophy of technology labels such phenomena 'technofixes' – that is, attempts to concoct a superficial technological solution to what is essentially a human problem.[45] Another example of a technofix might be the use of artificial insemination in captivity in order to preserve endangered species. Clearly, the real problem that endangered species face is not a lack of reproductive vigour – rather, it is generally the destruction of habitat through human pollution, human population pressure or humanity's predatory behaviour. Hence, any attempt to fix such a problem through technological means represents a superficial effort at best, because the solution addresses the symptoms of the problem rather than the root causes.

Should computer professionals be forced to think through the ethical basis, origins and implications of the work they undertake (even if society and governments do not)? Should they accept money to solve pseudo-problems or to create high-tech fixes for the symptoms of more fundamental problems? Should they be aware of the extent to which their work relies upon value judgements, not only in design and implementation terms (is this software feature a good/bad/useful/complicated/cost-effective one?), but also in terms of the values embedded in the design specification itself and those that are implicitly held by the client or sponsor?

Notes

1 'AI in medical diagnosis and aviation', *Software Engineering Notes*, vol. 11, no. 2, 1986, p. 5; 'Dispute over drug death', *The Australian*, 8 September 1987.
2 Michael Schrage, *The Washington Post – National Weekly Edition*, vol. 3, no. 40, 1986, p. 6.
3 Herbert A. Simon, *Models of Thought* (Yale University Press, 1979).
4 Terry Winograd, 'Understanding natural language', *Cognitive Psychology*, vol. 3, pp. 1–191; Terry Winograd, *Understanding Natural Language* (Academic Press, New York, 1972).
5 John Haugeland, *Artificial Intelligence: The Very Idea* (MIT Press, Cambridge, MA, 1986).
6 Donald Michie and Rory Johnston, *The Creative Computer: Machine Intelligence and Human Knowledge* (Penguin Books, Harmondsworth, 1985), pp. 17–18.
7 John Searle, 'Minds, brains and programs', in John Haugeland (ed.), *Mind Design* (MIT Press, Cambridge, MA, 1982); John Searle,'Minds, brains and science', *The 1984 Reith Lectures* (British Broadcasting Corporation, London, 1984).
8 Joseph Weizenbaum, *Computer Power and Human Reason: From Judgement to Calculation* (W. H. Freeman, San Francisco, 1976).
9 Kenneth Colby, F. Hilf, S. Weber and H. Kraemer, 1972, 'Turing-like indistinguishability tests for the validation of a computer simulation of paranoid processes', *Artificial Intelligence*, vol. 3, pp. 199–221; Kenneth Colby, 'Modeling a paranoid mind, with open peer commentaries', *Behavioural and Brain Sciences*, vol. 4, 1981, pp. 515–33.
10 W. Daniel Hillis, 'Intelligence as an emergent behaviour; or: the songs of Eden', in Stephen R. Graubard (ed.), *The Artificial Intelligence Debate: False Starts and Real Foundations* (MIT Press, Cambridge, MA, 1988). See also Chris Reynolds, 'The search for the intelligent computer', *New Scientist*, 16 September 1989.
11 'Complex barriers to speaking real English', *The Australian*, 14 April 1987.
12 Hubert L. Dreyfus and Stuart E. Dreyfus, *Mind Over Machine: The Power of Human Intuition and Expertise in the Era of the Computer* (Basil Blackwell, Oxford, 1986).
13 For some of the known physiological properties of brains, see, for example,

David L. Waltz, 'The prospects for building truly intelligent machines', in Graubard, *The Artificial Intelligence Debate*.

14 Alex Goodall, *The Guide to Expert Systems* (Learned Information, Oxford, 1985).

15 Avron Barr and Edward A. Feigenbaum, *Handbook of Artificial Intelligence* (William Kaufmann, New York, 1981), vol. 2, pp. 106–15.

16 Edward H. Shortliffe and Bruce Buchanan, 'A model of inexact reasoning in medicine', *Mathematical Biosciences*, vol. 23, 1975.

17 Arnold Kraft, 'XCON: an expert configuration system at Digital Equipment Corporation', in Patrick H. Winston and Karen A. Prendergast (eds), *The AI Business* (MIT Press, Cambridge, MA, 1984).

18 Martin Fischler and Oscar Firschein, *Intelligence: The Eye, The Brain and The Computer* (Addison Wesley, Reading, MA, 1987).

19 Richard Forsyth, 'The anatomy of expert systems', in Masoud Yazdani and Ajet Narayanan (eds), *Artificial Intelligence: Human Effects* (Ellis Horwood, Chichester, UK, 1984), pp. 186–99.

20 Donald Michie, *On Machine Intelligence* (Ellis Horwood, Chichester, UK, 1986); I. Mozetic, N. Bratko and N. Lavrac, 'An experiment in automatic synthesis of expert knowledge through qualitative modelling', *Proceedings of the Logic Programming Workshop*, Albufeira, Portugal, June 1983.

21 Edward Warner, 'Expert systems and the law', *High Technology Business*, October 1986, pp. 32–5.

22 Ibid.

23 Richard M. Lucash, 'Legal liability for malfunction and misuse of expert systems', SIGCHI Bulletin, vol. 18, no. 1, 1986, pp. 35–43.

24 Edward Feigenbaum and Pamela McCorduck, *The Fifth Generation: Artificial Intelligence and Japan's Computer Challenge to the World* (Addison Wesley, Reading, MA, 1983); Karen Fitzgerald and Paul Wallich, 'Next-generation race bogs down', *IEEE Spectrum*, June 1987, pp. 28–33.

25 David L. Waltz, 'The prospects for building truly intelligent machines', in Graubard, *The Artificial Intelligence Debate*.

26 Ibid.

27 Jacob Schwartz, 'The new connectionism: developing relationships between neuroscience and artificial intelligence', in Graubard, *The Artificial Intelligence Debate*.

28 Terry Winograd, *Understanding Computers and Cognition: A New Foundation for Design* (Ablex, Norwood, NJ, 1986).

29 Donald Michie and Rory Johnston, *The Creative Computer*. In their latest example of AI hype, *The Rise of the Expert Company: How Visionary Companies are Using Artificial Intelligence to Achieve Higher Productivity and Profits* (Times Books, New York, 1988), Edward Feigenbaum, Pamela McCorduck and H. Penny Nii make the extraordinary claim that 'Almost everywhere, expert systems were speeding up professional work by at least a factor of ten. Speed-up factors of 20, 30 and 40 were common. And today's expert systems, powerful as they are, are still Model-Ts!' See also William Ascher, 'Limits of "expert systems" for political-economic forecasting', *Technological Forecasting and Social Change*, vol. 36 (1989), pp. 137–51.

30 Edward Warner, op. cit. (n. 21).

31 Jeffrey Rothfeder, *Minds Over Matter* (Prentice-Hall, New York, 1985); Barbara Garson, *The Electronic Sweatshop: How Computers are Transforming*

the Office of the Future into the Factory of the Past (Simon and Schuster, New York, 1988).

32   Richard Pree, 'The human mind stored forever', *The Australian*, 1 December 1987.

33   Isaac Asimov, Patricia Warrick and Martin Greenberg (eds), *Machines That Think* (Penguin, Harmondsworth, 1985).

34   Geoff Simons, *Is Man a Robot?* (John Wiley, Chichester, UK, 1986).

35   Margaret Boden, 'AI and Human Freedom', in Yazdani and Narayanan, *Artificial Intelligence*.

36   J. David Bolter, *Turing's Man* (Pelican, Harmondsworth, 1986).

37   Elizabeth Corcoran, 'Strategic computing: a status report', *IEEE Spectrum*, April 1987, pp. 50–4.

38   Tom Foremski, 'Artificial intelligence: military cash keeps it in line', *Computing Australia*, 21 September 1987.

39   Donald Michie and Rory Johnston, *The Creative Computer*, p. 71.

40   Igor Aleksander and Piers Burnett, *Thinking Machines: The Search for Artificial Intelligence* (Oxford University Press, Oxford, 1986).

41   Richard Pree, 'The human mind stored forever'.

42   Hubert L. Dreyfus, *What Computers Can't Do* (Harper and Row, New York, 1979).

43   Alex Kozlov, 'Rethinking artificial intelligence', *High Technology Business*, May 1988, pp. 18–25; Lawrence Hunter, 'AI's Limits', *Technology Review*, July 1988, pp. 74–6; Helen Meredith, 'Narrower focus for expert systems', *The Australian*, 9 May 1989.

44   Theodore Roszak, 'Smart computers at insecure stage', *New Scientist*, 3 April 1986, pp. 46–7.

45   Perry Morrison, 'Limits to technocratic consciousness: information technology and terrorism as example', *Science, Technology and Human Values*, vol. 11, 1986, pp. 4–16; Alan Drengson, 'Applied Philosophy of Technology: reflections on forms of life and the practice of technology', *The International Journal of Applied Philosophy*, vol. 3, no. 1, 1986, pp. 1–13.

8 Computerizing the Workplace

Computers and Employment – Computers and
the Quality of Worklife: 'De-skilling' – Productivity
and People: Stress, Monitoring, Depersonalization,
Fatigue and Boredom – Health and Safety Issues:
VDTs and the RSI Debate – Suggestions for Further
Discussion

It looks as if humans will be replacing robots for some straightforward work
in modern factories. A psychologist told this cautionary tale at the British
Association's conference in Bristol. Dr Toby Wall of Sheffield University said
engineers had been asked to design a new factory to make bicycle pedals, using
an existing shopfloor with two parallel conveyor tracks. The engineers lined one
conveyor with the latest computer-controlled machine tools making the parts,
and the other with computer-controlled assembly machines for the pedals. At
the end, they positioned a robot to pick up finished parts and place them on
the track. The system worked. But eventually the engineers removed the robot
at the end of the line and put a *human* operator in its place. The reason, they
explained, was because the task made such little use of the robot's potential
and capabilities.

UK press report[1]

Computers and Employment

Work still remains central to the lives of millions of people. Despite frequent predictions of paid employment's early demise due to the imminent
arrival of the 'leisure' society, people in many respects appear to be working as hard if not harder than ever. According to a recent Harris survey,
the amount of leisure time enjoyed by the average US citizen shrunk by a
staggering 37 per cent between 1973 and 1989. Over the same period, the
average working week, including travel-to-work time, grew from under
41 hours to nearly 47 hours. US Bureau of Labor Statistics (BLS)
figures also show that the proportion of Americans holding down two
jobs is increasing and more seem to be doing more work at home and
taking part-time or temporary jobs. Other US opinion polls have also
shown a marked preference among respondents for longer hours and
higher incomes over more leisure and less pay. Much the same sort of

thing seems to be happening in European countries like West Germany, where the sacred weekend is being sacrificed for weekend working in some industries and in Australia, where 24-hour working is being re-introduced, for example, in the coal industry. The Japanese, of course, continue to work longer hours than anybody else and rarely take anything more than very short holidays.[2]

The impact of new technologies in the workplace is an issue which has caused controversy throughout history – the most famous example being the Luddites, who went around the North of England in 1811–12 smashing new textile machinery which they thought would decimate employment in the textile industry (it didn't). When the microchip first came to public attention in 1978–9, equally dire predictions were made about the impact of this latest 'new' technology on employment levels right across manufacturing industry and commerce. There were even calls in some quarters to reject outright the introduction of microprocessor-based technology in the workplace because of its job-destroying potential. In the context of rapidly rising unemployment in OECD countries, especially those of Europe, these concerns seemed reasonable and the 'debate' on computerization was largely structured in terms of its employment impact.

Now the employment debate is pretty much 'off the boil' for three main reasons. First, the introduction of computers into the workplace has been much slower than expected because of a host of financial, technical, human and organizational problems (including 'oversell' by the computer industry). The employment impact has been correspondingly less severe and/or less obvious, while trade union opposition to new technology – with one or two exceptions, like Fleet Street in London – has been negligible to non-existent. Second, unemployment has ceased to increase at such an alarming rate and indeed it is falling steadily in many OECD countries. In the US, it remains remarkably low on average. Third, the realization – particularly in the US and in Europe – that the 'baby boom' generation's entry into the workforce is now largely complete and that the arrival of the 'baby bust' generation in the 1990s will actually see some shortages of labour developing has helped take some of the heat out of the employment debate.

In a major US report which reflects the way in which guarded optimism has replaced pessimism in discussions of the employment impact of computers, Richard Cyert and David Mowery say that there is no evidence to support fears of mass unemployment due to technological change. Some contributors to their authoritative 1987 study, *Technology and Employment: Innovation and Growth in the US Economy*, which was commissioned by the US National Academy of Sciences, suggest that new technology ultimately creates more jobs than it destroys, although they say that there will ,be lengthy and painful periods of adjustment for certain groups of workers; other contributors to the volume repeat the familiar, orthodox refrain that job losses are more likely to result from the slow adoption of new technology rather than the too-rapid adoption.[3]

However, there is little doubt that the computerization of factories and offices has led to the steady erosion of employment opportunities, particularly those for less skilled manual workers and for clerical workers. An important British government-backed survey of 2,000 or so workplaces, *Workplace Industrial Relations and Technical Change* (1987), found that computers *are* replacing workers on a considerable scale – but in the medium rather than the short term. Author W. W. Daniel says that the introduction of new technology led to increases in manning in about one case in ten of those studied but to decreases – and often substantial decreases – in about one case in five. Although there were important variations between sectors, those workplaces using advanced technology to replace *manual* workers saw the biggest decreases when observed over a four-year period. Job losses were also greater in the private as opposed to the public sector. However, most of the employment reductions took place through natural wastage over a period of time rather than through redundancies in the short term.[4]

Job losses have been particularly severe in traditional manufacturing industries, where competition from the newly industrialized countries (NICs) and the process of deindustrialization have made matters much worse. The US Bureau of Labor Statistics reports that the US economy generated no less than 31 million new jobs between 1972 and 1988 and it will add another 21 million before the year 2000. The *net* gain (jobs created minus jobs lost) amounted to 18.2 million between 1974 and 1984, compared with a net *loss* of 2.8 million jobs over the same period in Britain, France and West Germany combined. But although the total number of manufacturing jobs in the US will actually grow by a million or two by 1995, employment in manufacturing industry as a proportion of the total US labour force will shrink to a mere 8 per cent. Employment growth will be overwhelmingly in the service sector. Old-style 'smokestack' industries like steel and cars in 'rust bowl' states like Pennsylvania, Indiana, Ohio and Michigan will never again employ the thousands that used to toil in their huge manufacturing plants. Manufacturing employment in future will be small-scale, high-tech and dispersed across the North American continent. As MIT's David Birch shows in his recent book, *Job Creation in America* (1987), small is beautifully fertile: of America's net employment gains since

1981, virtually all were generated in small firms employing less than 20 people.[5]

Job generation in the high-tech sector itself is impressive, but the high-tech sector remains small relative to aggregate employment. Even in the US, high-tech industries account for a mere 3 per cent of the non-agricultural workforce and this figure will grow to only about 4 per cent by 1995. To illustrate the point still further, it has been pointed out that the US automobile industry still employs twice as many people as the entire high-tech sector. According to BLS figures, high-tech industries in the US will generate between 750,000 and 1 million jobs by 1995, but this is still less than half the jobs lost from US manufacturing industry in the period 1980–3 alone. The majority of jobs in the future will in fact be in 'low-tech' or 'no-tech' occupations such as cashier, caretaker and security guard.[6]

A major study by Stanford University's Henry Levin and Russell Rumberger concluded that 'neither high-technology industries nor high-technology occupations will supply many new jobs over the next decade. Instead, future job growth will favor service and clerical jobs that require little or no postsecondary schooling and that pay below average wages.' They calculated that employment in jobs related to high-tech would grow by 46 per cent in 1995, but this would account for no more than 6 per cent of all new jobs created in the US economy.[7]

But even these figures seem optimistic compared to the results of a 1988 study by a Wellesley, MA, firm of consultants which covered 18,000 information technology, biotechnology and telecommunications companies. Of these, only 40 per cent increased employment over the previous year – for an average gain of 7.2 per cent. Although some companies in this volatile sector recorded employment gains of 50 per cent or more in one year, the majority of companies actually *reduced* employment. All this added up to a modest overall employment gain predicted for the whole high-tech sector in the 1990s of around 3 per cent a year.[8]

One trend that could further reduce job-generation in the high-tech sector is the growing tendency of US companies to export routine data processing jobs to cheap labour countries using the latest satellite and telecommunications technology. Just as US car companies are setting up high-tech manufacturing plants across the border in Mexico, so corporations like Travelers, New York Life and McGraw-Hill are sending data across the Atlantic for processing in Ireland, where some 3,000 programming and data-entry jobs have been created. As *Business Week* gleefully reported, 'With unemployment at 20 per cent, wages for Ireland's well-educated workers are rock-bottom.'[9] Indian programmers have also been used extensively by US companies and India is currently building a high-quality satellite link to boost this transnational trade in offshore programming.

While there is wide agreement about the high-tech sector's inability to create large numbers of jobs in the future, there is fierce debate about the service sector's continuing ability to generate jobs and about the nature and quality of service sector employment. With 75 per cent of the total US workforce of around 105 million now in the service sector, and with service sector employment growing at an annual rate of about 9 per cent in the early 1980s, the future of service sector employment is clearly an important issue.

In fact there are three major debates about the future *quantity* of service sector employment which have become intertwined. First, the assumption that jobs in the 'knowledge' or 'information' industries will continue to grow as they have done in the past has been questioned by various researchers. For example, in their book, *The Knowledge Industry in the United States: 1960–1980* (1986), Michael Rubin and Mary Huber show that the 'knowledge' sector of the US economy – education, research and development, communications, information services, etc. – only grew from 29 per cent of US GNP in 1958 to 34 per cent in 1980. What's more, its growth rate had slipped since 1972 to roughly the same as the rest of the economy.[10] This seems to negate the earlier work of Marc Porat and more especially Fritz Machlup, whose book, *The Production and Distribution of Knowledge in the United States* (1962), really started all the theorizing about coming 'information' societies and 'post-industrial' societies – a notion popularized in particular by Daniel Bell in *The Coming of Post-Industrial Society* (1973).

Second, the idea that the service sector can continue to create jobs while the manufacturing sector steadily withers away has also been challenged by academics such as Berkeley's Stephen Cohen and John Zysman, who argue forcefully in *Manufacturing Matters: The Myth of the Post-Industrial Economy* (1987), that the US does not have a post-industrial economy, nor is it ever likely to have one and, furthermore, it had better not try to acquire one. Pointing out that manufacturing in the US has in fact maintained its share of GNP (if not employment) over the past 40 years, Cohen and Zysman say that it is a mistake to view the process of social development as so many inevitable 'stages' of progress up from agricultural society to industrial society and thence to post-industrial society.[11]

Moreover, they say, it is the higher-paid manufacturing jobs that support many low-paid service sector jobs. The service sector cannot therefore continue to expand *ad infinitum* without a strong, underlying industrial base. And because manufactured goods are more tradeable than services, the US cannot succeed or indeed survive as a world power without being successful as an exporter of manufactured goods. Consequently, the notion that the US should somehow accept 'deindustrialization' as inevitable, 'give up' on manufacturing entirely and rely on importing cheaper manufactured goods from the NICs is not only misleading but positively dangerous. Shifting production overseas will further damage US industry by robbing it of the latest in products and production technology. This process is sometimes referred to as 'hollowing out'.

A quite different perspective on the service sector is provided by Dartmouth College's James Brian Quinn, Jordan J. Baruch and Penny Cushman Paquette, who point out that many service industries are coming to resemble manufacturing industries, with their centralized, large-scale and capital-intensive facilities, standardized output (for example, through franchising) and automated distribution techniques.[12] Moreover, service sector pay is fast catching up with manufacturing wages and more services are being exported. All this means, say Quinn et al., that a US economy dominated by services can continue to support real increases in income and wealth for a long time to come. Indeed, most of the economic growth, the opportunities for entrepreneurship and the applications of information technology, they say, will arise in the service sector over the next 20 years. The real danger, they say, is that business and governments will misinterpret the trends and waste money trying to shore up certain troubled 'rust bowl' manufacturing industries.

Third, the very industrialization of the service sector which Quinn et al. describe may also put pressure on service sector job creation once computer technology penetrates in a big way. For example, David Roessner of the Georgia Institute of Technology has forecast that clerical employment in the US banking and insurance industries will have peaked by about 1990 and will decline rapidly in the following decade. Even under the most conservative assumptions, he says, absolute reductions in clerical employment of 22 per cent in insurance and 10 per cent in banking are expected by 2000.[13] Likewise, a 1987 UK study of 247 large companies for the Confederation of British Industry and the Institute of Administrative Management suggests that up to 750,000 white-collar jobs will have to go from inefficient British firms if they are going to be able to compete with efficient UK and US companies. Most of the companies in the survey made 'the control of personnel costs' (i.e., getting rid of people) the most important way of increasing short-term profitability and the most favoured method of doing this was by computerization.[14]

While doubts have been raised about the quantity of jobs likely to be created in the service sector, there has been growing criticism of the *quality* of many new service sector jobs – despite the evidence of people such as Quinn et al. Service sector jobs *are* generally less well-paid and they offer fewer fringe benefits. A huge proportion are in fact part-time jobs or *temporary* jobs, typically taken by married women, which offer no health care, life insurance or pension entitlements. America now has 19 million part-time workers, representing nearly one-fifth of the entire workforce. Four-fifths of these part-timers work in sales, clerical, service or unskilled labour occupations which are basically low-paid, dead-end jobs. Involuntary part-time work grew four times as fast as full-time or voluntary part-time work in the 1980s. The number of temporary jobs also grew five-fold between 1982 and 1988 to total 1 million. These employees are typically paid less, receive fewer benefits and, of course, have absolutely no job security. Some say this trend to part-time and temporary working is creating a new group of second-class citizens variously called 'contingent' as opposed to 'regular' workers (in the US) or 'periphery' as opposed to 'core' workers (in Europe). Core workers are 'functionally flexible': in return for security and decent conditions, they are expected to do whatever the company commands. Periphery workers are 'numerically flexible': they are hired to do a specific job when trade is looking up to – and fired when no longer required.[15]

Finally, just as continued growth of the service sector may not generate a proportionate number of jobs because of computerization or industrialization of that sector, so, too, there are fears that any upturn in manufacturing will not be accompanied by significant employment growth. Economists call this phenomenon 'jobless growth': it is a paradox which comes about because new capital investment and the resulting improvements in productivity reduce the demand for labour even as output is increased.

Two recent studies seem to confirm this view: first, David Howell of the New School for Social Research, New York, suggests that the increasing use of robots will displace large numbers of jobs in manufacturing industry, although the impact will be concentrated in a small number of industries and occupations and the magnitude of the impact will be fairly small compared with the effects of economic cycles. Most of the jobs 'lost' – or rather job opportunities *eroded* – in this way will be unskilled and semi-skilled rather than scientific and technical, he says.[16]

Second, a British study of the world clothing industry by Kurt Hoffman and Howard Rush for the Geneva-based International Labour Office argues that increasing automation will reduce employment by as much as 30–40 per cent (or 1 million jobs in the US and Europe) over the next ten years. In particular, they say, the use of flexible manufacturing systems (FMS) and computer-based systems in finishing, inspection and production control after the mid-1990s will severely erode employment opportunities and fundamentally change the global business of making clothes.[17]

The message from these studies is clear: we cannot assume that a computer-based economy will automatically provide enough jobs for everyone in the future. Computer professionals should be aware of this pressure on employment when designing and implementing systems which will reduce job opportunities for those most in need of them.

Computers and the Quality of Worklife: 'De-skilling'

As a good-will gesture, Irv Klein and Jonah Kaufman hired several mentally handicapped adults to work in their 13 McDonald's restaurants on Long Island, New York, last year. The experience was so successful they recruited 34 more. The franchise owners found the new hires to be reliable, hardworking individuals.

With unskilled workers in dwindling supply, service companies are increasingly looking to the mentally retarded to man mops and grills. The fast-food industry, where the annual employment turnover rate is 200%, welcomes their loyalty. Of the 40 mentally handicapped adults hired by McDonald's on Long Island, only four have left. Says Kaufman: 'These people never come in late and are rarely sick.'

Kentucky Fried Chicken employs 28 mentally handicapped workers at company-owned restaurants in Virginia and is stepping up recruitment in Georgia and Kentucky. Flo Barber, a company human resources director, points out that these workers don't mind the chores that teenagers often find boring.

Marriott Corp . . . says the productivity of retarded employees is the same as that for nondisabled workers.

Fortune magazine.[18]

If we should be wary of computerization that decreases the *quantity* of work available, we should be equally concerned about the implementation of systems that may degrade the *quality* of working life. This can happen through (1) 'de-skilling' the workforce by reducing the control, responsibility and job satisfaction of skilled operators and/or (2) increasing the stress, depersonalization, fatigue and boredom experienced by employees and/or (3) creating health and safety hazards for the workforce such as eyestrain, tension headaches, backache and perhaps even miscarriages and birth defects. Each of these important aspects of computerization in the workplace will be considered in turn.

In its most recent form, the argument that automation 'de-skills' workers goes back to the publication in 1974 of Harry Braverman's *Labor and Monopoly Capital: The Degradation of Work in the Twentieth Century*, a book which generated a great deal of new speculation about technology and the 'labour process', and attracted a group of followers who became known as the 'labour process' school of thought. Essentially the 'labour process' theorists argue that every attempt to introduce new technology and redesign jobs is really an attempt by profit-motivated employers to increase their control over the workforce in order to exploit them further. Skilled workers are an ever-present threat to management, so the argument goes, because they are in a position to set their own pace of work and thus they effectively control the work process. It can be seen that the 'labour process' theory is basically an updated version of the old Marxist idea that the workplace is essentially a battleground between capital and labour, a forum where the class struggle is fought out.

Very much in the Bravermanian tradition, Harley Shaiken argues in *Work Transformed: Automation and Labor in the Computer Age* (1985) that computers 'de-skill' workers and thus degrade the quality of working life. He contends that managers don't like skilled workers because they are semi-autonomous: they therefore seek to remove skill from workers and transfer it to machines. In manufacturing plants, this transfer of skills to machines creates more jobs for less-skilled machine 'minders' but less jobs for skilled workers. Moreover, he says, despite the promise that new technology can improve the quality of working life, many of the new jobs being created in futuristic factories are every bit as tedious, fast-paced and stressful as old-style assembly-line jobs. Shaiken's views find support in the work of, for example, Noble in the US and Cooley, among others, in the UK.[19]

The contrary view on automation is probably best exemplified by Larry Hirschhorn, who argues in *Beyond Mechanization: Work and Technology in the Post-Industrial Age* (1984), that the notion that computers de-skill workers and degrade work is actually the opposite of the truth. First, he points out that 'robots can't run factories': the proven unreliability (see chapter 5) of most IT equipment, he says, actually *increases* the dependence of managers on their skilled workforce and not vice versa. Second, if robots can't run factories, then neither can the traditional manager: 'The new technologies introduce new modes of machine failure, new flaws in the control systems themselves, and new challenges to the design of jobs. In such settings, workers must *control the controls*.'[20] In consequence, human resource specialists must develop new forms of work design which foster co-operative rather than adversarial behaviour, he says. Without a 'vigilant, committed and curious' workforce, he says, major system failures such as that which happened at Three Mile Island will occur with increasing regularity. Managers cannot 'command' workers to behave in new ways. They must transcend inherited patterns of authority and win over the workforce so that they take a new interest in, and responsibility for, their actions. Far from de-skilling the workforce, computer technology demands that employers of the future need to constantly improve staff quality through learning and retraining if they are to survive and prosper.

Support for Hirschhorn comes from the British survey, *Workplace Industrial Relations and Technical Change* (1987). This found that manual manufacturing jobs involving the operation of new technology were generally associated with substantially *more* interest, *more* skill, *more* responsibility and *more* variety than the old-style jobs they replaced. Both the managers and the shop stewards (union representatives) in the survey seemed to agree on this, although both also appeared to agree that the impact of computerization was slightly negative in terms of its impact on autonomy (as measured by the level of supervision), control over the pace of work and how the job was done. In the case of office jobs, a similar consensus between managers and shop stewards emerged that new technology was associated with higher levels of interest, skills, responsibility and variety, but there was a modest divergence of opinion on autonomy, the pace of work and how the job was done. In these last three dimensions, shop stewards saw the impact of computers as modestly negative, while managers saw it as marginally positive.[21]

Between the proponents and opponents of 'de-skilling' is a fairly large group of agnostics who steer a middle course between the somewhat crude conspiracy theories of the labour process school and the naive, Panglossian view that all technology changes are for the best in this, the best of all possible worlds. For example, in summarizing a British symposium, *Information Technology in Manufacturing Processes* (1983), Graham Winch says there was a consensus that employers are not by any means simply motivated by a desire to 'control' their workforce. The choice of new technology is dictated by competitive market pressures and traditional managerial ideologies as much as power relations in the workplace. Some de-skilling may occur, but this need not necessarily be so: '. . . there is no single tendency towards de-skilling or re-skilling', he writes.[22]

Likewise, two British academics who have written extensively on technology management, David Buchanan and David Boddy, reject the view that computerization necessarily leads to either de-skilling or re-skilling. In *Managing New Technology* (1986), they argue forcefully that computers can be used to complement 'distinct and valuable' human skills rather than to replace them. There is no inevitable or uniform 'impact' or 'effect' of new technology on the nature of work and it is misleading to even think in terms of 'impacts': 'Bored and inefficient employees are the result of decisions about how their work is organized', they write.[23]

A number of other authors and researchers have also made this point that a particular type of technology does not determine what particular form of work organization will be adopted or quality of worklife will be achieved. They argue that the use of technology is a matter of strategic choice and often a matter of *negotiated choice* at that (negotiated, that is, between management and the workforce). For example, in his authoritative study of the 'impact' of computers in offices, *New Office Information Technology: Human and Managerial Implications* (1987), Canadian professor Richard Long concludes that paper-using organizations can either use new technology to enhance human abilities and skills, to increase user discretion and autonomy and generally to improve the quality of worklife – or it can be used to do the exact opposite. For example, the controversial practice of computer monitoring can be either beneficial or detrimental to employee discretion and satisfaction, depending upon how it is implemented. Computer professionals need to recognize that 'new office systems are not just technical systems, but behavioural systems which depend for success on the effective integration of both their social and technical components.'[24]

In a similar vein, Rob Kling and Suzanne Iacono of the University of California, Irvine, emphasize the role of choice in office computerization, arguing that specific interventions can lead to either increased flexibility in worklife and streamlined work groups, or regimented work organization and muddled work procedures. Kling and Iacono don't agree with the 'optimists' or the 'pessimists', whose views on the quality of office worklife are seen as overly deterministic. They say they don't expect to see any single form of 'office of the future' emerging, but a variety of forms depending upon managerial philosophies.[25]

At the same time, Ian McLoughlin and Jon Clark have introduced a new argument that computerization generates contradictory imperatives which both 'de-skill' *manual* work tasks but at the same time 'upskill' *mental* tasks associated with the operation of new technology. In *Technological Change at Work* (1988), McLoughlin and Clark argue from their case studies of the introduction of new technology in various organizations that computers and information technology exercise an *independent* influence on work tasks and skills. In rejecting what is seen as the 'technological determinism' of both the 'labour process' and the 'negotiated choice' theorists, they say (cf. Hirschhorn) that computers by their very nature 'generate more complex tasks which require mental problem-solving and interpretative skills and abilities and an understanding of system interdependencies' and that they 'involve a fundamentally different relationship between the user and the technology compared to mechanical and electro-mechanical technologies.'[26]

This account of computerization also finds an echo in the work of Harvard's Shoshana Zuboff, who argues that information technology is characterized by a fundamental duality. On the one hand, she says in her book, *In the Age of the Smart Machine* (1988) – which is based on eight case studies of organizations – that computers can be used by employers simply to replace people following the traditional nineteenth-century labour-substitution logic. On the other hand, their capacity to generate vast amounts of information about the underlying processes of production and administration enables employers to educate or 'informate' their workforce so that they can do their jobs better. 'The informated organization', she writes, 'is a learning institution . . . learning is a new form of labour' and this learning environment is based on egalitarian principles.[27]

Bellcore researchers Robert Kraut, Susan Dumais and Susan Koch, after studying the impact of a computerized record system on the working lives of customer service representatives in a large utility company, argue that the actual process of computerization is far more complex than the idealized rhetoric and simplistic models of de-skilling or upgrading imply. On the one hand, they found that office automation technology reduced job pressure and increased 'the happiness and mental health' of the primary users. On the other hand, they say that the new record system made the service representatives' jobs less satisfying and deskilled them by making them less complex, interesting and challenging, and by making their previous skills and training less relevant. The technology also decreased work satisfaction and involvement with work colleagues. They therefore conclude that monolithic or unidirectional models of technological impact are incorrect: 'These data demonstrate the oversimplicity of earlier work portraying office automation in either starkly negative or positive terms.'[28]

Productivity and People: Stress, Monitoring, Depersonalization, Fatigue and Boredom

A major lesson of the IT story so far is that the productivity pay-off from computerization has been somewhat disappointing. In manufacturing, commerce, government and elsewhere, productivity gains have often been hard to discern, despite massive spending on IT equipment. Much of the evidence on productivity remains anecdotal, but now more systematic studies are beginning to appear which throw new light on the productivity problem.

The first comes from the world of banking. Banks and other financial institutions were among the first to automate their operations – some electronic funds transfer (EFT) systems date back to the 1950s. So it should be possible to monitor the beneficial impact of computerization in the financial sector over a reasonable time period, reasoned Richard Franke of Loyola College, Maryland. But what he found was – to put it mildly – surprising. Franke reports that the adoption of computers by the US financial industry has been associated with massive increases in fixed capital, but *not* with proportionate increases of output either in total or per unit of labour. In fact, while capital productivity in US banks rose steadily in the quarter-century to 1957, it began to *decline* steadily after 1958 with the onset of computerization. This decline in capital productivity continued for another quarter-century. Productivity was particularly poor in the 1970s, yet by 1980 no less than a full half of all bank fixed capital expenditure went on computers and peripherals! Expected increases in capital and labour productivity and decreases in the growth of labour and capital inputs simply did not materialize.

However, a multivariate analysis did indicate the beginnings of an improvement in productivity in the 1980s, he says, and this may suggest that the financial industry is at last learning how to get the benefits out of automation. Drawing a parallel with the Industrial Revolution of eighteenth-century Britain, where it took a full 50 years for the economic benefits of technological transformation to become apparent, Franke believes that a similar thing might be happening with the current technological revolution. He therefore concludes that the information technology revolution has been characterized so far more by technical success than by economic success. In fact, the adoption of computer technology initially leads to decreased capital productivity and profitability, he says, and it takes time before the necessary changes in work organization can be successfully implemented to take advantage of the new technology. 'According to this assessment', he writes, 'it will be early in the 21st century when the accumulated experience in producing and using the equipment of the second technological revolution leads to the more effective utilization of human and capital resources and to major increases in output . . . Only with time can enterprises adjust to become productive.'[29]

In a second study of manufacturing automation, Tim Warner of York University, Ontario, reviews the evidence for increased productivity from the use of computers in factories. In 1987, US companies spent $17 billion on robots, CAD-CAM and FMS systems, he says. But according to US Bureau of Labor Statistics figures, the annual increase in US manufacturing productivity has been a paltry 3 per cent – far below that of Japan and South Korea, and even lower than that of Britain, France and Italy.

Warner looks in some detail at the three main ways in which information technology has been deployed on the factory floor: FMS or advanced manufacturing technologies; CAD systems; and computerized information and control systems. These in turn are looked at in the context of four

North American case studies. In each case, the company concerned had a problem (such as an inferior product, declining market share, slow response times, etc.) which it attempted to rectify by the adoption of information technology – or as Warner puts it, 'throwing computer power at the problem'.

But, says Warner, in every case this was the *wrong* thing to do. Heavy expenditure on a high-tech 'fix' merely compounded the problem. Far more could have been achieved, he says, by, for example, redesigning products in order to reduce the number of parts. Again, managing the work-flow in factories in a more intelligent way could have achieved very considerable savings. The point is that these were changes to the internal environment: automation, he says, is and must always be secondary. Warner points out that the Japanese have achieved large increases in productivity through, for example, the use of Just-In-Time (JIT) systems, which do not involve the use of high-tech. And there are many other conventional improvements to work organization that should be considered *before* the use of information technologies. 'A naive faith in technological silver bullets', he writes, 'diverts manufacturers from the hard task of rebuilding their operations from the ground up . . . Rather than reducing waste, an information technology approach adds to it by burdening an already inefficient system with the cost of computation', says Warner.[30]

A third batch of studies has focused on productivity in the office, where lavish spending on computers is also being questioned. In fact, according to US Bureau of Labor Statistics figures, overall office productivity in the US is no higher than it was in the late 1960s. Recent research by the Brookings Institution think-tank and by investment bankers Morgan Stanley has also found it hard to discern any improvements in office productivity, yet capital expenditure on computers has zoomed. While it is possible to find many individual success stories and while it is plainly evident that many commercial sectors are now wholly dependent on computers to service their customers, it seems that demonstrating the economic benefits in macro terms is much more difficult.[31]

Indeed, new technology in the office has created a new set of problems: documents which once went through one draft now go through an excessive number of re-drafts, each one taking time and money to produce – and incidentally boosting the consumption of paper (so much for the 'paperless' office!); employees tend to spend hours 'playing' with spreadsheets or generating electronic junk mail; the time gained by the automation of routine tasks is often wasted on office gossip; expensive equipment lies under-used for long periods, especially when it has been purchased for 'display' purposes on executive desks – in a modern version of Thorstein Veblen's 'conspicuous consumption'; with hardware and software being upgraded so often that secretarial staff now have to spend many hours being regularly 'retrained', whereas in the past learning to type was a once-in-a-lifetime task, and so on and so on. In these and a thousand other ways, the benefits of computerization can be dissipated.

Researchers who have studied the problem of white-collar productivity offer many explanations for the poor pay-off from computers. One suggestion is that *stress* in computerized offices is costing millions of dollars in lost working hours and reduced productivity. In the US, for example, the Office of Technology Assessment (OTA) has estimated that stress-related illnesses cost businesses between $50 billion and $75 billion per year. Workers' compensation claims based on job stress have more than doubled since 1980 and now account for approximately 15 per cent of all occupational disease claims.[32] In her book, *The Electronic Sweatshop* (1988), Barbara Garson even argues that computers are transforming the 'office of the future' into a kind of stressed-out 'factory of the past'.[33]

In Britain, a 1986 Department of Education and Science (DES) report estimated that stress in offices was costing the UK economy millions of pounds a year – and those in closest contact with new technology were most at risk. Author of the report, Sue Cox, writes that automation is often seen as the solution to a messy office problem. But automating a mess only creates an automated mess, she says. Her report found that many workers were inadequately trained for new technology and they needed help in coping with the stress arising out of change. Stress in the modern office led to loss of job satisfaction, low morale, absenteeism and poor management–labour relations.[34]

Yet it seems the Japanese deliberately set out with the intention of increasing levels of stress in order to maximize productivity. In a study of the famous Toyota–General Motors NUMMI (New United Motors Manufacturing Inc.) car plant at Fremont, California, Mike Parker and Jane Slaughter argue convincingly that even the much-vaunted Japanese 'team' concept of management is actually based on boosting stress. This is achieved by the regular speeding-up of production lines, the process of *kaizen* or 'continuous improvement' and the constant testing of the production system to breaking point. Even the 'just-in-time' (JIT) parts production system has been introduced, they say, to ensure that workers do not build up buffer stocks in order to take a rest. It's therefore not surprising that even the highly selected US employees of Japanese car plants are starting to complain of 'burn-out'.[35]

This linking of stress and the contemporary workplace is a growing theme in management literature. As Boddy and Buchanan put it,

The concern with work organization in the late 1980s and into the 1990s is thus based on pressures arising from stiffer trading conditions in domestic and international markets, from the realization that stress has more impact on job performance than dissatisfaction, and from the introduction of new computing and information technologies which lead to a rethink of work flows and work roles in manufacturing and administration. A de-skilled, unmotivated, uncommitted and inflexible workforce is not competitive when careful attention to costs, quality and delivery schedules is fundamental to capturing and retaining changing and unpredictable markets. The effective management of human resources has for these reasons become even more of a key factor in sustaining competitive advantage and work organization has for these reasons become a crucial management consideration.[36]

Another issue causing considerable controversy at present is that of the computerized monitoring of employees. According a recent Office of Technology Assessment (OTA) report to the US Congress, between 25 and 30 per cent of US clerical employees are now under surveillance in this way.[37] In the past, employees were monitored directly by progress-chasers, foremen and supervisors. But these days monitoring can be done surreptitiously by microchip. Computerized monitoring is constant, reliable and cheap. Supervisors are no longer limited by what they can observe with their own eyes. A complete record of employee performance exists in the print-out.

Supporters of computer monitoring point out that managers are under ever-increasing pressure to improve productivity and competitive performance. Computer monitoring provides clear, accurate performance measures and enhances the ability of managers to motivate employees. Many companies have also suffered from industrial espionage and employee thefts. Because of the growing sophistication of manufacturing processes and office information systems, mistakes are more costly and computer systems are more prone to employee sabotage. In the US in particular, a dramatic increase in drug use at work and the spread of AIDS have, it is said, forced employers to take more interest in the behaviour and private lives of employees.

Critics charge that computerized employee monitoring represents an intolerable invasion of privacy and disregards human rights. It undermines trust, reduces autonomy and fails to measure *quality* rather than quantity. They say that the practice itself causes stress and, perhaps most damning of all, it is actually counter-productive because employee morale declines and with it productivity.

In an important study of the phenomenon, Canadian researchers Rebecca

Grant, Christopher Higgins and Richard Irving found that monitoring had a dramatic effect on employee attitudes towards productivity and customer service.[38] The research took place in a claims-processing division of a large North American insurance company, where Grant et al. compared the behaviour of monitored employees with that of unmonitored employees.

Generally, they report that the effect of computerized monitoring was to degrade the quality of the product offered to the customer and the work environment in the process. Whereas no less than 85 per cent of *unmonitored* employees rated work quality (customer service and teamwork) as the most important factor in their jobs, as many as 80 per cent of *monitored* employees said production quantity was most important. According to the researchers, monitoring promoted this bureaucratic behaviour: monitored employees not unreasonably perceived that if a work task was not being counted, then it didn't count. But they did not necessarily see this to be a fair measure of an employee's worth. They also realized that customer service was sacrificed and tasks requiring special attention were side-lined as a result of monitoring. Those who had internalized the new standards were happier in knowing what was expected of them. Those who felt the new quotas eliminated the intrinsic satisfaction of providing good service commented on the stress of being 'watched' all the time.

What is to be done about the growth of computer monitoring? MIT's Gary Marx and Sanford Sherizen have proposed a code of ethics to control the use of monitoring and to safeguard privacy. Their proposed guidelines include: (1) Applying to monitoring the same protection that applies to pre-employment background checks – that is, permit only information to be collected which is directly relevant to the job. (2) Requiring employers to provide employees with advance notice of the introduction of monitoring as well as appropriate mechanisms for appeal. (3) Requiring people to verify machine-produced information before using it to evaluate employees. (4) Providing workers with access to the information themselves and provide mechanisms for monetary redress for employees whose rights are violated or who are victims of erroneous information generated by monitoring systems. (5) Applying a 'statute of limitations' on data from monitoring. The older the data, the less its potential relevance and the greater the difficulty employees have in challenging it.[39]

There is also a set of environmental problems connected with modern offices. For example, there is serious concern about air quality in large office buildings due to inadequate air-conditioning systems. After years of complaints, rumours, absenteeism and high turnover, medical researchers have now identified something called 'sick building syndrome' which results in drowsiness, headaches, eye irritation, sore throats, and so on.

Sick building syndrome is caused simply by a lack of fresh air and the accumulation of fungi, bacteria, dust and debris in ventilation ducts. The air-conditioning systems of high-rise office buildings have been found to contain fibreglass, asbestos, pollen, spores, carbon dioxide, tobacco smoke, formaldehyde from resins, ozone from photocopiers, toluene from cleaning fluids and trichloroethane from office supply fluids, among other irritants and suspected carcinogens. According to the US Environmental Protection Agency, indoor pollution levels can be 1,000 times that of out-doors.[40]

Further aggravating the situation are problems with the design of offices and office furniture, such as the fashion for 'open-plan' systems which reduce the amount of space available per employee at the expense of efficiency, job satisfaction and increased stress. Poorly designed seats, tables and workstations which do not conform to ergonomic principles have been blamed for eyestrain, headaches, neck and shoulder ache, and wrist and elbow disorders, as we shall see in the next section.

Peter G. Neumann has also identified a number of other quality of work issues specifically associated with computerization. For example, he suggests that computers can bring out personal anxieties and phobias, which are often exacerbated by people being told that 'the computer' is to blame rather than its designers or operators. Computers can increase fatigue and boredom, he says, because so many tasks associated with computers are highly repetitive, such as data entry, tape library maintenance and audit-trail watching. Computers can lead to a reduced ability of people to control systems and the placing of unquestioning, blind trust in technology: 'Because of factors such as enormous complexity and poorly conceived human interfaces, people often have great difficulties understanding and controlling computer-based applications – especially in real time. The opportunities for accidental misuse or intentional abuse are greater. When something goes wrong, the problems are often very difficult to diagnose.'[41]

But perhaps most important of all from the ethical point of view, computers increase the sense of depersonalization: 'Interactions with computers tend to depersonalize both the user community and the application itself. The resulting sense of anonymity can inspire a lack of respect for the system and its resources, and a diminished sense of ethics, values, and morals on the part of the affected people. The depersonalization can increase the temptations to commit misdeeds, diminish human initiative, and cause the abdication of decision-making responsibility. The sense of ethical behaviour seems much more diffuse, even though in principle it should be no different from ethical behaviour in general.' Neumann says that while there are obvious quantitative differences between computer technology and other technologies, collectively these seem to make a qualitative difference. Computers create a wholly new set of problems in the workplace.

There is a growing awareness that these sorts of human factors and quality of work issues play a major role in determining the success or failure of systems. As Long points out, a major study by the Rand Corporation of 2,000 US companies that had implemented new office systems revealed that at least 40 per cent had failed to achieve their intended results. Yet less than 10 per cent of the failures were attributed to technical difficulties – the majority of the failures were attributed to human and organizational problems.[42] Companies are therefore (slowly) rediscovering that people and not machines are their most valuable resource and that they can best improve their competitive performance by getting humans and technology working together in harmony. Many managers are realizing what better managers figured out years ago: that you need to get the people side of the equation right if you want to get the most out of the latest technology. This is more profitable for the employer and often better for the psychological well-being of the employees involved.

In his study of UK banks, Steve Smith shows that conventional automation has not been very successful either in economic or social terms. It has failed to boost efficiency, it has disrupted work systems and it has alienated the workforce from the banks and from each other. He writes: 'Technologists have under-estimated the value and importance of skill, knowledge, flexibility and career . . . contrary to scientific management, efficiency actually improves and control is made easier if the "labor process" is as coherent as possible. There should be a presumption in favor of skills, pride in the job, staff flexibility, apprentice-based careers and intuitive knowledge.'[43] The answer therefore seems to lie in the development of more human-centred systems, that is, systems which seek to retain and enhance human skills, control and discretion, rather than taking them away from the worker. As indicated by Hirschhorn, Zuboff and McLoughlin and Clark, instead of splitting jobs into innumerable minor tasks, a more human-centred approach is to give workers more knowledge of, and responsibility for, the entire production process – and this is made easier by information technology. Human-centred systems therefore make both economic and social sense.

Health and Safety Issues: VDTs and the RSI Debate

Video display terminals (VDTs) were first introduced in the 1960s, but it was not until the 1970s that they really became common in workplaces. Now there are about 15 million in daily use in the US alone – and millions more are being added to the world stock of VDTs every year. But as their use has become more widespread, so have the allegations that VDTs cause eyestrain, headaches, backaches, stiff necks and sore wrists. More serious complaints are that VDTs can cause cataracts, miscarriages and birth defects. In management, trade union and feminist circles, the alleged health and safety hazards of VDTs have become a big issue.

Yet on both sides of the VDT debate it is remarkable how little is really known about VDT safety – despite a string of reports and studies which have appeared in the last decade. The first was the US National Institute for Occupational Safety and Health (NIOSH) report which was published in 1980: this stated that there was 'cause for concern' about possible physical and psychological hazards arising out of prolonged VDT use. At the three major sites studied, VDT workers reported more instances of eyestrain and stiff necks, as well as higher levels of stress, irritability, depression and anxiety. But the NIOSH report left open the question of whether the high levels of stress reported and the associated psychological problems were caused by the nature of the job or by the use of VDTs – or both. A new NIOSH report was due out at the end of 1989.

The consensus of a 1981 National Academy of Sciences (NAS) conference was that the application of ergonomics – in the form of better lighting, improved seating and more appropriate screen technology – would only go some way toward solving both the physical and psychological problems of VDT users and that job stress was a major causal factor. But a 1983 National Research Council (NRC) report appeared to conclude the opposite: namely that most of the physical problems associated with VDT work *could* be cured by ergonomics: 'Our general conclusion', said study group chairman, Edward Rinalducci, 'is that eye discomfort, blurred vision and other visual disturbances, muscular aches and stress reported among VDT workers are probably not due to anything inherent in VDT technology.'[44]

The NRC findings did nothing to quell further speculation that VDTs were a problem – particularly from labour unions and feminist groups in the US like 9 to 5 and the National Association of Working Women. In 1985, a Japanese study of 13,000 workers reportedly found a high level of miscarriages, premature births and still-births among VDT operators, while a Swedish study of 10,000 programmers concluded that there were no statistically significant differences between the pregnancies of women who had experienced low, medium and high levels of exposure to VDTs. Likewise, Professor Kenneth Foster of the University of Pennsylvania found no connection between the use of VDTs and reproductive problems – nor did he believe that any strong connection was likely to exist. And a Canadian government study of 51,885 births and 4,127 abortions found that congenital defects in infants were not related to whether women had used a VDT during their pregnancy.[45]

Meanwhile a 1987 Japanese study by Professor Satoshi Ishikawa of Kitazato University found that 90 per cent of VDT users reported eyesight problems, 17 per cent suffered from eyeball degeneration, 27 per cent reported stiff shoulders and necks, and 13 per cent complained of insomnia. Swedish researchers reported a link between electromagnetic radiation from computer terminals and foetal deaths and deformities in pregnant mice, while a US Office of Naval Research group reported a significant increase in abnormalities among chicken embryos exposed to low frequency magnetic fields. A University of Maryland study also suggested a link between the electrostatic (as opposed to electromagnetic) radiation emitted from VDTs and the appearance of some types of dermatitis. In July 1989, Cal-OSHA, California's Occupational Safety and Health Administration, came out with a report compiled by two dozen experts who failed to agree on whether new regulations were necessary to govern the use of VDTs, other than periodic rest-breaks and regular eye tests.[46]

But probably the most important report on VDT hazards to emerge in recent years came in June 1987 from the Kaiser-Permanente Medical Care Program in Oakland, California. Kaiser-Permanente studied 1,600 women clerical workers who had become pregnant since 1984 and found that expectant mothers who had spent more than 20 hours per week at terminals were more than twice as likely to suffer a miscarriage as other clerical employees. However, the difference was not statistically significant. Job-related stress and poor working conditions for the VDT users could also not be ruled out as intervening variables, said the researchers. Nevertheless, the director of the study, Edmund Van Brunt, was quoted as saying that he believed the research did indicate an association between VDT use and miscarriage and it was this alleged link that was widely reported in the media right around the world. With indications that some pregnant women were quitting their jobs on the spot as a result of the Kaiser-Permanente study, the report's authors were forced to retract – or at least repeat the statistical qualifications. For example, Michael Polen, one of the three researchers, told *Fortune* magazine: 'I regret that our study has increased the level of fear, and I think that's unwarranted. All we can say for sure is that we need more studies.'[47]

In the same month that the Kaiser report was published, another major event occurred in the history of VDT health and safety: Suffolk County, a suburban area on Long Island, New York, passed a bill that would for the first time regulate the use of VDTs in the workplace. The controversial bill, sponsored by Democrat John Foley, was enacted one year later in

June 1988, after a 13 to 5 vote and a stormy passage which included the county chief executive, Patrick Halpin, using his veto over the bill under pressure from the county's business community, who had threatened to pull out of the area. At one point, Halpin warned that Suffolk County risked becoming an 'economic island' to be avoided by major employers. The act applies to businesses that operate more than 20 VDTs and provides for 15 minute breaks every three hours for employees who use the terminals for more than 26 hours a week – hardly a revolution. In addition, employers must pay for 80 per cent of the cost of eyeglasses and annual eye tests; and by 1990 all new VDT equipment installed in Suffolk County will have to feature adjustable chairs, detachable keyboards and non-glare screens. The act finally became law in January 1989, although four large employers in the county still felt so strongly about the additional costs imposed on them that they challenged the law in the New York State Supreme Court. As many as 25 US states are reportedly considering whether to enact similar legislation and in New York City itself, councillor Miriam Friedlander introduced a Bill almost identical to the one passed in Suffolk County.[48]

If not enough is known about VDTs and their alleged hazards, then so-called Repetitive Strain Injury (or RSI) is an even more unknown quantity. For centuries, manual workers such as cobblers, blacksmiths, textile workers and butchers have suffered from strained ligaments and joints, which have sometimes necessitated leaving their jobs. One such painful affliction is carpal tunnel syndrome – a nerve block involving the carpal ligament in the palm of the hand. For years, too, writers have complained of 'writers' cramp' and sports' lovers have suffered from epicondylytis or 'tennis elbow' and tenosynovitis or 'golfers' wrist' from over-indulgence in their favourite sport. But in recent years there has been evidence that the excessive use of computer keyboards can also lead to a new, modern form of industrial injury: RSI.

In fact, the term RSI seems to have originated in Australia, where it is used to describe a variety of painful and disabling afflictions which appear to be caused by repetitive movements of the hands and arms. Typists and word processor operators seem particularly vulnerable since they can make up to 45,000 keystrokes per hour (although the average is much less). This can irritate or inflame tendons (tenosynovitis or tendonitis) leading to unpredictable and excruciating pain. Yet a majority of reported RSI cases in Australia cannot be traced to tendons or indeed to any other parts of the human body. A majority, it seems, are 'conversion illnesses' such as hysterical blindness or shell-shock which can be psychological (or even sociological) in origin.[49]

Australia itself suffered a strange epidemic of RSI in the 1980s, beginning in 1981 with nearly 100 reported cases, rising to about 200 cases in 1983 and reaching a peak of over 900 cases in 1984, only to 'disappear' – or rather decline steadily from around 750 cases in 1985 to less than 200 reported cases in 1987.[50] Most of the complainants were women office workers in government employment whose jobs involved spending long hours on computer keyboards. For example, of 560 reported cases in Western Australia prior to 1985, 22 per cent involved data processing operators, 19 per cent were word-processing operators, 18 per cent were secretary stenographers and 12 per cent were typists.

In attempting to find out the cause of Australia's RSI epidemic, Sara Kiesler and Tom Finholt of Carnegie-Mellon University, Pittsburgh, have suggested that poor ergonomic design of equipment is associated with RSI, while work practices such as speed-ups, heavier workloads, greater monotony, fewer rest breaks, non-standard hours and so on are also related to the incidence of RSI. In particular, they say, those using keyboards for prolonged, rapid and repetitive tasks such as data entry or word processing seem more prone to RSI than computer programmers, computer scientists and journalists who use keyboards in a more leisurely and varied way. But this could mean either of two things: that RSI sufferers get sick from physically doing the job or that they get sick from *having* such a boring, dead-end, monotonous and low status job. Yet RSI not only varies between countries, as the Australian experience indicates, it also appears to vary between workplaces within Australia where similar types of people are doing similarly boring and repetitive jobs using similar equipment.[51]

The key question, therefore, is why did RSI suddenly become a problem of epidemic proportions in Australia in the 1980s? Kiesler and Finholt put forward four main reasons: first, that there is historical precedent for RSI-type compensation claims in Australia and a long history of union involvement in workers' health issues; second, RSI became a *cause celebre* of Australian unions and feminist groups as soon as new technology started being introduced into Australian offices in the early 1980s; third, RSI received official validation from the Australian medical establishment, who seemed quite confident in diagnosing it early on (it is also compensatable with or without physical symptoms being present); and fourth, the Australian media followed the RSI story in some detail, thereby communicating the medical 'facts' to a wider audience. Put these four factors together, say Kiesler and Finholt, and RSI rapidly became a socially legitimate disease which was a perfectly respectable one to have. It also provided an alternative to continued boring, repetitive work in an unpleasant, stressed environment. It was, they say, 'a legitimate ticket out of the pink ghetto' for hundreds of women clerical workers.

'We do not intend to suggest that RSI is a scam to promote the practice of medicine or that Australian workers use RSI claims to defraud their employers', they write. 'We believe that they legitimately have symptoms of RSI. We speculate that if the work environment were better and if jobs were more satisfying, RSI complaints would not be as important. The epidemic in Australia ostensibly involves RSI, but we hypothesize that it is really related to bad work conditions and an unfulfilling work life. The ambiguous nature of RSI makes it the perfect candidate for many workers as they seek an approved exit from the computing pool while preserving benefits and some salary.'[52] Kiesler and Finholt therefore conclude that RSI is an extreme example of how the social, organizational and political context of work and technological change defines and influences the nature of health problems. Illnesses and injuries like RSI do not occur in a vacuum, they say. They are created by society.

Suggestions for Further Discussion

You may wish to think about the following, hypothetical scenario.

It is designed to illustrate many of the common problems that software designers (and their clients) encounter during the development of a new computer-based information system.

Liverwurst Literature Inc. was a small but successful publishing company that derived its major source of income from subscriptions to a range of magazine titles. With the entry of a major foreign company into the market, however, Liverwurst decided that it needed to expand its operations if it was to remain competitive and looked at the range of changes that would have to be implemented in order to boost its competitiveness. The company quickly found that its existing subscription processing system was inadequate to meet the anticipated levels of processing. As a result, management decided that a new computer-based system was needed to overcome the limitations of the existing, largely manual system. The following describes the chain of events associated with this process and its outcomes.

Before considering the computerized system and its development, it is important to understand how the manual system operated. The steps in the system were as follows:

Original System

1 Incoming post was directed to the postal clerk where payments received were sorted out. The remaining items were divided into

- orders
- non-orders (i.e. complaints, changes of address, etc.)

At this stage, items were manually counted and totalled to serve as a control for subsequent steps. These later steps were handled by staff working in the subscriptions department.

2   The first task in the subscriptions department was to sort the orders by transaction type (new, continuing, gift, etc.) and code them accordingly. Batches of each transaction type were assembled for the next stage of processing, the data processing stage.

3   A manual card processing system was used to carry out the major data processing tasks. The data entry section filled in the order cards and verified them – they were then passed on to the data processing clerk who typed them into a file on a microcomputer, sorted them and printed out the list of orders. What the data processing phase produced was an initial set of bills, mailing labels, notices and subscriber cards, etc. This phase also detected any invalid inputs.

4   Subscriber cards resulting from the stage 3 process were then taken and manually inserted into the alphabetically ordered card file boxes. This file was periodically used as a basis for the production of monthly mailing labels, annual renewal notices, etc.

A schematic representation of the system is:

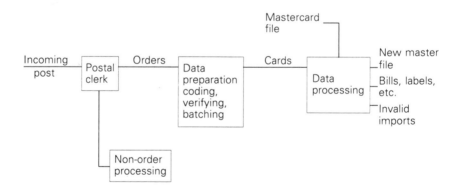

This labour-intensive system became increasingly slow, expensive, unreliable and unable to keep up with the seasonal peaks in subscription processing. Delays and customer complaints prompted the management to follow the lead of many larger-circulation periodicals and automate their subscription processing. Nevertheless, there were several positive aspects of the system:

1 It produced a high level of operator involvement. Workers felt they had a level of expertise which made the system work despite its problems – that is, they felt that the company required and valued their skills.

2 Workers were highly familiar with the system and knew where problems were likely to occur. Hence, their fault diagnosis was surprisingly quick. This was helped by having a good grasp of the functionality of the system. Its physical layout provided them with a good 'mental model' of how it worked.

3 Both (1) and (2) can be explained in large part by the extent to which the existing procedures had been co-designed by the workers. Many of the original co-designers still worked for Liverwurst and were able to provide specialist advice or important information when needed. That is, a great deal of relevant expertise and specialist knowledge relevant to the system were already 'in house'.

4 Although the existing system was heavily routinized such that most workers performed repetitive 'piece' work, nevertheless, the physical form of the system provided direct, observable feedback to all workers on the amount of work that had been completed that day and how much was left to be processed. It was also possible for workers to predict a 'lag' in the processing so that they could take a quick break or help another worker who had an excessive amount to do. That is, some amount of autonomy and choice existed.

The Development Process

Because the company itself did not have the appropriate computer skills to develop the new system, management opted to employ a team of consultants who appeared to have a good track record in software development. The consultants' previous training and experience were focused on deriving program solutions from clearly formulated programming problems. In the case of Liverwurst Literature, they analysed the situation, identified the part that had a programming solution and applied that solution to the problem.

Being mindful of the cost ceiling that the company had given them, the consultants decided that the adaptation of an existing off-the-shelf solution would be most cost-effective. That is, they believed that customizing this package to meet the unique needs of Liverwurst was the most efficient way of implementing the required system. Their approach focused on processing the data and took a top down form, i.e.:

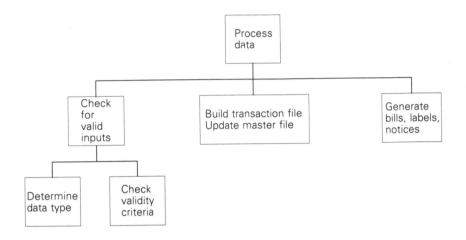

The software solution fitted into the original system in the following way:

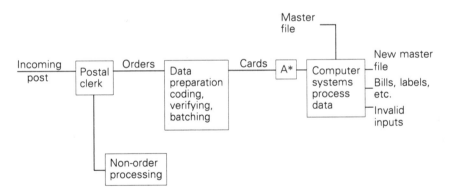

* A is a program to add the new entries to a master file held on disk.

In the process of developing this system, the consultants *did* look at the existing system but they *did not* analyse its strengths and deficiencies either from a pure processing point of view or from a worker point of view. They did not attempt to compare existing computer-based systems in similar applications with the system they intended to provide. They did not have any formal or informal discussions with workers as to how the existing system could be improved or how the anticipated system could best be grafted on to the current one. They did not attempt to validate the system with the workers as it was being developed. Their attempts at requirements specification were not comprehensive. Their testing procedures in the early stages of development were inadequate and several bugs proved impossible to eliminate without rebuilding the code from scratch. As a result of this, a key member of the programming team resigned in mid-project, principally because she believed her warnings in regard to specification and testing had not been heeded. This person was the most knowledgeable in the team and her departure meant that whatever likelihood there had been of delivering a bug-free product was now gone.

The Outcome

When the product was eventually delivered, it proved necessary to place the system over several floors. This happened because the noise of some of the printers and card readers was too great for them to be placed near the clerical workers and acoustic baffles were too expensive. As a consequence of this, workers frequently had to move floors to obtain output or input. They were also unable to see if other workers were overloaded. The system did not provide any system statistics that were available to workers (only to the analysts) and hence there was little feedback on how much had been accomplished and how much of the day's processing was left.

As part of their contract, the consultants agreed to be involved in a 'teething' period in which the bugs in the system were ironed out and operators were trained in its use. However, this period was very short and only the simplest problems with the system were rectified while the trainers and analysts remained in-house. After their departure, the expertise of the operators had increased markedly and the range and complexity of the problems they faced became enormous. The operators soon found that telephone diagnoses were of little help.

In addition, the error-checking and input-validation procedures involved in the new system were inadequate. A trivial error would often cause the program to reject entire batches of input or cause an update run to stop completely. When this happened, the transaction input listing had to be found and manually checked for errors. This also involved another cumbersome process of updating the transaction file.

Faced with this problem, the management imposed additional levels of control on the manual processing steps that preceded the computer processing. This required the use of more complicated input forms and control sheets to handle exceptional conditions. These changes resulted in:

- the need for more, not less, personnel
- increased costs
- more delays, and
- reduced staff morale.

On the latter point, workers began expressing the view that whereas previously they had had a good 'model' of the system and how it worked, the training carried out by the consultants had not provided this for the new system. Hence, the ability of operators to predict failures, diagnose faults and 'cover' for weaknesses or bottlenecks were not part of the new system.

Whereas the physical layout of the previous system gave them feedback on work progress and allowed them to have some control over their own work routines, they now had little understanding of how the day's work was progressing or when they might be able to assist another worker. This problem was exacerbated by the location of the system over several floors.

Workers expressed the view that their skills had been downgraded and that their new tasks required little initiative, no thought and even less skill or involvement in the goal that their work was intended to meet. They recognized that old skills had to be discarded and new ones learnt, but they also pointed out that if they had been involved in the system design from the start, they could have designed tasks and work roles that would have preserved some autonomy, responsibility and pride in their skills.

In sum, because of these technical and workforce difficulties, for the new system as a whole:

- Costs went up rather than down
- Reliability and quality of service went down
- More clerical people were required
- Employee morale went down
- Employee turnover went up.

Cases like this *do* happen, and perhaps more frequently than many of us are willing to admit. Obviously, there are issues of considerable ethical significance here, including system designers' responsibilities to both their clients and users, who may have conflicting goals. For workers, the quality of their worklife and task satisfaction may be just as important as the salary packages they receive. For employers, however, efficiency and competitiveness translate into profitability (and employment).

The major issue therefore is how to maximize profitability and corporate efficiency without creating an unbearable working environment for employees. One possible solution would be to incorporate workers into the design process, system implementation and fine tuning. After all, the experts in these matters are often the workers themselves.

In addition, we should question the after-delivery practices of this company and its responsibilities in delivering a quality product through a reliable and professional development process. Without such professional practices, many commentators question whether the software industry can truly take on the status of a profession in the manner that, say, law and medicine have. 'Fly-by-night' companies, shoddy products and ridiculous disclaimers are more in the realm of the used-car business than a profession filled with educated and intelligent people.

If computer professionals wish to be accorded the status (and not just the money) of other professions, then their social awareness and ethical values must be upgraded substantially.

Notes

1 *The Financial Times*, diary section, undated.
2 George C. Church, 'The work ethic lives!', *Time*, 7 September 1987; 'Americans are still having a love affair with work', *Business Week*, 18 January 1988; James Graff, 'Weekend work', *Time*, 19 December 1988; Alan Goodall, 'Holiday a dirty word in Japan', *The Australian*, 24 December 1988; Walter Kiechel III, 'The workaholic generation', *Fortune*, 10 April 1989; and Nancy Gibbs, 'America runs out of time', *Time*, 24 April 1989.
3 Richard M. Cyert and David C. Mowery (eds), *Technology and Employment: Innovation and Growth in the US Economy*, Panel on Technology and Employment, Committee on Science, Engineering and Public Policy (National Academy Press, Washington, DC, 1987). See also Allan Hunt and Timothy Hunt, *Clerical Employment and Technological Change* (W. E. Upjohn Institute for Employment Research, 1987).
4 W. W. Daniel, *Workplace Industrial Relations and Technical Change*, Report of the UK Workplace Industrial Relations Survey, co-sponsored by the Department of Employment, the Economic and Social Research Council, the Policy Studies Institute and the Advisory, Conciliation and Arbitration Service (PSI/Frances Pinter, London, 1987), pp. 278–82.
5 Louis S. Richman, 'Tomorrow's jobs: plentiful, but . . .', *Fortune*, 11 April 1988; J. A. Alic, 'Employment and job creation impacts of high technology', *Futures*, August 1986, pp. 508–13; David Birch, *Job Creation in America* (Free Press, New York, 1987).
6 'America rushes to high-tech for growth', *Business Week*, 28 March 1983; Ian Anderson, 'New technology will not provide jobs', *New Scientist*, 10 May 1984; Richard Brandt, 'Those vanishing high-tech jobs', *Business Week*, 15 July 1985; 'Is the US becoming a nation of sales clerks?', *Business Week*, 18 May 1987.

7 Russell W. Rumberger and Henry M. Levin, 'Forecasting the impact of new technology on the future job market', *Technological Forecasting and Social Change*, vol. 27, 1985, pp. 399–417.

8 'High-tech leads the way in job growth', *Business Week*, 19 December 1988.

9 Harley Shaiken, 'High-tech goes third world', *Technology Review*, January 1988; 'How satellites are beaming jobs to Ireland', *Business Week*, 21 March 1988; 'Will a "Tradeport" soon link Beantown and Bombay?', *Business Week*, 12 December 1988.

10 Michael R. Rubin and Mary T. Huber, *The Knowledge Industry in the United States: 1960–1980* (Princeton University Press, Princeton, NJ, 1986).

11 Stephen S. Cohen and John Zysman, *Manufacturing Matters: The Myth of the Post-Industrial Economy* (Basic Books, New York, 1987).

12 James Brian Quinn, Jordan J. Baruch and Penny Cushman Paquette, 'Technology in Services', *Scientific American*, vol. 257, no. 6, December 1987.

13 J. David Roessner, 'Forecasting the impact of office automation on clerical employment, 1985–2000', *Technological Forecasting and Social Change*, vol. 28, 1985, pp. 203–16.

14 'White-collar job cuts on the way in the UK', *The Australian*, 7 April 1987, reprinted from *The Times*.

15 Sar A. Levitan and Elizabeth A. Conway, 'Part-timers: living on half-rations', *Challenge*, vol. 31, no.3, May–June 1988; Louis Uchitelle, 'Reliance on temporary jobs hints at economic fragility', *The New York Times*, 16 March 1988, p. A1; and Michael A. Pollock, 'The disposable employee is becoming a fact of corporate life', *Business Week*, 15 December 1986.

16 David R. Howell, 'The future employment impacts of industrial robots', *Technological Forecasting and Social Change*, vol. 28, 1985, pp. 297–310.

17 Kurt Hoffman and Howard Rush, *Microelectronics and Clothing: The Impact of Technical Change on a Global Industry* (Praeger, New York, 1988).

18 'Hiring the handicapped', *Fortune*, 26 September 1988.

19 Harley Shaiken, *Work Transformed: Automation and Labor in the Computer Age* (Holt, Rinehart and Winston, New York, 1985); Harley Shaiken, 'The automated factory: vision and reality', in Tom Forester (ed.), *Computers in the Human Context* (Basil Blackwell, Oxford, and MIT Press, Cambridge, MA, 1989); David F. Noble, *Forces of Production* (Knopf, New York, 1985); Mike Cooley, *Architect or Bee?* (Langley Technical Services, Slough, UK, 1980); Stephen Wood (ed.), *The Degradation of Work?* (Hutchinson, London, 1982); David Knights, Hugh Willmott and David Collinson (eds), *Job Redesign* (Gower, Aldershot, UK, 1985).

20 Larry Hirschhorn, 'Robots can't run factories', in Forester, *Computers in the Human Context*, p. 301; Larry Hirschhorn, *Beyond Mechanization* (MIT Press, Cambridge, MA, 1984). Even Shaiken comes close to conceding this – see, for example, the last paragraph of of his piece in Forester, *Computers in the Human Context*, p. 299.

21 W. W. Daniel, *Workplace Industrial Relations*, pp. 151–66.

22 Graham Winch, 'New technologies, new problems', in Graham Winch (ed.), *Information Technology in Manufacturing Processes* (Rossendale, London, 1983), p. 7.

23 David Boddy and David A. Buchanan, *Managing New Technology* (Basil Blackwell, Oxford, 1986), pp. 84–112.

24 Richard J. Long, *New Office Information Technology: Human and Managerial*

Implications (Croom Helm, London, 1987); Richard J. Long, 'Human issues in new office technology', in Forester, *Computers in the Human Context*, pp. 328–9 and p. 332.

25   Rob Kling and Suzanne Iacono, 'Desktop computerization and the organization of work', in Forester, *Computers in the Human Context*, p. 351.

26   Ian McLoughlin and Jon Clark, *Technological Change at Work* (Open University Press, Milton Keynes, UK, 1988), pp. 116–17.

27   Shoshana Zuboff, *In the Age of the Smart Machine* (Basic Books, New York, 1988).

28   Robert Kraut, Susan Dumais and Susan Koch, 'Computerization, productivity, and quality of worklife', *Communications of the ACM*, vol. 32, no. 2, February 1989.

29   Richard H. Franke, 'Technological revolution and productivity decline: the case of US banks', in Forester, *Computers in the Human Context*, pp. 281–90, reprinted from *Technological Forecasting and Social Change*, vol. 31, 1987, pp. 143–54.

30   Timothy N. Warner, 'Information technology as a competitive burden', in Forester, *Computers in the Human Context*, pp. 272–80, reprinted from *Sloan Management Review*, vol. 29, no. 1, Fall 1987.

31   See, for example, William Bowen, 'The puny payoff from office automation', *Fortune*, 26 May 1986.

32   Curt Suplee, 'The electronic sweatshop', *The Washington Post*, Outlook Section, 3 January 1988, p. B1.

33   Barbara Garson, *The Electronic Sweatshop: How Computers Are Transforming the Office of the Future into the Factory of the Past* (Simon and Schuster, New York, 1988).

34   Sue Cox, *Change and Stress in the Modern Office* (Further Education Unit, Department of Education and Science, London, 1986).

35   Mike Parker and Jane Slaughter, 'Management by stress', *Technology Review*, October 1988; Louis Kraar, 'Japan's gung-ho US car plants', *Fortune*, 30 January 1989.

36   David Boddy and David A. Buchanan, p. 105.

37   *Federal Government Information Technology: Electronic Surveillance and Civil Liberties*, Office of Technology Assessment, US Congress (Washington, DC, 1985).

38   Rebecca A. Grant, Christopher A. Higgins and Richard H. Irving, 'Computerized performance monitors: are they costing you customers?', *Sloan Management Review*, Spring 1988, pp. 39–45.

39   Gary T. Marx and Sanford Sherizen, 'Monitoring on the job', in Forester, *Computers in the Human Context*, reprinted from *Technology Review*, November/December 1986. See also Michael W. Miller, 'Computers keep eye on workers and see if they perform well', *The Wall Street Journal*, 3 June 1985, p. 1.

40   Curt Suplee, 'The electronic sweatshop'.

41   Peter G. Neumann, 'Are risks in computer systems different from those in other technologies', Software Engineering Notes, vol. 13, no. 2, April 1988, pp. 2–4.

42   Long, *New Office Information Technology*, p. 327.

43   Steve Smith, 'Information technology in banks: Taylorization or human-centred systems?', in Forester, *Computers in the Human Context*, pp. 377–90, reprinted from *Science and Public Policy*, vol. 14, no. 3, June 1987.

44 Tom Forester, *High-Tech Society* (Basil Blackwell, Oxford and MIT Press, Cambridge, MA, 1987), p. 215.
45 Kenneth R. Foster, 'The VDT debate', in Forester, *Computers in the Human Context*, reprinted from *American Scientist*, vol. 74, no. 2, March–April 1986, pp. 163–8; 'VDUs and Health', *Futures*, June 1987, p. 362.
46 'VDTs "Cause Eye Problems"', *The Australian*, 1 December 1987; 'Studies underline hazards of computer terminals', *New Scientist*, 13 August 1987, p. 33; David Kirkpatrick, 'How safe are video terminals?', *Fortune*, 29 August 1988; *Software Engineering Notes*, vol. 13, no. 4, October 1988, p. 19; 'VDT committee split on recommendations', UPI report in *The Australian*, 20 June 1989. See also 'VDTs linked to deformation of contact lenses', *The Australian*, 29 August 1989 on a new British study and 'VDTs cleared of causing miscarriages', *The Australian*, 19 September 1989 on the latest British and Canadian studies.
47 Christine Gorman, 'All eyes are on the VDT', *Time*, June 27, 1988; and David Kirkpatrick, 'How safe are video terminals?', p. 44.
48 Jack Bell, 'US county moves to protect VDT workers', *The Australian*, June 30 1987; Ben Brock, 'Storm erupts over pioneer law to protect VDT workers', *The Australian*, 21 June 1988; 'VDT safety law comes into force', *The Australian*, 17 January 1989. In the last week of 1989, the New York State Supreme Court invalidated the Suffolk County law and outgoing New York City Mayor Ed Koch vetoed the Friedlander Bill.
49 Sara Kiesler and Tom Finholt, 'The mystery of RSI', *American Psychologist*, December 1988, pp. 1004–15; see also 'A newsroom hazard called RSI', *Columbia Journalism Review*, January/February 1987.
50 Mark Ragg, 'Plague of RSI suddenly "Disappears"', *The Australian*, 7 September 1987.
51 Kiesler and Finholt, 'The mystery of RSI'.
52 Ibid., p. 1012.

Appendix

Autonomous Systems: the Case of 'Star Wars'

Although very few examples are currently in existence, the proposed construction of complex systems that have no role for human involvement and decision-making – so called 'autonomous systems' – is a development that disturbs many computer professionals. What makes such systems different from more commonplace ones is the possibility that they will be given almost complete responsibility for a task, with human input, verification and decision-making playing almost no role at all. Such a development raises several important ethical issues, especially in the light of the difficulties experienced by software engineers in building reliable systems (see chapter 5).

Perhaps the most controversial of autonomous systems is the proposed Strategic Defence Initiative (SDI) – the famous 'Star Wars' program that was announced by former President Ronald Reagan in March 1983. In addressing problems associated with Star Wars, we need to know what SDI actually is, how it works and wherein its difficulties lie. As an interim answer to the latter and as a framework for what is to follow, it appears that its difficulties lie in the dangers associated with a hair-trigger, autonomous system that controls powerful energies, as well as the ethical (and legal) difficulties this raises for human decision-making processes; the practical difficulties (perhaps impossibilities) that lie ahead of SDI; and the ethical problems associated with spending on a program that probably cannot either in practical and or theoretical terms be made to work.

The basic concept behind SDI is the construction of a layered defence system designed to protect the United States from inbound nuclear warheads. As press reports have indicated, the proposal requires extremely sophisticated co-ordination of radars, satellites and as-yet-undeveloped weapons systems in order to destroy warheads in the three phases of their delivery. The first phase is the 'boost' phase – the initial few minutes of launch – when the main rocket motors of the missile are at full thrust with their large exhaust plumes making them easy to detect by instruments aboard satellites. Although many commentators have not always emphasized the point, it is clear that for Star Wars to have any chance of success at all, then the highest priority must be attached to destroying missiles in the boost phase simply because each missile 'bus' can contain as many as 12 or 13 warheads. Hence, destroying a missile at this point of an attack effectively eliminates 12 or 13 possible targets at one stroke. If they are not destroyed in this phase, then once they are separated from their bus they become 12 or 13 extra targets that have to be tracked and destroyed. Misses at this stage therefore would create much greater difficulties for the other layers of the defence.

The second phase of delivery is the 'mid-course' phase in which the warhead-holding bus has separated from the launch vehicle and is coasting toward its targets, dropping off warheads one by one to fall upon their targets. In this phase, searching for buses and warheads, allocating priorities to different weapons systems and the verification of target destruction becomes an exponentially more difficult task for the defence. Not only do the huge numbers of data sources have to be integrated (different kinds of radars, satellite data streams, data uplinks and downlinks, etc.), but weapons systems with different physical capabilities (rail guns, lasers of various sorts, nuclear weapons – with different versions of all of these existing on the ground and in space) have to be *managed*, so that holes in the defence are not created by, for instance, several weapons shooting at the same target. And of course while all this is happening, a constant update of the situation has to be kept with successfully-destroyed targets being noted, new targets being identified, tracked and assigned while missed targets are 'tagged' for the last phase of the defence to deal with.

The last phase in the proposed Star Wars design is called the 'terminal' defence phase. Here, the warheads have re-entered the atmosphere and are falling toward their targets at a speed of several thousands of miles per hour. Some US warheads have the ability to take evasive action in their approach to the target (MARVs – manoeuvrable re-entry vehicles) and it is likely that if and by the time that SDI is actually implemented, Soviet warheads will have a similar capability. Furthermore, many of these potential targets would not be real warheads but merely inflatable decoys that simulate most of the characteristics of a real warhead. And in the great tradition of counter-counter-counter-intelligence, some warheads are designed to look like decoys while some decoys are designed to look like warheads pretending to look like decoys and so on. In summary, the terminal defence is tasked with the tracking, evaluation, and destruction of warheads and decoys that have survived the first two layers of the system and which are only moments away from impact. Again, as the plan stands, a combination of lasers, projectiles or kinetic energy weapons and possibly nuclear explosions will be directed against these surviving warheads before they can destroy their military or civilian targets.

Perhaps the major danger that has been identified with this system, however, is the likelihood that it will be required to be placed on a hair-trigger. In other words, because the destruction of missiles during the boost phase of launch (the first two minutes) is at an absolute premium, so that warheads are destroyed in clusters rather than singly, the system itself cannot be subject to any human input or control. In effect, the system has to be placed in an 'automatic' mode, looking for missile launches and dealing with them as it sees fit. There is simply no time for humans to be informed and certainly no room for precious seconds to be spent in human decision-making.[1]

Now there are obvious problems with this, not least among them the possibility of false alarms causing laser weapons and perhaps even small atomic bombs to be accidentally used. Our earlier references to some of the classic false alarms in the strategic defence systems of the United States should be enough to convince us that such false alarms are extremely likely. Indeed, given that much of the hardware and software that composes our present systems is rather dated and 'thought' to be understood, we might expect that the chances of false alarms are even higher with the kinds of new technologies needed in SDI.

Perhaps a final point in support of this criticism lies in the history of the development of anti-ballistic missiles in both the USSR and USA. In the 1950s and 1960s both of the superpowers built long-range and short-range missile systems for the destruction of ballistic nuclear warheads, with some missiles being tipped with small A-bombs. Eventually, both because the short-range system was placed on a hair-trigger and because cost-benefit calculations revealed that the US would suffer an accidental nuclear atmospheric burst every few years, the American system was scrapped. Although the Soviet system is still in service close to Moscow, it is certainly not operating on a hair-trigger and partly as a result it is thought to be incapable of providing any worthwhile defence for the Russian capital.[2]

Before discussing the software engineering impediments to SDI and their ethical implications, we need to consider for a moment the real physical difficulties that face such a system. To begin with, there appear to be immense problems associated with the physical possibility of developing the weapon components themselves. It is known, for instance, that ground-based lasers will have great difficulty keeping their beams in focus because of the distorting effect of the atmosphere. We know that placing chemical lasers aboard orbital battlestations is extremely problematic because their energy requirements are enormous. This will create difficulties not only logistically in terms of getting the necessary materials in space, but also in providing battlestations that can be fired enough times to make any difference to the thousands of warheads that would be involved in a full-scale attack. Moreover, it is known that laser weapons will require an improvement of several orders of magnitude in intensity, power output and aiming capability before they become a threat to a target of almost any form. We also know that several of the proposed weapons systems have very different physical characteristics – differences that would make co-ordination of the defence even more complex. For example, although lasers would hit a target almost instantaneously, kinetic energy weapons such as rail guns would take much longer for their projectiles to impact. The defence would have to take account of these differences when assigning weapons and determining priorities.

Moreover, the structure of SDI in an organizational and logistic sense reveals several fundamental difficulties. For example, if battlestations in space are regarded as the primary mode of defence, then one must provide very large numbers of them simply because a satellite that is placed in anything other than geostationary orbit will track across the earth's surface. At many points in that orbit, a satellite will be unavailable to the defence, simply because it happens to be on the other side of the globe. And if one places battlestations in geostationary orbit so that they remain over the one point, the distance involved (22,000 miles high) creates enormous difficulties in aiming the weapon. Warheads in their protective cones are less than two metres long and, at 22,000 miles, no matter what technology is involved, that will always remain an extremely small point to aim at. Furthermore, for obvious reasons, ranges of this order absolutely prohibit the application of projectile-type weapons. Indeed, even if one designed the system to use ground-based lasers that directed their beams via orbiting mirrors (one such proposal exists), similar problems remain in that large numbers of mirrors would have to be launched and maintained (their surfaces would become coated with dust from micrometeorites) and some form of feedback mechanism would have to be developed so that corrections to a mirror's orientation improved its aim in relation to the target.

Perhaps the most obvious and damning argument against SDI, however, is that it may become a technological monolith that can be easily duped by the simplest of counter-measures. For example, to foil laser weapons, Soviet missiles and warheads could be provided with highly reflective coatings or foils which would deflect the beams. An even more obvious countermeasure is for the Soviets to launch their missiles in lower trajectories. Although this would diminish their range to some extent, it would also deny SDI the precious moments it would need to destroy missiles in their boost phase. Other critics have also pointed out that American orbital battlestations could be effectively neutralized by the Soviets if they 'parked' mines or explosive-bearing satellites next to them, simply waiting for the appropriate moment to eliminate the chain of orbital weapons.

More importantly, this list of counter-measures does not include those that are already to hand. Jamming of radars and communications is quite common in modern warfare and the techniques involved are extremely sophisticated. It is not difficult to anticipate that large-scale jamming and even the detonation of nuclear weapons in the atmosphere (which scrambles communications on a massive scale and disables electronic equipment via an electromagnetic surge called EMP) would be used by the Soviet Union in order to help confuse any space-based defence. Lastly, it appears quite clear that even without the interference of these countermeasures, SDI would be hard-pressed to deal with a full-scale attack consisting of several thousand warheads, let alone the additional thousands of decoys and other intelligent 'penetration aids' that would inhibit the effectiveness of the defence.

Undoubtedly, SDI poses several ethical dilemmas and indeed moral dilemmas for those involved in its development. Even before SDI in an autonomous form becomes a reality, some US citizens have expressed extreme concern about the autonomous or semi-autonomous nature of the existing 'launch-on-warning' capability of the strategic forces of the United States. That is, a launch-on-warning (colloquially, 'use 'em or lose 'em') policy provides that in the event of a nuclear attack, the United States will retaliate upon detection of the attack, before warheads have impacted and damaged the capacity of the US to respond.

In a noteworthy case, Clifford Johnson of Stanford University has charged that such a policy is unconstitutional, since the President is unable to be involved in the decision-making process because of time constraints. In effect, Johnson claims that this decision-making capacity has been embedded within a computer system and that as a result, the constitutional power of the President and Congress to declare war has been unlawfully removed. Despite winning in a lower court, Johnson's claim was eventually rejected on the grounds that although the US *does* have a launch-on-warning capability, it is claimed by the government that such a capability has not been implemented as policy and hence, this unused capability was not a claim over which the government could be sued. Johnson however appears to be furthering his efforts by obtaining evidence that purportedly shows that the US is already poised in a launch-on-warning state.[3] It may be that as its autonomous nature becomes more apparent, SDI itself will become the next target of these accusations.

Yet even if we disregard the autonomous nature of SDI in its grander forms, there remains an even deeper ethical problem associated with the development of the system. As we have already noted in chapter 5, there are extreme limits to the practical and theoretical capabilities of software engineers to provide error-free systems. Those limitations should be even more obvious in the context of SDI – a system which easily surpasses the complexity of any which has so far been built or even proposed.

We would therefore be well advised to heed the views of David Parnas and other critics who have pointed out the extreme difficulties that face SDI in terms of software engineering and the possibility of it meeting its design specification. One of the major difficulties is the impossibility of completely testing the system in any real sense, since its full use can only occur in the face of a nuclear attack. Furthermore, a system of this scale requires that certain assumptions be made about the characteristics of both attacking and defending weapons. These may change at any time (particularly the weapons characteristics of the attackers) and such variability poses great problems for modifying and updating such a large and complex system.[4]

These points have been confirmed by other computer scientists in various media releases. In a report in the *New York Times* of 27 May 1986, Charles Mohr quotes from a letter by computer scientist Jim Horning:

To date no system of this complexity has performed as expected (or hoped) in its full-scale operational test; no one has advanced any reason to expect that an SDI would either. A huge system that is intended to be used at most once and cannot be realistically tested in advance of use, simply cannot be trusted.

Other experts have expressed similar viewpoints. Among the most damaging was a statement signed by 36 of 61 experts who attended a workshop at Pacific Grove, California on 16–19 March, 1986:

The effective defence from nuclear annihilation of the lives, homes and property of the American people, as embodied by the Strategic Defense Initiative (Star Wars), requires highly reliable computer systems of unprecedented complexity. As experts in reliable computing, we strongly believe that a system meeting these requirements is technologically infeasible.[5]

The last-ditch defence that proponents of a system like SDI tend to make is to argue that the kind of thinking we have engaged in here is simple Luddism and that the landing of man on the moon was also thought to be impossible.

Let us handle the initial accusation first. We should be clear that the term 'Luddism' in its normal usage refers to a rejection of technology (generally all technology, although the original Luddites were only opposed to the technology that threatened to displace them from their employment as textile workers). Most reasonable people are prepared to accept technology in its various forms into most aspects of their lives, while in other areas they may deem the risks too great (e.g. some people refuse to travel by air or reject the use of electronic funds transfer). These people cannot be accused of Luddism because they do not reject *all* technology (though they may reject some), while others may reject some technologies on quite rational grounds. For example, one may refuse to live next to a nuclear power station because scientists remain deadlocked over what constitutes a safe level of exposure to radiation. Why take a risk if one doesn't have to? Hence, these people, too, cannot be regarded as Luddites. We may regard the stance taken here to involve a *rational* appreciation of what we can expect computer-based systems to achieve for us, and what they cannot achieve. Indeed, one could argue that a sense of limitations is a primary component of any intelligent discussion of computation and technology and its costs and benefits. Without a sense of limits, we cannot even begin to determine where our research efforts should be placed, nor even what form our endeavours in this area should take.

In answer to the second point – that the Apollo missions were also once regarded as impossible – we need to point out the huge differences between what the moon project set out to achieve and what SDI is intended to achieve. Landing a person on the moon is a task composed of several components that are *static*. To be blunt, it involves transporting people to the moon, landing them, allowing them to survive long enough to perform something useful, removing them, transporting them back to an earth orbit and achieving re-entry. Now, these are all extremely difficult tasks, but the point is that they are static. The position of the moon is known at any time to within a distance of a few centimetres. It does not attempt to dupe or foil our systems. It does not change location suddenly or attempt to hide. Moreover, the huge system which was the Apollo program itself could be tested thoroughly and incrementally. Indeed, all of the earlier Mercury and Gemini missions can be seen to be stepwise refinements and increments toward the final goal of Apollo 11. SDI can never be developed in this incremental fashion, since the launch of several thousand warheads or decoys is logistically and economically unthinkable.

Unlike SDI, the software and hardware of the Apollo program did not have to face the possibility of being frequently and radically redesigned or rewritten because of a change of goal characteristics or simple, unexpected counter-measures. Hence, with SDI it is not a just a question of developing the appropriate technologies (although this in itself may be insuperable), it is really a question of proposing a goal that is constantly shifting and which would require redesigns of a monolithic system that will be hard-pressed to even meet a single, static goal of this scale. We may observe (as is already happening) that as the scope and difficulty of the task becomes more apparent to the system's implementors, the goals of SDI itself will become less and less extreme. To some extent this has already happened with the US government making vague noises about implementing a partial defence first. Undoubtedly, the research dollars will be spent, but as the realities become apparent, we may predict that the scope and scale of the project will diminish.

In his book on SDI, Ben Thompson has noted that the cost of the Star Wars project is in the region of $1,000 billion or more, while the cost of the entire Apollo moon project was a mere $25 billion. By mid 1989, some $17 billion had already been spent on Star Wars and there were no realistic prospects of deploying any Star Wars system within a decade.[6] Even after inflation, the difference in cost and scale is staggering. If this is the case, and given the criticisms levelled at SDI in terms of simple functionality, can software practitioners ethically work on such a project? Can they assume that they are merely pursuing research which, like much basic research, may or may not end up by being applied in real applications? Perhaps we should dig much deeper into matters of a moral kind by pointing out that the bulk of research scientists in the developed world (computer scientists included) carry out research for the military.[7]

In particular, if our methodologies are unable to guarantee that SDI will work properly (or even at all), then we should ask ourselves whether we are being ethically responsible by pursuing this kind of research and development. (Should researchers take the money under this pretence?) We might also ask, as Clifford Johnson has, whether it is ethically, legally and even logically sound to place the responsibility for the lives of millions into the decision-making processes of a machine. Should we only entrust such responsibilities to humans, especially if, in the end, the behaviour of the computer systems we create cannot be properly understood? If, as we have argued, the behaviour of the 'entity' controlling our nuclear weapons is unpredictable and potentially catastrophic in its effects, might not this entity just as well be human as anything else? Can the realities involved in the deaths of millions be understood by anything other than a human being?

Notes

1   Mike Norton, 'World War Three: the Pentagon plans for the nuclear aftermath', *Computing Australia*, 25 May 1987, pp. 30–1.
2   Ben Thompson, 'What is Star Wars?', in E.P. Thompson (ed.), *Star Wars* (Penguin, Harmondsworth, 1985).
3   *Software Engineering Notes*, vol. 11, no. 5, 1986, p. 16; Mary Madison,

Peninsula Times Tribune (Palo Alto, CA), 9 March 1985; *Software Engineering Notes*, vol. 10, no. 2, 1985, pp. 9–11; David Kadlecek, *The Guardian Weekly*, 20 August 1986, p. 9.

4   David L. Parnas, 'Software aspects of strategic defence system', *Communications of the ACM*, vol. 28, no. 12, 1985, pp. 1326–35; *Software Engineering Notes*, vol. 11, no. 3, 1986, p. 8.

5   *Software Engineering Notes*, vol. 11, no. 3, 1986, p. 8.

6   The attempt to revitalize SDI via the 'brilliant pebbles' concept, announced by Defense Secretary, Dick Cheney, in April 1989, has also come under fire – for example, from Jonathan Jacky, 'Throwing stones at "brilliant pebbles"', *Technology Review*, October 1989.

7   Bruce Van Voorst, 'Will Star Wars ever fly?', *Time*, 26 June 1989; see also Joseph Weizenbaum, 'Not without us', *Science for the People*, November/December, 1986, pp. 18–20 and 37.

Index